Border Writing

Theory and History of Literature
Edited by Wlad Godzich and Jochen Schulte-Sasse

For other books in the series, see p. 141

Border Writing
The Multidimensional Text

D. Emily Hicks
Foreword by Neil Larsen

Theory and History of Literature, Volume 80

University of Minnesota Press, Minneapolis and Oxford

Published by the University of Minnesota Press
2037 University Avenue Southeast, Minneapolis, MN 55414
Printed in the United States of America on acid-free paper

Library of Congress Cataloging-in-Publication Data

Hicks, D. Emily.
  Border writing : the multidimensional text / D. Emily Hicks ; foreword by Neil Larsen.
    p. cm. − (Theory and history of literature ; v. 80.)
  Includes bibliographical references and index.
  ISBN 0-8166-1982-4
  ISBN 0-8166-1983-2 (pbk.)
  1. Literature, Modern−20th century−History and criticism.
2. Boundaries in literature. 3. Alienation (Social psychology) in literature. 4. Minorities in literature. I. Title. II. Series.
PN771.H44 1991
809'.04−dc20   90-24072
                                                              CIP

A CIP catalog record for this book is available from the British Library

The University of Minnesota is an
equal-opportunity educator and employer.

To my son

Guillermo Emiliano

Contents

Acknowledgments

This book was made possible by many people whose lives have traversed various borders and who have shared their knowledge with me. I would like to thank Daniel J. Martínez, Sharon McCormack, Lloyd Cross, and Chili Charles, for their contribution to my understanding of the holographic paradigm; Stanley Aronowitz, Abbe Don, Terry Cochran, and Rocío Weiss, for their intellectual and emotional support throughout this project; Fredric Jameson, Sylvia Wynter, Gayatri Spivak, Carlos Blanco, Rosaura Sánchez, and Gustavo Segade, for their patient teaching; Victor Zamudio and the members of the study group with Herbert Marcuse on aesthetics; Gloria Anzaldúa and Alurista, for their contribution to my understanding of border culture; the Centro Cultural de la Raza, for providing the context in which I was able to do most of this research; Guillermo Gómez-Peña, Marco Vinicio Gonzáles, María Eraña, and all those who have supported *The Broken Line/La Línea Quebrada*; all the participants of the Border Culture Residency in Banff, including Angel Cosmos, Jessica Hagedorn, Marina Grzinic, Trevor Gould, and Marlene Nourbese Philip; my students and colleagues at San Diego State University and the Universidad Autónoma de Baja California; BAW/TAF (Border Art Workshop/Taller de Arte Fronterizo), 1986–89; *Las Comadres*; my family on both sides of the border, from San Francisco to Mexico City; and finally, Wlad Godzich.

Foreword
Neil Larsen

In keeping with a growing trend in critical theory, Emily Hicks's *Border Writing: The Multidimensional Text* takes as its implicit point of departure the following problem: how are we now to think about, produce, and/or consume culture without succumbing either to the tainted universalism embodied in Enlightenment notions of "civilization" or to the equally suspect particularisms lurking in notions of "national culture"? Or, to put it more succinctly: how to think about culture without nation? For what is perhaps the dominant current of cultural studies, this problem is "solved" through a tacit mapping of the cultural domain to correspond to that abstract universal ("postmodern," "postcontemporary," "postindustrial," etc.) within which it is only "counter-" or "sub-"culture(s) that command critical interest. The paradox here is that the many "countercultures" do not appear to add up to *a* counterculture, and neither are we quite willing to be pinned down about what that culture *is* that the multiple forms of opposition are counter *to*. (Masculine culture, white Anglo culture, heterosexual culture, business culture, no doubt, but are these really cultures any longer, and even if they are, do they reduce to a single dominant culture and not merely to its absence as a universal?)

But as soon as the cultural studies map is redrawn to include the extracultural boundaries between imperial center and imperialized periphery (or between "First" and "Third" worlds, the "Second" having now been effectively divided between these two), this "solution" quickly becomes obsolete. For here we are faced with the seemingly unavoidable fact that, once drawn up against the dominant (non)culture of imperialism, postcolonial "national" culture coincides with sub- and counterculture. Even if it is conceded that the national culture of, say, Peru or Sri Lanka reenacts its own subimperial forms of marginalization (as witness in the exclusion and oppression of Quechua-speaking and Tamil ethnic groups), the category itself suffers no real damage. It is, after all, the imperialists who drew the postcolonial maps, often with the expressly political aim of dividing national-cultural entities. Or it may be claimed—as Mariátegui did on behalf of Peru's indigenes—that the oppressed and marginalized "sub-"national culture represents what is merely the embodiment of an authentically national culture still shackled by postcolonial forms of cultural alienation.

So in answer to the question posed earlier, the response of a Third World or postcolonial "cultural studies" has, overall, been to deny that culture and nation can, finally, be disentangled. Indeed, the very structure of an imperialist division of labor, its imposition of a (paradoxically) *universal* law of unequal development, would seem to dictate this response. For the identical socioeconomic trends (increasing concentration of capital coupled with universal commodification) that have worked to undermine and finally explode the unity of the national-cultural in settings such as the United States and Western Europe (Japan may be another matter) would seem to require, or at least to thrive upon, the maintenance of a colonial/postcolonial reserve of superexploitable and yet-to-be-commodified labor in which the older sociocultural bonds—above all that of the national-cultural—remain in suspension. In this situation, it is said, the "nation" can become a place of resistance to imperialist encroachment—whence the still frequently reiterated political reasoning that the generally reactionary character of a dominant cultural-nationalism becomes "progressive" as soon as it is taken up by a dominated or "dependent" national grouping.

This persistent haunting of a would-be transnationalized cultural studies by specters of the national-cultural—a kind of eternal return, within the postmodern, of the postcolonial—can be registered in the recent efforts by critics such as Fredric Jameson and Edward Said to temper the postmodern urge to globalize late capitalist culture with reminders that national liberation movements, hence cultural nationalism, have not simply closed up shop because Paris- or California-based intellectuals have lost interest in them.[1] Thus, the fact that authors such as Gabriel García Márquez, Wole Soyinka, Jamaica Kincaid, and Anita Desai can continue to produce compelling narrative fictions rooted, at one level at least, in an authentically national-cultural experience, is not simply to be explained as a consequence of a postcolonial pristinity still unsullied by an "incredulity toward metanarratives." Such a tragic view of things is not only patronizing; it obscures the important sense in which the postcolonial writer's ability to draw on the cultural experience of a national "public sphere" represents a conscious resistance to postmodernism's affirmative alienations. Could it not be that the Elias Khourys and Euzhan Palcys are, in addition to being as hip as anyone to the "precession of simulacra," people with something genuinely new to teach us?

In this respect, of course, the Jamesons and Saids (and one should mention here as well, inter alia, Neil Lazarus, Barbara Harlow, and John Beverley and Marc Zimmerman)[2] merely take up questions of cultural politics that have long occupied postcolonial artists and critics themselves. In Latin America (the post-colonial region about which I personally am least ignorant), the debate over the national-cultural and its role in resisting imperialism has its modern beginnings in the essays of José Martí, who, together with his more conservative genera-tional cohorts, Rubén Darío and José Enrique Rodó, was quick to take up the cul-tural issues posed by the decline of the older, European colonial presence in Latin America and the concomitant rise of North American imperialism. There follows a long succession of culture critics who, in the wake of Latin America's major twentieth-century revolutions, take up this question anew, including intellectu-als as politically divergent as José Vasconcelos, José Carlos Mariátegui, Gilber-to Freyre, Fernando Ortiz, Ernesto ("Che") Guevara, Octavio Paz, and Ernesto Cardenal.

This is not the occasion even for summarizing, much less recapitulating, the many theories of anti- and postcolonial culture that have gained currency in Latin America since Martí's "Nuestra América." In my own work on modernist and avant-garde culture in Latin America, however, I have found it useful to identify two, effectively alternative paradigms of postcolonial oppositional culture: the "transcultural" and the "anthropophagous."[3] The first, stemming from the anthro-pology of Fernando Ortiz, and redeployed by Angel Rama as a category of narra-tive composition and analysis, proposes that the Latin American narrative text (and by extension the producer of a local, autochthonous culture) avoids the dou-ble bind in which one either settles for a direct imitation of metropolitan imports or seeks to expunge all "foreign" cultural influences. Instead, the narrative text must treat the local or regional culture itself as a species of language or code, within which to, as it were, speak or rearticulate or, in this sense, "transculturate" the exotic cultural dominant. Rama cited as successful enactments of this proce-dure the "neoregionalist" narratives of José María Arguedas, João Guimarães Rosa, and García Márquez.

The one severe problem plaguing this model, according to my analysis of it, is that it privileges cultural production without factoring in consumption as an equally critical phase of cultural activity. As a possible solution to this, the an-thropophagous paradigm, first explicitly outlined in the "Manifesto antropofago" of the Brazilian vanguardist Oswald de Andrade, advocates a practice of (in my own wording) "consumptive production," whereby the metropolitan cultural im-port, rather than being simply recoded and then abruptly reinserted into the same, exclusive network of cultural distribution, undergoes an even more radical sub-version by being directly appropriated as simply one motif of a dynamic, post-colonial *mass* culture that can consume without losing its national-cultural iden-tity. But for this, of course, a postcolonial (and distinctly post-Adornian) "culture industry" is required—a need met, in Brazil, by that country's massive film and television enterprise.

But however they measure up against each other, both of these paradigms can claim a certain level of success in Latin America. The fiction "boom" of the 1960s and 1970s, together with the establishment (in Brazil mainly, but also in Mexico, Cuba, Argentina, and Venezuela) of local film, television, and music industries, proves, if nothing else, how far Latin America has come from Martí's nightmare vision of a complete and abject cultural dependency. Even North American literary and popular culture feels the transcultural/cannibalizing pull from its southern "backyard"—as witness cultural phenomena ranging from the magical realist *Milagro Beanfield War* to the Afro-Brazilian-Andean-disco syncretism of lambada.

The fact remains, however, that this indisputable cultural triumph—postcolonial Latin America's conquest not only of a decisive portion of its own but also of a certain sector of a metropolitan cultural terrain—has not, as its earlier political visionaries imagined it would, been matched by a corresponding social and political emancipation from imperial bonds. Although undoubtedly propelled by concrete social and political gains—none of the aforementioned cultural accomplishments would have been thinkable without the breakthroughs of the Mexican and Cuban revolutions—these gains themselves, with the possible exception of Cuba's now endangered and vestigial socialism, have led merely to new forms of imperial/local elite condominium. And this, in turn, raises the question of whether cultural nationalism itself, even when "overdetermined" by anti-imperialism, may not in the end render service as the *ideology* of a postcolonial capitalism more interested, finally, in increasing its market share than in liberating the masses without whose labor and sacrifice and political allegiance no national liberation is possible.

The reality of this gap between the emancipatory promise of postcolonial cultural nationalism and its actual historical record, even though it is not often consciously acknowledged, has, I think, had a pervasive effect on Latin American cultural politics in the last two decades or so. I believe this can be registered in the growing pressure to, so to speak, de-essentialize cultural nationalism by rethinking the postcolonial itself as a sort of "unfixity" whose historic task is not simply to free itself from colonial dependency but to subvert the very notion of an underlying, shared or universal standard of "culture"—a standard that itself validates the claim to "independence." My use of terms here suggests the key influence of poststructuralist doctrines in furthering this trend, and indeed, the connection is an important one (as we shall see in a moment). But, as I have suggested elsewhere,[4] the impulse to rethink cultural nationalism along nonessentialist lines has its more local origins in the cultural theory of Latin Americans such as the Cuban poet and critic Roberto Fernández Retamar, whose writings of the late 1960s and early 1970s[5] were already calling for a rejection of a "universal" literary culture and holding up Latin America's "hybrid" cultures as models for a new, postimperial order of limitless regional differences. A theologically inspired "philosophy of liberation," based mainly in Argentina, and whose best-known advocate has been Enrique Dussel,[6] had, meanwhile, been developing along similar lines for at least twenty years. Now that metropolitan-based intellectuals—going back at least as far as Sartre, but comprising more recently such poststructuralist thinkers as Tzvetan Todorov, Michel de Certeau, and Gayatry Spivak—have taken up this theme, the suspicion is readily generated of yet another First World attempt to construct a utopian alter image of itself out of the imperialized Other. There is, to be sure, a good deal of truth to this suspicion, but one must not overlook the extent to which the crisis of national liberation and of its ancillary forms of cultural nationalism in both Latin America and much of the rest of the postcolonial world have opened up a kind of ideological space for the confluence of poststructuralist doctrine and the cultural opposition to imperialism.

It is in this context, then, that the contribution and significance of *Border Writing* can, I think, best be appreciated. In keeping with the trend in cultural-political theory I have described above, Hicks's interest in Latin American literature and culture stems not from a desire to gain its admittance into the European/North American-dominated canon, but rather from that of mobilizing the former for the seemingly more radical, postnationalist drive to smash the canon altogether. Cultural nationalism recognized the existence of a rigid cultural hierarchy, but sought to reverse, or at least to suspend, the value judgment that hierarchy implied. "Border writing," according to Hicks, seeks rather to undermine "the distinction between original and alien culture." Moreover, Hicks proposes that this imperative is not to be understood as a mere application of poststructuralist strictures regarding "identity thinking," but arises in fact from cultural and artistic transformations that in Latin American are to be encountered in actual practice: "To recuperate now a long tradition of experimentation with the uncritical use of European poststructuralism is unnecessary."

The originality of *Border Writing* is that, rather than simply affirming the—as I have elsewhere termed it—"subversive particularity" of Latin American culture in the abstract, it seeks to demonstrate how this abstract possibility is realized in practice through specifically semiotic and psychic mechanisms operating in and through a discrete set of literary texts. These mechanisms are classified in a variety of ways (e.g., "multidimensional perception," "nonsynchronous memory," a holographic duality of "interference patterns") but they all revolve around the central figure of the "border"—"border writing," "border text," "border subject," "border culture." In using this figure, Hicks is, in effect, attempting to come up with a kind of spatial marker, both literal and figurative, for the postnationalist cultural space whose existence she both posits and celebrates.

Of course both the transcultural and cannibalizing texts cross cultural borders as well—borders between codes and even modes of consumption—but always with the final aim of redrawing the national cultural border *around* the text or consuming/producing subject in a final return to categories of national-cultural identity. Hicks's theory of "border writing" aims not at a mere complication of this essentially *mediational* poetics (a further transculturation of the now increasingly traditional forms of transculture) but rather at undermining the mediation itself — at continually drawing the border *within* and across both the local and the global text/culture. Or, as Hicks herself phrases it, "[Border writing] allow[s] for a description of the mediations of a logic of nonidentity." Where previously a text by, say, Arguedas has been interpreted as merely an improved device for forging a self-identical postcolonial subject out of a hybrid historical, social, and cultural experience, in its reinterpretation as "border writing" it functions in exactly the opposing sense as a means for deconstructing the colonial/postcolonial, center/periphery binarisms as such. In crossing borders, the 'border text' nevertheless thinks, speaks, writes *from* the border itself. Polarities are not simply reversed. They are internalized and then endlessly reproduced.

The bulk of *Border Writing* is devoted to tracing the effects of this process in texts by García Márquez, Cortázar, and Valenzuela. Here, as I see it, the results do not quite measure up to the basic ingenuity of the theoretical hypothesis. Hicks's reading of Cortázar, in particular of *Rayuela* and *Libro de Manuel*, as border writing — buttressed by analogies to Stockhausen's "interactive" method of composition — are perhaps the most successful. Cortázar's narratives certainly resist any effort to endow them with transcultural or cannibalistic properties, a fact that, in recent years, has seemed to encourage a subtle tendency to read Cortázar as somehow less "authentic" than, say, a García Márquez or even a Borges. Hicks's insistence on Cortázar as a writer always sensitive to the double edge of "identity" politics in whatever guise performs the useful task of thwarting this move.

The attempt to read García Márquez's *Cien años de soledad* as "border writing" itself borders on the inauthentic, however. Granted that this text enacts a sort of "nonsynchronous memory" in which the colonial and the postcolonial, the archaic and the hypermodern collide without any opportunity being provided for their "rational" mediation, the reader's vicarious experience of this border crossing is itself reterritorialized in the generational saga of the Buendías. The unity of postcolonial national experience, even if it must relinquish any pretense to a heroic or tragic sense of its own significance (García Márquez remains, for me at least, a subtle but inveterate satirist), is nevertheless preserved in a genealogical structure.

Like Cortázar's, Valenzuela's fictions seem on the whole to fit the "border" paradigm better than they do that of a radicalized but identity-seeking cultural nationalism. However, Hicks's assertion (in chapter 2) that in texts such as "Cambio de armas" Valenzuela not only foils the nationalist/masculinist imaginary but forces the reader to consider a new form of agency freed from European notions of the subject as self-conscious strikes me as, at the very least, undecidable. If, as Hicks claims, "it is necessary that Laura's act [i.e., the heroine's possible assassination of her male captor/torturer/lover] emerge from a conjuncture of history and agency, not from her deliberation as a self-conscious subject," it is hard to see how Valenzuela's narrative itself instructs the reader in this necessity. The fact that Laura's "act" is not preceded — at least on the surface of the narrative — by some brilliant flash of hypermnesia leading to a return to full consciousness of history (both her own and that of the "nation" during the "dirty war" of the 1970s and early 1980s) might after all imply that it is simply a freak occurrence, irrational and unrepeatable, and hence an "agency" only in a fortuitous sense. Where, moreover, does "history" enter into it? The reader must evidently supply it, but what if the (non-Argentine) reader herself has not crossed that particular border? And must agency, in order to reencounter history and politics on some trans-subjective, activist terrain, necessarily evade the question of consciousness? Hicks's tendency to reduce the latter concept to its existentialist meaning in Sartre's *Nausea* — a meaning she then, quite correctly, rejects for its abstract individualism — leads her, unnecessarily it seems to me, to seek its replacement by a hypothetical "border subjectivity," which, even if it really exists, requires a considerable act of imagination to be detected in texts such as "Cambio de armas."

The question of how to know with any certainty whether or not a "border effect" is truly obtained in narratives such as Valenzuela's (although perhaps not of any importance to an orthodox poststructuralism that embraces undecidability as both an inevitable and an optimal state) points, I think, to the intrinsic problem with any theory of the text as endowed with multiple perspectives. This is that there is nothing in the logic of such a theory to explain why the interpreting subject for whom the effect itself is devised might not, in practice, undo the effect by resolving the multiplicity of perspectives in her or his unifying gaze. Even if armed with a clear understanding of the holographic image as an illusion of three-dimensionality produced by the mixing of interference patterns, my contemplation of such an image does not, by that fact alone, escape the illusionist effect of a three-dimensional representation. Of course the claim might be lodged, a la Baudrillard, that *all* objects of perception have now been reduced to the virtual status of holograms. But Hicks seems, wisely, to aver this sort of reasoning. The basic idea here — and it is one with solidly modernist credentials — is that by multiplying the levels of representation, or, if one prefers the Barthesian schema, by pluralizing the various reference codes, one achieves a non- or transrepresentational access to the "real." "The 'real' can be known through reflexive activity in relation to it. Art provides the possibility of gaining access to such reflexive knowledge." Supposing the real to be, on its most profound level, such a multiple, nonuniform entity, this process might perhaps really do the thing it claims. But, then, if the extratextual or uncoded object already exists in a state of spontaneous deconstructedness, why should it be necessary to mirror this condition through a conscious and purposive fragmentation of perspective?

This intrinsic difficulty becomes even clearer if we pose it in terms of the Deleuzo-Guattarian politics (as formulated in the *Anti-Oedipus*) to which the idea of border writing is most closely affiliated. Ronald Bogue has nicely synthesized this politics as follows: "The only means of overcoming the paranoiac impulse is to intensify the schizophrenic tendency of capitalism to the point that the system shatters, and this can only be achieved through the creation of group-subjects that form transverse connections between deterritorialized flows that are no longer subject to the constraints of commodity exchange."[7] In this sense, the production and reproduction of border subjects in and through the border text might justify itself as simply a facet of this overall drive to "intensify the schizophrenic tendency of capitalism." But even if one were to accept the essential premise here that capitalism is vulnerable to the simple intensification of one of its own spontaneous tendencies, it is hard to see how, in transposing this uncontrolled, anarchic impulse into the controlled and evidently purposive schizophrenia of the "multidimensional text," its very emancipatory potential would not be counteracted. Any effort to guide or set in motion the process of intensifying the schizophrenic tendency would seem, by virtue of its own "paranoiac" intentionality, to contradict this tendency.

But these sorts of problems are, of course, no longer specific to Hicks's particular hypothesis regarding what is, after all, the possibility that Latin American literature and culture might be incubating a sort of border poetics. They stem, in my view, from the basic futility of trying to outflank the oppressive logic of cultural nationalism by postulating the capacity of purely abstract-discursive and (in the case of *Border Writing*) aesthetic mechanisms to produce a postnationalist "border subject." This is a utopian project, in the best and worst senses of the word. It reproduces the classical ideological pattern of severing the transformation of consciousness from the constraints imposed by the transformation of social being. Thus, for example, in her discussion of the idiomatically "border" reality of the *maquiladoras* (foreign-owned assembly plants located in Mexico just across the U.S. border and employing an overwhelmingly female work force at starvation wages), Hicks is moved to ask "what possible definition of the subject would be mirrored by the object produced in such an environment?" But, we must ask, do "objects" (here the economic, social, and political reality of the *maquiladoras*) in fact "mirror" an independent and preexisting border subject, as the wording here suggests? Is it not the subject here that mirrors the object? Elsewhere, in summing up the textual politics of Valenzuela's *Cola de lagartija*, Hicks writes:

> Symbols, or metaphors, the end product in the production of meaning, must be created by Argentines themselves. They must occupy and self-

manage the location at which meaning is produced, the border region between the political unconscious and the political conscious. They must gain control over this production process such that even if the "real" remains elusive, as individuals they will have access to new images, and as subjects, they will effect changes at the level of signifiers, speech, and language.

To suggest, of course, that progressive social change is possible without, on one level, wresting control over the "production of meaning" is to fall into a justly discredited form of economic determinism. And perhaps, in fairness, this is what Hicks really wants to convey here. But can such a thing be deemed possible in the first place, in view of the unconscious, presubjective plane on which meanings are, in Hicks's Lacanian framework, thought to be produced? Moreover, to suppose that by merely having "access to new images" and effecting changes "at the level of signifiers," etc., events such as Argentina's "dirty war" might be avoided — is this not finally to reduce the "dirty war" itself to a sort of symbol, to question its very existence as something 'real'?

If the direct production of border subjects, whether through the spontaneous "flows" of deterritorialization or through aesthetic interventions, is finally a utopian delusion, what then, we must ask, is the alternative to cultural-nationalist decay? Here, I think, Samir Amin, in his recent work *Eurocentrism*, has at least produced the framework for an answer.[8] Amin places the development of cultural-nationalism (or, as he simply terms it, "culturalism") in the context of a Eurocentric "universalism" hatched in the European "Renaissance" and systematically formulated in the nineteenth century. Two historical factors effect its decline. One is the objective demystification of Eurocentric universalism brought about by its own twentieth-century pathologies: imperialism, with its world wars and its condemnation of the masses living on the imperial periphery to perpetual exclusion from the benefits of "civilization." The other is the rise of a social universalism, enabled by universal commodification itself, and first articulated by Marxism.

According to Amin, however, this Marxist or socialist universalism (comprising a cultural universalism as well) did not immediately free itself from a residual Eurocentrism contained in the conception that, even *qua* socialism, "Europe was the model for everything" (*EU*, 126). It is partly as a result of this that, in our own period, "existing" capitalisms and socialisms effectively converge in a social formation dominated by "economism," or the theory of society as governed by economic "laws" independent of conscious social agencies. This combined reality, then — the decline of the older, capitalist, Eurocentric universalism, coupled with the difficult, contradictory emergence of a new, genuinely social universalism embodied in the vision of a classless society — results in what Amin terms the current "impasse" in which "capitalist ideology remains dominant on the world scale" but is matched by "inverted Eurocentrisms" on the periphery. "Without a truly universalist perspective founded on the critique of economism and enriched by the contributions of all peoples," writes Amin, "the sterile confrontation between the Eurocentrisms of some and the inverted Eurocentrisms of others will continue in an atmosphere of destructive fanaticism" (*EU*, 146).

The clear implication here is that it is only along the slow and tortuous route of revolutionary-political movements, guided by an authentically universalist and emancipatory worldview, that the impasse can be broken down. Transcending cultural nationalism on the level of both theory and culture can only be the result, in any lasting sense, of transcending cultural nationalism as a political and social practice. From this perspective, the project of a border writing (or border subject, border culture, etc.) must be seen as an ambiguous one, reflecting the configuration of the impasse itself—unable to continue existing on either side of the border but still unwilling to give up the border itself for fear that this will place it back in the domain of Eurocentrism's false universe.

But must we then avoid even the anticipatory practices and rhetoric of a post-nationalist, social universalism until the impasse is practically a thing of the past? I think not, and here is the point on which I dissent most pointedly from Hicks's border writing hypothesis, even while participating in its underlying sympathies. The reality that produces border subjects also tells us a certain amount about what a future, and at least *trans*national culture might entail. That the emergent face of this culture still hides behind the mask of capitalism's universal consumerism is beyond question. But to the extent that activities other than consumption (or the desire for it) become the centrally shared experiences of heretofore distinct "nationalities" (e.g., the wide degree to which black and Hispanic musical, linguistic, and purely social idioms are adopted by middle- and working-class white youth in the United States), one surely glimpses its features. Of what purpose is the border effect here, unless it is to preserve the opportunity for reinserting cultural nationalism just when it appears to be decisively yielding its sway? (The same question can, it seems to me, be posed of certain forms of "multiculturalism," in which, as Amin puts it, "all aspirations for universalism are rejected in favor of a 'right to difference' . . . invoked as a means of evading the real problem" [*EU*, 146].)

Moreover, I suggest that it is possible to extend the general interpretive thesis of a border writing beyond the vanguardist and ambiguous class politics of texts by García Márquez, Cortázar, and Valenzuela, to comprise somewhat older literary traditions of a more social-universalistic character. I have in mind here especially the tradition of the "proletarian novel" in Latin America, a tradition including such national-cultural anomalies as B. Traven (a "border crosser" if there ever was one) as well as the more national-culturally grounded texts of socialist realists such as Icaza and the Jorge Amado of the 1940s and early 1950s. In Amado's trilogy *Os subterrâneos da liberdade* (a work long neglected thanks to the cold war/"boom"-inspired aversion for its supposed "Zhdanovite" qualities), we find, for example, innumerable border crossings, albeit here on the level of the referent per se, rather than that of its various "codes." The fascism of Getulio Vargas's *Estado Novo* emerges—in an interesting variation on the standard Latin American "dictator" novel—as a preeminently international phenomenon, in which politics on the level, say, of rivalry between U.S. and Nazi imperialism takes concrete shape in an intricate plot comprising characters from virtually every level of Brazilian class society. In the end, of course, Amado's own Third International brand of nationalism takes hold in the trilogy's final cultish celebration of Prestes as a Brazilian national savior, but along the way many of the representational limits imposed by Latin American cultural nationalism are convincingly overcome. That this tradition is not, moreover, entirely a thing of the past can be verified in the more contemporary narratives of the late Manuel Scorza. In this Peruvian author's epic cycle of social-indigenist novels (collectively entitled *La guerra silenciosa*), Amado's feat is basically repeated, but here in a narrative style incorporating many of the more innovative discoveries of the intervening "boom." In works such as *Redoble por Rancas*, Scorza's mercilessly sardonic replay of the battle of Junín (interspersed with scenes of the modern destruction, by Peruvian armed forces, of the indigenous community named in the title) makes the more aestheticist and historically ambiguous reappraisal of Bolívar in García Márquez's *El general en su laberinto* look tepid by comparison.

Such works, it seems to me, at least bear witness to what has evidently been the slow, but ongoing, emergence of a poetics of a postnational, social universalism in Latin America, although this may never have been a conscious aim per se. Emily Hicks—even if, for ideological and theoretical motives of her own, she prefers to locate this poetics elsewhere—nevertheless insists on such a postnational aegis as her own conscious point of departure. And that, I think, is the particular virtue of the work that follows.

Introduction
Border Writing as Deterritorialization

As the functional expression of the self-conscious attitude of a writer juxtaposed between multiple cultures, border writing must be conceived as a mode of operation rather than as a definition. What makes border writing a world literature with a "universal" appeal is its emphasis upon the multiplicity of languages within any single language; by choosing a strategy of translation rather than representation, border writers ultimately undermine the distinction between original and alien culture.[1] Border writers give the reader the opportunity to practice multidimensional perception and nonsynchronous memory (Bloch, "Nonsynchronism and the Obligation to Its Dialectics," 22–38).[2] By multidimensional perception I mean quite literally the ability to see not just from one side of a border, but from the other side as well. In Roland Barthes's terms, this would mean a perception informed by two different sets of referential codes. Such a writing practice arises out of border culture, an essential characteristic of which is the specific configuration of cultural practices that rob the discursive mechanisms of their power to dissimulate an identity between cultural theory and its praxis; that is, the functional unity between any specifiable aesthetic and its programmatic implementation has been replaced by a relationship of nonidentity.

Border regions produce cultures that have certain common features. The Mexico-U.S. border provides a set of general categories: the *pollo* (the border crosser), the *mosco* (the helicopter of the U.S. Immigration and Naturalization Service), the *migra* (the U.S. immigration officer), the *coyote* (the person who brings the *pollo* across the border), the *turista* (the North American visitor to Mexico), and the *cholo* or *chola* (the young bicultural inhabitant of the border region). The *coyotes* and the *cholos/cholas* are the most bicultural because their lives depend on their ability to survive in the interstices of two cultures.

Latin American culture in particular is essentially heterogeneous, a culture that articulates borders between widely disparate traditions. The contemporary culture of Mexico, for example, emerges from what can be considered a multilayered semiotic matrix: the Mixteco Indians, Spain, the Lacandonian Indians, McDonald's, ballet folklórico, and punk rock. The heterogeneous cultures of Latin America exist in the spaces that emerge between a desire for memories of pre-Colombian cultures, a respect for the continuing traditions of indigenous cultures, and a problematic relationship with Spanish and other European cultures and the New World culture of the United States. As a result, much contemporary Latin American literature is a literature of borders: cultural borders between Paris/Buenos Aires and Mexico City/New York, gender borders between women and men, and economic borders between dollar-based and other-currency-based societies. Border writing, in a Latin American context, presents the cultures of Europe and the United States in their interaction with Latin American culture rather than as fundamental cultural models. In border writing, the subject is decentered and the object is not present or immediate but displaced.[3] Border writers re-present that attitudes toward objects as they exist in more than one cultural context. For example, the *maquiladoras* advertise the opportunity to produce commodities in what Jean Baudrillard would call "hyperspace." Corporations are encouraged to manufacture in factories built along the Mexican side of the border. Mexican workers enter the plant from the Mexican side where they live, whereas most of the management crosses the border from the United States into Mexico to go to work. In this way, a "grotesque" element of border life, the crossing of thousands of undocumented workers, can be diminished by eliminating the need to "cross the border." Nonetheless, the question must be raised as to what possible definition of the subject would be mirrored by the object produced in such an environment.

One view of the decentered subject is suggested by Paul de Man in "Phenomenology and Materiality in Kant."[4] He argues that Immanuel Kant's notion of the architectonic assumes, in rhetorical analytical terms, a consideration of the limbs of the body apart from any use. This leads him to a provocative conclusion: the dismemberment of the body corresponds to dismemberment of language "as meaning-tropes are replaced by fragmentation" into words, syllables, and letters (121–44). This dismemberment of language bears a similarity to Gilles Deleuze and Félix Guattari's notion of deterritorialization. That is, one could argue that the nineteenth-century European notion of the subject is replaced in the work of the border writer by fragmentation in cultural, linguistic, and political deterritorialization.

Yet, in border writing, we can no longer speak of a clearly defined "subjective" or "objective" meaning. Rather, there is a refusal of the metonymic reduction in which a white, male, Western "subject" dominates an object. The core of border writing is the border metaphor, which may be compared to Walter Benjamin's "dialectical image," where there is a joining of the subjective and the accidental to create objective meaning.[5] Instead of the "accidental," however, there is a broader view of the object that presents it within a historical—although not necessarily linear—past. This is the border "object" to which the Chicana poet Gina Valdés refers in "Where You From?": "my mouth still / tastes of *naranjas / con chile / soy del sur / y del norte.*" The subject in this poem is dominated by the nostalgic memory for an object. Trinidadian writer Marlene Nourbese Philip also writes about the border object; by mimicking a grammar lesson in her poem "Universal Grammar" (*She Tries Her Tongue, Her Silence Softly Breaks*), she exposes the complicity between language and violence: "The tall, blond, blue-eyed, white-skinned man is shooting an elephant / a native / a wild animal / a Black / a woman / a child."

What the postmodern subject is or is not, and how the debates relate to the culture being produced outside of Europe, is touched upon by Gilane Tawadros in her essay "Beyond the Boundary: The Work of Three Black Women Artists in Britain." She writes that "the diasporan experience constitutes a critical distance which Jameson claims has been abolished in the space of postmodern society."[6] Furthermore, in Philip's view, there is also a "re-membering" in the work of some Caribbean writers that is distinct from both deterritorialization and reterritorialization.[7]

Deleuze and Guattari have discussed the nonunified subject in relation to the writings of Kafka. They posit that the "statement" never refers back to a "subject" and that even the most individual "enunciation" is a particular case of "collective enunciation" (*Kafka*, 84). In their discussion of *The Trial*, they argue that "ultimately, it is less a question of K as a general function taken up by an individual than of K as a *functioning of a polyvalent assemblage of which the solitary individual is only a part*, the coming collectivity being another part, another piece of the machine—without our knowing yet what this assemblage will be: fascist? revolutionary? socialist? capitalist?" (85).

I propose considering Franz Kafka, a Czech Jew who lived in Prague and wrote in German, as an example of a writer of border literature. Deleuze and Guattari call him a writer of "minor" literature. Border writing emphasizes the differences in reference codes between two or more cultures. It depicts, therefore, a kind of realism that approaches the experience of border crossers, those who live in a bilingual, bicultural, biconceptual reality. I am speaking of cultural, not physical, borders: the sensibility that informs border literature can exist among guest workers anywhere, including European countries in which the country of origin does not share a physical border with the host country.

Who, then, might be the audience for border writing? Philip writes, in "Who's Listening: Artists, Audiences and Languages," that we each complete a novel, play, poem, or painting differently depending on factors as diverse as age, gender, class, and culture. She goes on to question the validity of the response of a reader who is a stranger to the traditions that inform a work. Like Kafka, who as a writer experienced the deterritorialization of language, the reader of border writing may experience a deterritorialization of signification; to read a border text is to cross over into another set of referential codes. The reader of border writing will not always be able to perceive the "logic" of the text at first. Nor will she be able to hear the multiplicity of discourses within a single language—the four keys in a sequence of four chords, or the multiple sets of referential codes. For this reason, Argentine writer Julio Cortázar had to invent the *lector cómplice*; similarly, much of border art and culture is considered with the active participation of the audience. A greater demand is made on the reader of border texts. In Derridean terms, the Ear of the Other must be heard; some readers of border texts may become border crossers.

The border crosser is both "self" and "other." The border crosser "subject" emerges from double strings of signifiers of two sets of referential codes, from both sides of the border. The border crosser is linked, in terms of identity, activity, legal status, and human rights, to the border machine, with its border patrol agents, secondary inspection, helicopters, shifts in policy, and *maquiladoras*. According to Deleuze and Guattari, a machine may be defined as (1) a system of interruptions and breaks; (2) possessing its own set of codes; and (3) connected to other machines (*Anti-Oedipus*, 36–41). The border machine, which produces the border subject, is subject to "flows" that depend on the labor needs of California growers; its codes are continually changing, as they are connected to and determined by the political and juridical machines of Washington and Mexico City.

All of the above has been obscured by the term "magic realism," which has been used to refer to border writing. The term comes from art history, where it has described Arnold Böcklin and Giorgio de Chirico, both of whom have been associated with surrealism. David Young and Keith Hollaman note in *Magic Realist Fiction* that the first use of the term in relation to Latin American literature may have been in 1954 by Angel Flores. Gregory Rabassa rejected it in 1973 because it "gave too much credence to realism as a norm" (Young and Hollaman, 1). Many critics, however, including Jean Franco, continue to use "magic realism," often as a means of identification. Has it outgrown its usefulness? For in the absence of any definitive critical analysis of the historical and political context of Latin American literature, the term "magic realism" can only serve to depoliticize the text. Fredric Jameson draws attention to this problem in *The Political Unconscious*: "Thus, in the first great period of bourgeois hegemony, the reinvention of romance finds its strategy in the substitution of new positivities (theology, psychology, the dramatic metaphor) for the older magical content . . . from Kafka to Cortázar" (134). Restated, border writers rely on more than one set of referential codes. The "dramatic metaphor," whether the "dialectical image" of Kafka, the "magic realist" image of Cortázar, or the "i-mage" of Philip[8] nevertheless maintains certain elements of "the older magical content."

Because of its dependence on the literary categories of dominant cultures, the term "magic realism" necessarily obscures important issues such as narrative non-linearity, the decentered dimensional perspective. Rather than elaborating the term "magic realism," I want to analyze the border metaphor. I also want to consider the appropriateness of applying European postmodernist terminology to border writing by juxtaposing certain border texts with the category of "deter-ritorialization" of Deleuze and Guattari. Finally, I will propose a model of analyzing the border text, a multidimensional model drawn from holography.

Although border studies, along with cultural studies, is currently a rapidly expanding field, only J. Nelly Martínez has discussed Latin American literature in terms of a multidimensional or holographic model, and most Anglo critics of Latin American literature still refer to García Márquez and others as magic realists. Nevertheless, unlike the term "magic realism," which maintains the binary opposition of magic/real, the term "border writing" connotes a perspective that is no longer dominated by nonborder regions. It hints at the subversive nature of this writing, a writing that disrupts the one-way flow of information in which the United States produces most of the mass-media programming in the world and thereby controls the images of itself as well as those of other countries. North American critics of Latin American literature must realize that to continue to stress the "magical" or even certain postmodernist aspects of Latin American literature is to deny the larger, broader understanding of reality that informs these texts. Long before French poststructuralist criticism had been imported to U.S. literature departments, artists and writers in Latin America were already "appropriating" images and "decentering" the subject. We need only consider a few examples such as the Mexican artist Posada in the nineteenth century, the Brazilian concrete poets in the 1960s, the writers of the "boom," and the artists of the *neo-gráfica* movement in Mexico. To recuperate now a long tradition of experimentation with the uncritical use of European poststructuralism is unnecessary. Gilane Tawadros makes a similar argument with regard to the work of black artists.

Independent historical developments have led to "postmodernism" in border writing. Harry Polkinhorn has stated that "Chicano writing at least in part short-circuited the power lines of transmission of the European avant-garde and broader modernist tendencies, which had much more of an impact on Latin American practitioners (viz. Ultraísmo to Huidobro, Estridentismo, Noigandre's Concrete Poetry of the de Campos and Pagnatari, Poem/Process, and later developments such as Espinosa's Post-Art group). By contrast with this richness of cultural embeddedness, Chicano literature was born ex nihilo, as it were, with connections less to a long tradition of oppositional art but more to one of oppressed social experience" (42).

The multiplicity of voices in the work of many Latin American writers has given the grotesque a place from which to speak. The grotesque, suppressed in the nineteenth-century European novel, is often confused by U.S. readers of Latin American literature with the "magical." What Mikhail Bakhtin in *Rabelais and His World* calls "the grotesque" has not been homogenized out of the metaphors deployed in border writing; indeed, the referential code of "the grotesque" is very important. In the border region, the notion of the grotesque is linked to relations of power. In the U.S.-Mexico border city of Tijuana, the U.S. tourist is fascinated and repulsed by "grotesque" culture: velvet paintings, ceramic sculptures of the Last Supper, and children selling chewing gum. The *tijuanenses* watch, amused and horrified, as surfers walk into the churches barefoot and drunk Marines stumble into shop displays on the street. The inclusion of the grotesque is already an anticentering strategy. Border writers are conscious of the gap or difference between the reader and the audience, and between the characters and the temporal setting (Derrida, *Writing and Difference*, 196–231). Border narratives are decentered: there is no identity between the reader and the individual character, but rather, an invitation to listen to a Voice of the Person that arises from an overlay of codes out of which characters and events emerge (Barthes, *S/Z*). There is a displacement of time and space.

The "magical" or "grotesque" content, in that it disrupts the rational, raises the question of linear narrative. How is the reader able to understand a nonlinear narrative? Laura Mulvey, Teresa de Lauretis, and Fredric Jameson among others have written on this issue. In "Visual Pleasure and Narrative Cinema," Mulvey argues that "sadism demands a story, depends on making something happen, forcing a change in another person, a battle of will and strength, victory/defeat, all occurring in a linear time with a beginning and an end" (14). The structure of the relationship between the sadist and masochist resembles that of the relationship between narrative structure and the reader. Jameson imagines an alternative to bourgeois, linear narrative in his discussion of Bakhtin's notion of the dialogic: "as rupture of the one-dimensional text of the bourgeois narrative, as a carnivalesque dispersal of the hegemonic order of a dominant culture" (*Political Unconscious*, 285). Border writers often engage in a metacommentary about "story." Cortázar and Argentine writer Luisa Valenzuela in particular address their roles as narrators. They also demand that their readers address their roles as readers.

What methodological tools or theoretical model might we use in approaching border writing? Recent demonstrations in which Anglo-Americans drive to the border and shine their headlights in the direction of Mexico constitute one of many examples of border behavior that defies unidimensional logic. When pressed, demonstrators have claimed that by pointing their headlights at Mexico, they will send a message to people in the United States about the seriousness of "the [immigration] problem." This border trope, of turning away from the addressee in the moment of sending the message, suggests that we require a model that will allow us to look in two directions simultaneously. The model of holography presents itself because it creates an image from more than one perspective. If we imagine the "real" to be a matrix of interactions between "subjects" and "objects" that can be partially translated, but which, in the final analysis, resists symbolization, then border writing might be conceived as a framing of certain crucial interactions: nature and technology, humans and nature, popular culture and mass culture, meaning and nonmeaning. The border metaphor summarizes these relationships by selecting two or more perspectives from which to "digitally sample" a portion of the matrix. In the same way that one part of a hologram can produce an entire image, the border metaphor is able to reproduce the whole culture to which it refers. Border metaphors are holographic in that they re-create the whole social order, but this is merely to say the "whole" in its fragmentation, as would Deleuze and Guattari (*Anti-Oedipus*, 42). In "The Absence of Writing," Philip discusses the "decontextualized" or deterritorialized "i-mage"-making power of the African in the New World (15).

To clarify the relationship between the border trope and holography, let us consider how a holographic image is formed. Holography provides a provocative multidimensional model for visualizing the production of deterritorialized meaning/nonmeaning. A holographic image is created when light from a laser beam is split into two beams and reflected off an object. The interaction between the two resulting patterns of light is called an "interference pattern," which can be recorded on a holographic plate. The holographic plate can be reilluminated by a laser positioned at the same angle as one of the two beams, the object beam. This will produce a holographic image of the original object. A border person records the interference patterns produced by two (rather than one) referential codes, and therefore experiences a double vision thanks to perceiving reality through two different interference patterns. A border writer juxtaposes the two patterns as border metaphors in the border text. The border metaphor reconstructs the relationship to the object rather than the object itself: as a metaphor, it does not merely represent an object but rather produces an interaction between the connotative matrices of an object in more than one culture. The holographic "real" is less solid, and as a result it cannot be dominated as easily as the monocultural or nonholographic real.

What is the relationship between the border machine and holography? What would a holographic system of interruptions and breaks be? What codes would the border machine as a holographic image possess? How would the holographic border machine be linked to other holographic border machines? Perhaps William Gibson gives us a clue in *Neuromancer:* the border machine and holography would meet in the matrix in border cyberspace. The border "cyber" would be piloting the machine with a double bicultural program in which the data base contained two sets of referential codes, one from each side of the border. Theodor

Adorno at the new frontiers within First and Third world cultures. Negative border praxis.

Many border tropes, metaphors, and images juxtapose traditional culture and technology; this juxtaposition forms the basis of a phrase used by more than one Chicano artist: "From Aztec to high tech." Border writing is rooted in a critique of technology. It is a "committed" art form in Adorno's sense of the term. Benjamin's problematic angel of history in *Illuminations* is helplessly propelled toward the storm of plutonium; the industrialized world is on the edge of a storm worse than the storm that destroyed Macondo. Deterritorialized children grow up near chemical-waste dumps in Los Angeles. Where some in the industrialized world would see "a chain of events," Benjamin's angel sees one single catastrophe, which now threatens to be nuclear holocaust. Where some see linearity, the angel sees a piling up of images. According to Kant, "The whole is articulated and not just piled on top of each other" (de Man, *Hermeneutics*, 128). Physicist David Bohm describes the whole in terms of the implicate order (Martínez). Why can't the angel see that the whole is articulated? The angel of history would like to warn us, to make whole what has been smashed, to translate the disaster, but its wings are caught up in the storm. The "storm" is like that text that links the puppeteer to the puppet. The image of "making whole that which has been smashed" — that is, of adopting a multi-dimensional perspective — recalls Benjamin's view of the task of the translator: "to piece together the fragments of a broken vessel" (*Illuminations*, 78). How are the translator and the angel of history alike?

For Deleuze and Guattari the task of the translator is "to make use of the polylingualism of one's own language, to make a minor or intensive use of it, to oppose the oppressed quality of this language to its oppressive quality, to find points of nonculture or underdevelopment, linguistic Third World zones by which a language can escape, an animal enters into things, an assemblage [*agencement*] comes into play" (*Kafka*, 26–27). Philip reminds us of the oppressive quality of her "own" language, English, a language in which she is forced to operate. What, then, is the task of the writer or artist? For Philip, it is to use language in such a way "that the historical realities are not erased or obliterated" ("The Absence of Writing," *She Tries Her Tongue*, 19). Another example of the exploration of border culture within the Third World can be found in the work of the young Cuban visual artists of the 1980s, including José Bedia and Magdalena Campos.[9]

According to Deleuze and Guattari, the three characteristics of "minor literature" are (1) the deterritorialization of language; (2) the connection of the individual to political immediacy — that is, everything is political; and (3) the collective assemblage of enunciation — that is, everything takes on a collective value (*Kafka*, 17). In addition, they consider Kafka to be what I call a border writer: "Not only is he at the turning point between two bureaucracies, the old and the new, but he is between the technical machine and the juridical statement. He has experienced their reunion in a single assemblage" (82). As a border writer, he is a Czech Jew, a minority, but writes in a major language, German. In a similar way, border writing is deterritorialized, political, and collective.

In order to expand the definition of "minor literature" to include border writing, Deleuze and Guattari's categories can be rewritten to consider: (1) the displacement or "deterritorialization" of time and space through nonsynchronous memory and "reterritorialization" (and not only through nostalgia in a pejorative sense); (2) deterritorialization or nonsynchrony in relation to everyday life; (3) the decentered subject/active reader/assemblage/agent/border crosser/becoming-animal; and (4) the political. When one leaves one's country or place of origin (deterritorialization), everyday life changes. The objects that continually reminded one of the past are gone. Now, the place of origin is a mental representation in memory. The process of reterritorialization begins. "Border" literacy, or the ability to read border literature, is a kind of border crossing as well as a democratic thought process; it avoids a single perspective, such as a middle-class, Western cultural bias. It takes a critical view of authority and supports the imaginative.

Border writing offers a new form of knowledge: information about and understanding of the present to the past in terms of the possibilities of the future. It refuses the metonymic reduction of reality to the instrumental logic of Western thought. As Valenzuela puts it, the word is sick: in order to heal it, the writer must free it from the teleological and bring it across the border into the architectonic (see Hicks, "La palabra enferma"). This historic journey will reterritorialize it. The global body needs to be healed. Border writing holds out this possibility, through its combination of perception and memory, of subverting the rationality of collective suicide, of calming the storm of progress blowing from Paradise — the ability to withstand the pull of the future destruction to which one's face is turned.

In "La palabra enferma," I argued that border writing is the trace of the *coyote*/shaman, basing this on Valenzuela's view of the role of the writer as a shaman who writes in order to cure the reader. We can also see from Deleuze and Guattari's notion of the machine that the writer is a smuggler or *coyote*. If the border is a machine, then one of its elements is the bicultural smuggler, and to read is to cross over to another side where capital has not yet reduced the object to a commodity — to a place where a psychic healing can occur.

Chapter 1
García Márquez:
Cultural Border Crosser

Border Reality in Macondo

Gabriel García Márquez grew up in Aracataca, Colombia, a company town that was built by the United Fruit Company, and had the same wooden shacks with roofs made of zinc and tin and the same contrasts of wealth and poverty as those described by William Faulkner, another border culture dweller. The imperialist presence of the banana company deterritorialized language or the production of signification. After leaving Colombia in 1955, García Márquez lived in Paris for three years, then in Venezuela and New York. In the early 1960s, he went to Mexico City, where he wrote *Cien años de soledad*.[1] Although from a new historicist perspective we might take issue with his distinction between the terms, García Márquez claims that *Cien años de soledad* is a metaphor, not a history, of Latin America ("Interview," 74). He describes the coastal region of Colombia as a place inhabited by those who were left after the respectable people had migrated to the interior, to Bogotá, that is, "bandits — bandits in the good sense — and dancers, adventurers, people full of gaiety" (74),[2] the descendants of "pirates and smugglers, with a mixture of black slaves" (74). With such a background during childhood, the distinction between the "magical" and the real was blurred. In the border culture of Colombia, everyday life is informed by Spanish culture, Indian culture, and African culture: thus the inspiration for *Cien años*.

The gypsies who come to Macondo are cultural border dwellers: they live in the interstices between different cities and countries. By bringing technology to Macondo, they place the town's inhabitants in the position of border dwellers vis-

1

a-vis Europe. The arrival of the banana company merely accelerates the process of border acculturation, producing its own set of border juxtapositions such as swimming pools filled with old shoes. But in *Cien años* the gypsies are border dwellers who seduce the inhabitants of Macondo, through marvelous objects, to think in terms of more than one culture. Thus, they are *coyotes* that bring the inhabitants of Macondo across the cultural border from the past into the technological age of the banana company.

Once the process of deterritorialization begins, Macondo is forever transformed. Memory is now a problem. Written language is necessary to remind inhabitants of the use of objects. Without their past, the inhabitants of Macondo accept everything as a given. They cannot perceive the strike because they have no historical memory. They deny its existence. They are convinced by the arguments of the company, which claims that there were no workers but only part-time employees.

The notion of deterritorialization is linked in Deleuze and Guattari's analysis to the notion of the machine and to the holographic model of the production of signification. Examples of machines in Macondo are the multiple-use machine and the language machine ("*Esta es la vaca, hay que ordeñarla todas las mañanas . . .* "; *CA* 47) ("*This is the cow. She must be milked every morning . . .* "; *OHY* 53).[3] From a holographic perspective, the need to label the cow arises out of the new "deterritorialized" reference beam (referential code) that coincides with the arrival of the gypsies. The arrival of technology is accompanied by the onset of amnesia. In *Anti-Oedipus*, Deleuze and Guattari explain the concept of the machine using the example of the relationship between the artisan and his or her tool. Together, the artisan and the tool form a machine, or a "body without organs" (9–16). In *Kafka*, Deleuze and Guattari describe the machine of Kafka's world: "The machine of justice is a machine metaphorically: this machine fixes the initial sense of things, not only with its rooms, its offices, its books, its symbols, its topography, but also with its personnel (judges, lawyers, bailiffs), its women who are adjacent to the porno books of the law" (81–82). The relationship between the personnel and the legal books, offices, and so on is one of a machine. With the arrival of the banana company, the inhabitants of Macondo are now connected to this new machine of justice that further deterritorializes their referential codes.

In the case of Macondo, the banana company for García Márquez is analogous to the insurance company for Kafka. The juridical machine of the banana company "fixes" the fate of the workers by making them totally invisible.[4] Because the inhabitants of Macondo have forgotten their past, they do not question the given. They have no basis of comparison and therefore accept the official story that there was no strike and that nothing happened.[5] The "decrépitos abogados vestidos de negro" ("decrepit lawyers dressed in black") argue that the workers do not exist and had never existed "sino que los reclutaba ocasionalmente y con carácter temporal" ("because they were all hired on a temporary and occasional basis") (*CA* 255, 256; *OHY* 279, 280). The representative of the company, Mr. Jack Brown, is discovered in a brothel when the workers go to look for him in order to present their demands. The next day, he appears in court "with his hair dyed black and speaking flawless Spanish" (*OHY* 279). In the Kafkaesque infinite regress, behind every Klamm or representative of the company, there is another Klamm. When José Arcadio Segundo Buendía tells people about the massacre of the strikers, he is told that " . . . no ha pasado nada en Macondo" (*CA* 261) (" . . . nothing has happened in Macondo"; *OHY* 285).[6]

The strike of the banana workers can also be linked with the distinction Deleuze and Guattari make between "the collective assemblage of enunciation" and the statement, which can be juridical. They in no way believe, however, that such enunciations ensure freedom: "one can't really tell if submission doesn't finally conceal the greatest sort of revolt and if combat doesn't imply the worst of acceptances" (*Kafka*, 82). One reading of *Cien años* could be that the endless civil wars in fact preserve the status quo. There is, however, an alternative to preserving the status quo: deterritorialization.

Deleuze and Guattari use Gregor as an example of what they call "becoming-animal." For him, it was better to become a bug than to remain a bureaucrat. Another kind of deterritorialization involves the crossing of borders. Ursula's discovery of a passageway between Macondo and the rest of the world might be considered such a border crossing. Using a nonlinear method, she "encontró la ruta que su marido no pudo descubrir en su frustrada búsqueda de los grandes inventos" (*CA* 38) ("she had found the route that her husband had been unable to discover in his frustrated search for the great inventions"; *OHY* 43). She may be credited with the deterritorialization of the inhabitants of Macondo. In *Kafka*, Deleuze and Guattari refer to other kinds of border crossings in their linking of dodecaphonic music with deterritorialization and the fall of the Hapsburg Empire (24).

The narrative structure García Márquez employs in the telling of the different responses to ice in the scene at the fair involves a flight from linearity not unlike the technique of that theory of musical opposition. His use of four logical possibilities, for example, relates his narrative structure to much of the experimental work in music and the arts, and to similar explorations of possibilities in works by Cortázar and Valenzuela. First, José Arcadio Buendía touches the ice, holding his hand there for several minutes. The dichotomy to be considered here is duration. Second, his son José Arcadio refuses to touch the ice. Third, Aureliano touches the ice and removes his hand immediately, saying "It's boiling." There is a reversal here between hot and cold. In terms of duration, this is a negation of the first case. Fourth, the father lays his hands on the ice again, and says, "Este es el gran invento de nuestro tiempo" (*CA* 23) ("This is the great invention of our time"; *OHY* 26). This synthesis of all the other cases is both a comment on "It's boiling" and a mediating gesture between touching quickly and removing immediately. It goes beyond a description and enters the realm of naming. Thus, the narrative structure of the ice story is nearly identical to that of composer Arnold Schoenberg's twelve-tone technique, in which a series of notes, in this case analogous to the basic plot of touching ice, forms the basis of the composition. The four possibilities for the forms of a tone row are, first, the original form, in this case the touching of the ice; second, the retrograde form of the opposite of the first, not touching the ice; third, the inverted form, touching the ice but removing the hand quickly and negating its most salient property by saying "It's boiling"; and fourth, the retrograde inversion, a combination and variation of the second and third, a laying of hands on the ice and the declaration that it is the greatest invention of our time.

The displacement of deterritorialization of time and space can also occur through multidimensional or nonsynchronous memory. Examples can be found at the level of verb tense and syntax in border writing. In the first sentence of *Cien años* the reader is told not only what someone will do in the future, but receives this information from a perspective in which this future is already past: "Muchos años después, frente al pelotón de fusilamiento, el coronel Aureliano Buendía había de recordar aquella tarde remota en que su padre lo llevó a conocer el hielo" (*CA* 9) ("Many years later, as he faced the firing squad, Colonel Aureliano Buendía was to remember that distant afternoon when his father took him to discover ice"; *OHY* 11). Just as in Marcel Proust's *Recherches du temps perdu*, in which a *madeleine* transported Marcel backward through time and space, through the memories it evoked, so in *Cien años* characters are freed from a single ordering or sequencing of reality through multidimensional or nonsynchronic memory. Objects take on additional meanings as they trigger unconscious responses. In his study of collage and montage in the works of early modernist poets, Andrew Clearfield writes that sequences can unfold in three ways, through logical, temporal, and spatial order. The first involves causality, conjunction, exclusion, or inclusion; the second involves chronology; the third involves grammatical or visual similarity or dissimilarity (7). In the context of border syntax, the three are combined and mutually disrupted in a fourth: holographic ordering. Holographic ordering proceeds by association across a cultural border. This is most clearly seen in the border trope, which is characterized by a turning away from the addressee. In terms of the border machine, holographic ordering is a desiring vector propelled both North and South.

The Border Machine

In "Aesthetic Formulation," Paul de Man writes about Kleist's essay "Über das Marionettentheater," in which one character, C, argues that mechanical puppets are more graceful than live dancers (267). Kleist argues that self-consciousness inhibits freedom of action. Puppets have no motion themselves; they are connected to the puppetmaster through a series of lines. Both are controlled by the text. The "quantified systems of motion" in this series of lines—the text—are tropes (286). In terms of the border model, this text is the border machine. The quantified systems of motion are border tropes, which emerge across a border between two systems of quantification. The dance/trap described by de Man can also be seen, in terms of Deleuze and Guattari's reading of Kafka, as a form of deterritorialization, a rhizome of bicultural tropes:

> The memorable tropes that have the most success (*Beifall*) occur as mere random improvisation (*Einfall*) at the moment when the author has completely relinquished any control over his meaning and has relapsed (*Zurückfall*) into the extreme formalization, the mechanical predictability of grammatical declensions (*Fälle*). But *Fälle*, of course, also means in German "trap," the trap which is the ultimate textual model of all texts, the trap of an aesthetic education which inevitably confuses dismemberment of language by the power of the letter with the gracefulness of a dance. This dance, regardless of whether it occurs as mirror, as imitation, as history, as the fencing match of interpretation, or as the anamorphic transformation of tropes, is the ultimate trap, as unavoidable as it is deadly. (290)

Thus, the marionette occupies two sides of a border, the borders between life/death, pathos/levity, and rising/falling. This privileging of the mechanical over human is analogous to José Arcadio Buendía's fascination with technology and mechanical toys. In Kleist's essay, a bear is argued to be the intermediary form between the lifeless puppet and the omnipotent god. In *Cien años*, Ursula functions as the intermediary form between the lifeless puppet, Colonel Arcadio Buendía tied to a tree, and the omnipotent god, revealed in Melquíades's text. Paradoxically, "gracefulness is directly associated with dead," because "articulated puppets can rightly be said to be dead, hanging and suspended like dead bodies" (287). This is the unavoidable and deadly border crossing that anyone who cannot bear the confines of the Oedipal must enter.

What are the effects of the border machine, with its *pollos, coyotes*, the *migra*, contraband, and so forth, on everyday life? In his article on border aesthetics and border identity, Nestor García Canclini mentions Michel de Certeau, who taught in San Diego during the last years of his life. He recalls an article in which de Certeau described California:

> . . . en California la mezcla de inmigrantes mexicanos, colombianos, noruegos, rusos, italianos y del Este de los EE.UU. hacía pensar que "la vida consiste en pasar constantemente fronteras." (10)[7]

[. . . in California, the mix of Mexicans, Colombians, Norwegians, Russians, Italians, and Easterners makes one think that "life consists in constantly crossing borders."]

Does the border machine affect everyone in the same way? García Canclini, commenting on de Certeau's view that life consists in the constant crossing of borders, points out that this crossing is much more difficult for Chicanos, African-Americans, and Puerto Ricans (11, note 6). Furthermore, is not every-day life itself the other side of a "border" between "significant" events, such as revolutionary activity, and "insignificant" events, such as milking cows? In *Cien años* we see the fantastic contradictions of colonialism or the relationship between developed and underdeveloped countries in the unreal elements of everyday life. The embryonic border machine enters into a culture in camouflage, as a magical object. Once it has disarmed everyone, it makes its new home in their everyday lives. Their sense of time changes, as they must allow for the time it takes to "cross the border." A new sense of time is created. It takes two forms: nonsyn-chrony and nostalgia. For the Anglo, the unreal is an anachronism preserved as the repressed in the unconscious. Not only is it what appears to the Anglo, who has lost a relationship to the past, to be the "magical" in "magic realism"; it is also what constitutes the negative space around what appears to the Latin American, who desires a relationship to the future, to be "magical" in technology.[8]

The reader's first contact with the marvelous in everyday life in *Cien años* is in the transformation of the village with the arrival of the gypsies. When José Arcadio Buendía is at the fair, looking at the wonders the gypsies have brought— parrots reciting Italian arias, a multiple-use machine that could sew on buttons or reduce fevers, an apparatus to make bad memories disappear—the narrator tells us that "José Arcadio Buendía hubiera querido inventar la máquina de la memoria para poder acordarse de todas" (*CA* 22) ("José Arcadio Buendía must have wanted to invent a memory machine so that he could remember them all"; *OHY* 24). In other words, the marvelous is linked to technology. The mere per-ception of technology involves the crossing of a psychic border and entrance into the border machine. To listen to the parrot reciting Italian arias is to become a *pollo*; the price paid to the *coyote* is the unbroken relationship to the past. Pietro Crespi provides another route of access to technology, in addition to that of the gypsies, in the form of "las cajas de música, los monos acróbatas, . . . la rica y asombrosa fauna mecánica" (*CA* 70) ("music boxes, acrobatic mon-keys, . . . the rich and startling mechanical fauna"; *OHY* 77) that he brings to the house of José Arcadio Buendía. The latter is distraught over the death of Mel-quíades and lives in "un paraíso de animales destripados, de mecanismos deshechos, tratando de perfeccionarlos con un sistema de movimiento continuo fundado en los principios del péndulo" (*CA* 70) ("a paradise of disemboweled animals, of mechanisms that had been taken apart in an attempt to perfect them

with a system of perpetual motion based upon the principles of the pendulum";
OHY 77–78).

The semes of technology in *Cien años* include the telescope and a magnifying
glass. The infusion of these new signifiers into the social text disrupts the existing
semiotic system. The border machine engulfs all pre-existing meanings, which
now must be "remembered." Before the intrusion of technology, the inhabitants
of Macondo used certain objects in their everyday lives and there was no possibility of "forgetting." With the disruption of everyday life, however, the link between an object and its use is broken. José Arcadio Buendía foresees the possibility that the use of things may someday be forgotten, so he sets out to label objects
around the village (*CA* 47, *OHY* 53). Before the entrance of technology, in the
era of "the collective assemblage of enunciation," there was no need for a statement such as *"This is a cow."* Only when the cow, or the banana, is no longer
itself but a commodity, does the sign "This is . . . " appear.

As García Canclini pointed out, not all border residents find border crossing
as easy as others. Not all *pollos* respond to the experience of crossing the border
in the same way; the responses, therefore, are nonsynchronous. Some choose to
return; others fall by the wayside. In some, there is a gesture toward "reterritorialization." In *Kafka*, Deleuze and Guattari develop a model of desire to discuss
reterritorialization in their juxtaposition of sound against the photograph. In *Cien
años*, an example is a family photograph, which stops desire and which one experiences lost in nostalgia. Fernanda embodies reterritorialization. In terms of the
border, the border crosser is involved in "deterritorialization" by crossing the border, but in "reterritorialization" to the extent that she or he clings to nostalgic images on the other side.

García Márquez records these effects, the differences in the responses of his
character to progress. José Arcadio Buendía is fascinated by technology. Rebeca,
the orphan who married José Arcadio, retreats into the past, evidenced by her attempt to pay for the restoration of her house with coins that have been withdrawn
from circulation. García Márquez tells us that the wife of Aureliano Segundo
"empezaba a hacer una mala madurez con sus sombrías vestiduras talares, sus
medallones anacrónicos y su orgullo fuera de lugar" (*CA* 218) ("was entering into
a sad maturity with her somber long dresses, her old-fashioned medals, and her
out-of-place pride"; *OHY* 238). At the same time, "la concubina [Petra] parecía
reventar en una segunda juventud, embutida en vistosos trajes de seda natural y
con los ojos atigrados por la candela de la reivindicación" (*CA* 218) ("the concu-
bine [Petra] seemed to be bursting with a second youth, clothed in gaudy dresses
of natural silk and with her eyes tiger-striped with a glow of vindication"; *OHY*
238).

At the end of the novel, Pilar Ternera, the fortune teller, is 145 years old, so
she is able to have a view of history and the family that begins with José Arcadio
Buendía and ends with her friendship with Aureliano, the father of the child with

the pig's tail. Her exaggerated age emphasizes the nonsynchronous elements in the novel, the many disruptions in linear time, and the disparate experiences of time in the characters.

The Border Family: Becoming-Animal

That *Cien años* should end with an orphan as the father of the last in the line — because Aureliano is an orphan until he discovers his identity — is a metaphor for the entire narrative structure of the novel. García Márquez has agreed that his book can be reduced to the following: "It is just the story of the Buendía family, of whom it is prophesied that they shall have a son with a pig's tail: and in doing everything to avoid this, the Buendías do end up with a son with a pig's tail" ("Interview," 74). This is reminiscent of the story of Oedipus, who did everything he could to avoid the prophecy, only to fulfill it. At the end of *Cien años* we are introduced to a character who has no idea who he is. Aureliano, the son of Meme, is able to construct his identity only by resorting to a reading of a text, his family history. His identity emerges from the history of incest. Thus, García Márquez challenges the notion not only of the unified subject, but also of the Oedipal family structure. This is a border family: as Deleuze and Guattari argue in *Kafka*, schizo incest results in becoming-animal (35–37).

In *Anti-Oedipus*, Deleuze and Guattari state that "the unconscious is an orphan, and produces within itself the identity of nature and man" (48). The transgression of the incest taboo is a product of the desire of the unconscious. This taboo itself is a result of the repression of a desire produced in the unconscious. Macondo was built upon this transgression: José Arcadio Buendía and Ursula Iguarán were married, in spite of the fact that they were first cousins. The fear of the grotesque, associated with the breaking of the taboo — the prophecy of the birth of a child with a pig's tail who will be devoured by ants — is manifested as reality when the child of Meme and Aureliano, related as aunt and nephew, is born. Unconscious desire, unable to be repressed, is accompanied by fear and an image — the child with a pig's tail. This image, a fiction, finally materialized. The child that is a result of incest is a border child.

Several passages in *Cien años* link smell and deterritorialization, or becoming-animal. The smell of the devil is linked to the memory of Melquíades in the mind of Ursula (*CA* 13, *OHY* 16). Aureliano finds Remedios "convertida en un pantano sin horizontes, olorosa a animal crudo y a ropa recién planchada" (*CA* 65) ("changed into a swamp without horizons, smelling of a raw animal and recently ironed clothes"; *OHY* 71). Pietro Crespi arrives "precedido de un fresco hálito de espliego" (*CA* 70) ("preceded by a cool breath of lavender"; *OHY* 77). Deleuze and Guattari also link homosexuality to their notion of deterritorialization (*Kafka*, 69). Two examples in *Cien años* are Pietro Crespi and José Arcadio. Pietro

Crespi is considered gay by José Arcadio because of his tight clothes. José Arcadio is attended by children who bring him hot towels, polish his nails, and perfume him with toilet water. His house is transformed into "un paraíso decadente" (*CA* 314) ("a decadent paradise"; *OHY* 342). These children kill him in order to get three sacks of gold. He is found floating "en los espejos perfumados de la alberca" (*CA* 317) ("on the perfumed mirror of the pool"; *OHY* 346).

In *Kafka*, Deleuze and Guattari argue that the process of becoming animal takes generations, as it does in *Cien años*: "the becoming-animal lets nothing remain of the duality of a subject of enunciation and a subject of the statement; rather, it constitutes a single process, a unique method that replaces subjectivity" (36). The text discovered at the end of *Cien años* similarly dissolves the distinction between the subject of enunciation and the subject of the statement; it is a "collective assemblage of enunciation." Deleuze and Guattari further argue that Kafka's "Metamorphosis" is "the story of a re-Oedipalization that leads him [Gregor] into death, that turns his becoming-animal into a becoming-dead" (36).

Each of the characters in *Cien años* is controlled by the text of Melquíades. Aureliano knows that he will never leave the room after he reads Melquíades's text, because "estaba previsto que la ciudad de los espejos (o los espejismos) sería arrasada por el viento y desterrada de la memoria de los hombres en el instante en que Aureliano Babilonia acabara de descifrar los pergaminos . . . " (*CA* 351) ("it was foreseen that the city of mirrors [or mirages] would be wiped out by the wind and exiled from the memory of men at the precise moment when Aureliano Babilonia would finish deciphering the parchments . . . "; *OHY* 383).

In terms of the border model, the *coyote* is the puppetmaster and the *pollo* is the puppet. Both are controlled by U.S. immigration policies, quotas, and the larger social text that articulates the relationship between the two countries. As Freud has made evident, for the unconscious there is no difference between reality and fiction. The unconscious in *Cien años* propels the narrative at two levels: first, by displacement or deterritorialization of time and space through memory; and second, in the final determination in the identity of the character.

After reconsidering the term "magic realism" in the context of *Cien años*, what conclusions can we reach? Is Macondo half real, half magic, partly developed, or partly underdeveloped? Do the elements that appear to be marvelous actually mark those points of resistance to the intrusion of technology? Might not "magic realism" be another name for the documentation of cultural domination? Those nonsynchronous elements we have found—women who refuse to respect the currency or fashion of the period—are they not articulating cultural codes that have defied technology and outside influences? Perhaps we have the whole thing backward. What could be more irrational than a banana plantation that takes the wealth out of the country where it is located? The only justification for such activity is imperialism. In this context, which group is more bizarre, the inhabitants of Macondo or the U.S. owners of the banana plantation?

Is *Cien años* a border text? Certainly it contains a special kind of "magic," a "circle of power" or a space of resistance that strategically displaces the conscious narrative structures of the reader such that in the act of reading, a remembering occurs: in memory, past knowledge is preserved. The form of memory depends on the reader; it can be nostalgic or historical. To view Latin America as "other" is to view it with nostalgia. From a holographic perspective, the need in Macondo to label objects arose out of the new "deterritorialized" reference beam (referential code) that coincided with the arrival of the gypsies. Just as the residents of Macondo had to learn new referential codes, so may the Anglo reader become aware of the referential codes she or he is lacking. *Cien años* may be a "realist" or "historical" novel in that it documents the mistreatment of workers by plantation owners and registers the cultural effects of technology. The term "border" or "multidimensional" can embrace both of these; border writing re-presents and translates from a multiplicity of perspectives.

Chapter 2
Beyond the Subject:
From the Territorialized to the
Deterritorialized Text

The Multidimensional Gaze: From Asco to Action

If writing is always a rereading, is not reading always a rewriting? Such a question points up the context in which border writing must be approached as a process of negotiation. If part of the "meaning" of a text may exist in the difference between the conscious and unconscious reference codes of the author and those of the reader, without excluding the logic or narrative strategies of the text itself, then the problem of the relationship of art and politics can be reformulated. This approach makes it possible to see how the work emerges from an interference pattern created by the interaction of the illusory referential codes of the writer and the sociohistorical semiotic context. As a result the reader is understood to interact with the text by (1) adopting some of the illusory referential codes presented in the logic of the text as short-term referential codes, and (2) retaining referential codes that are different from those of the author. Thus a text is created that differs from the one understood by the author. It follows that the politically committed artist can be understood best by a reading that is willing to engage in a kind of border crossing, that is, a critical consideration of the nonidentities between the referential codes of the writer, the reader, and the sociohistorical semiotic context.

In this chapter, I consider Jean-Paul Sartre's *La nausée*, Julio Cortázar's *Rayuela*, and Luisa Valenzuela's "Cambio de armas" because each confronts the decision to be engaged or to make a commitment, even if this engagement only takes the form of throwing the notion of commitment into question. These texts will be considered in terms of three characteristics of border writing, a writing that is (1) deterritorialized, (2) political, and (3) a product of collective enunciation.

Part of Cortázar's struggle with the notion of commitment was certainly shaped by his relationship to existentialism. The importance of existentialism, particularly Sartre's, was considerable in Latin America. Cortázar was profoundly impressed by *La nausée*, and in his review of the Spanish translation that appeared in 1948, he wrote in *Cabalgato*: "Hoy que solo las formas aberrantes de la reacción y la cobardia pueden continuar subestimando la tremenda presentación del existencialismo" ("Today only the aberrant forms of reaction [in sense of reactionary] and cowardice can continue underestimating the tremendous appearance of existentialism"). Sartre is not a deterritorialized writer, although he may have been searching for the "Third World zones" within his culture; Cortázar and Valenzuela are. Born in Brussels, Cortázar spent most of his life outside his own country, Argentina, living in Paris. Argentine writer Valenzuela currently lives in New York. I would like to address the subject-object relation in the work of these three writers. I do this believing that, like the continuing debates surrounding the "death" of painting in relation to other art forms, the debates surrounding the subjectivity of the non-white male remain significant. Roquentin, the protagonist in *La nausée*, cannot escape his sense of nausea before the object; Horacio, in *Rayuela*, is a transitional figure in this context, a decentered subject, but unable to take action; Laura, in "Cambio de armas," is able to "return the gaze" and to take action. Roquentin's "deterritorialization" exists in terms of his marginalization within his own culture, but he is neither able to cross over into political activity nor capable of understanding his "enunciation" in relation to collective enunciation. In this context, I will argue that the border texts of Cortázar and Valenzuela demand a different response from the reader from that demanded by the territorialized text. Technology produces a kind of deterritorialization of signification as well. The written labels on objects in Macondo were a result of the entrance of technology into the culture. Toward the end of this chapter, I will discuss technology and some of the cultural responses to it, including Cortázar's comic book *Fantomas contra los vampiros multinacionales*.

Valenzuela's "Cambio de armas" could be understood merely as a love story if the reader were not aware of the political context within which it was written, that is, if it is not understood as a border text. Margo Glantz's explanation of the image of the weapon in this story in terms of the look or the gaze is relevant in understanding the border gaze (the deterritorialized gaze). Glantz writes that "las armas están en la mirada desorbitada que busca con desesperación un reflejo" (The weapons [in *Other Weapons*] are in this case in the expression of the face that desperately searches for a reflection). Her observation is interesting in the light of Lacan's assertion that the true aim of seeing is not visual but a function in a largely unconscious discourse that can be glimpsed in the Gaze, the functioning of the whole system of shifts.[1] The functioning of the "whole system," that is, a double, or a multidimensional, critical view of power relations, is what the border crosser needs to develop in order to survive.

Jameson, in "On Magic Realism and Film," writes that in "magic realist" texts, the "libidinal apparatus separates objects" whereas the postmodernist text creates "images of simulacra of the past," that is, "a pseudo-past for consumption as compensation for a different kind of past" (312). In capitalism the problem is that the "scopic consumption of the veil has itself become the object of desire" (312). Valenzuela must fight this in the reader; she does it by presenting a different libidinal ordering.

What shifts occur in the codes in "Cambio de armas"? After the torturer's initial monitoring of Laura's activities, Laura begins to watch him through her concept—her hole, specifically, her vagina. In this altered relationship to her body, which registers political change directly, Laura experiences the world. In this, her life resembles that of the border crosser, whose fate is directly determined by the relationship between two political powers. In her essay "The Rhetoric of the Body," Nelly Richard writes:

> The body is the physical agent of the structures of everyday experience.
> It is the producer of dreams, the transmitter and receiver of cultural
> messages, a creature of habits, a desiring machine, a repository of
> memories, an actor in the theatre of power, a tissue of affects and feel-
> ings. Because the body is at the boundary between biology and society,
> between drives and discourse, between the sexual and its categorisation
> in terms of power, biography and history, it is the site par excellence
> for transgressing the constraints of meaning or what social discursivity
> prescribes as normality. (65)

Laura's deterritorialized or holographic body slowly overcomes her amnesia; object by object, she rebuilds her past.

In his article "Lacan, Poe and Narrative Repression," Robert Con Davis explains that according to Lacan's reading of Freud, one position must be cancelled or repressed in the act of watching/being watched (985). Three scenes of looking can be distinguished in Valenzuela's novel *Cola de lagartija*. In the first, Luisa attempts to establish mastery. Next, the sorcerer watches her. Finally, Navoni watches the sorcerer. The chain continues as Luisa observes the process, and we, the reader, observe her observing. In *Cola de lagartija*, the active reader is challenged to stare back. In "Cambio de armas," the chain is broken and this model is no longer adequate. The revolutionary/shaman puts on the mask and removes herself from the chain of watchers and those watched.

The notion of the "active gaze" can be contrasted with that of the revolutionary/shaman. The protagonist of *Libro de Manuel*, whom Jaime Alazraki in his essay "Cortázar—Towards the Last Square of the Hopscotch," calls "a sort of outgrowth of Horacio Oliveira," attempts to go beyond the decision of Horacio and to engage in political concerns. The Serpent Club is replaced by a group of persons interested in politics; women are no longer silent nor are they excluded. As Jean Franco points out in *An Introduction to Spanish American Literature*, Cortázar himself describes the reader of *Rayuela* as an "espectador activo" (328). Using Barthes's terminology from *S/Z*, Cortázar insists that *Rayuela* is a writerly text. *La nausée* is not a writerly text; "Cambio de armas" certainly is.

The problem of the relationship between art and politics, the writer and her or his political commitment, must be radically recast in the case of "Cambio de armas." A twentieth-century First World starting point in the discussion might be Bertolt Brecht. In *Brecht: The Man and His Work*, Martin Esslin claims that Brecht's politics were either destructive to his artistic work or irrelevant to it. Another viewpoint was held by Sartre, whose work centered on the problem of what he called, in *Critique of Dialectical Reason*, "engagement." For him, freedom consisted in taking responsibility, that is, of engaging oneself in the world. This perspective is more applicable to Valenzuela's work, but it is still inadequate, although it may provide some insight in relation to Anglo referential codes.

In the case of Valenzuela, the word has been doubly wounded, first, by the political repressive discourse of the fascist regime, and second, by the mass media. The facilities of perception on the part of the North American reader have been truncated by the absence of political debate in the United States and by the media. Valenzuela intends to cure the word, her country, and the reader. She is successful to the extent that the reader is able to consider the interaction of these various referential codes. For example, López Rega is an actual historical figure who in fact predicted that in the 1970s, a river of dry blood would run beneath the Argentine pampa; when he came into power, there was a river of fresh blood.[2] This historical referential code is probably unfamiliar to the Anglo reader, who has less access to information about Latin America through the mass media.

In his model, Sartre places the subject in the situation of having to find its way out of the practico-inert, as he will call it in *Critique of Dialectical Reason*, and into conscious political activity. For the woman in "Cambio de armas," the question of conscious political activity is meaningless. Instead, the reader must consider the notion of agency with a stronger link to Argentine history than to the European subject.

Border Subject/Speaking Subject

The border "subject" is a "body with organs" operating within the border machine, with its *pollos, coyotes, migra*, and contraband.[3] I will discuss the work of Sartre, Cortázar, and Valenzuela in terms of the border "subject" and the reversal of the subject-object relationship. Cortázar will be a transition in this mapping, between Sartre (self-other) and Valenzuela (the return of the gaze). The "subject" in border writing, however, can no longer be conceived as a unified subject nor a subject who thinks it is acting on its own. We must remember that the subject, as defined by European-based philosophy, labors under the illusion of acting on its own. I will discuss the work of Sartre, Cortázar, and Valenzuela from the perspective of the speaking "subject," the subject who has returned the gaze. Such a notion of the subject functions as a prototype of "engagement," one in which there can be neither a unified subject nor a subject who thinks it is acting on its own. The introjection of the social order, experienced as the taking of personal responsibility for the alienation inflicted upon the social individual by the socioeconomic system in its highly mediated and complex operations, results in the salient and related phenomena in European thought in the twentieth century. And yet, the literature of the Third World provides indisputable evidence that a new formulation of the subject is still necessary.

Even the "unified" subject was in fact a fissured one. First, in the realm of psychoanalysis, we find Freud's positing of the death wish in *Beyond the Pleasure Principle*. Otto Rank, in *The Double*, interprets the death wish for the brother as a wish for self-punishment as well. This is the basis, in part, of the double phenomenon in European literature, which René Girard explores in *Deceit, Desire and the Novel*. Second, in the realm of European philosophy, the Sartre of *La nausée* sees the human experience of absurdity and nausea as leading to inaction. Third, language is increasingly seen as the "house wherein man [*Mensch*] dwells" and in which she/he is the "guardian" (Kern, 108). Authenticity and proximity to Being are equated, and, in the work of Heidegger, their accomplishment is to bring about the uncovering of the Truth of language and the Truth of Being.[4]

These metaphors must be seen as a response to the development of capitalism and the ripening of the technological age as well as to the reenactment or reformulation of the subject-object dichotomy that is fundamental in Western thought. The former, in its tendency to result in the reification of the subject, actually exacerbates the latter. Ironically, even the European critiques of this dichotomy have only served to reify the subject even further.

The problem of alienation presents itself in Cortázar's work in the form of the alienation of Horacio from Argentina, instanced metaphorically in a physical being, Traveler. The self-other problematic Horacio experiences with La Maga remains characterized by his constitution of her as other. Sartre likewise holds to the inevitability of the other as alterity. Neither he nor Cortázar conceptualizes fragmentation and alterity within a logic of nonidentity. In Sartre's model, the subject has to find its way out of the practico-inert and into conscious political activity. But in resigning themselves to the forms of appearance, i.e., fragmentation, neither Horacio nor Roquentin is able to find a way out. For the woman in "Cambio de armas," on the other hand, the question of conscious political activity has itself become meaningless. Instead, the reader must consider the notion of agency with a stronger link to history than to the set of categories specified under the European concept of subjectivity. Laura alone among these characters, through remembering, is able to act and thus to embrace her freedom. Valenzuela creates an ideal speech situation: Laura, Roque, and the reader.

Although *La nausée*, *Rayuela*, and "Cambio de armas" may be seen as different points on a scale between politically committed art and art for art's sake, what links them is their juxtaposition of the codes of isolated individual and political commitment. Laura, through memory, achieves a new epistemological relationship to the world and embraces her freedom. In *Rayuela*, on the other hand, Horacio is invited by Ronald to engage in "unas confusas actividades políticas" (*Rayuela* 473) ("some vaguely political activities"; *Hopscotch* 425).[5] This invitation leads to an argument about action and passivity; through labyrinthine rationalizations Horacio finally discovers himself to be an onlooker. He questions the morality of action and recalls certain communists in Buenos Aires and Paris who were "capable of the worst villainy," but redeemed themselves "in their own minds," at least, by "*la lucha*," who had "to leave in the middle of dinner to run to a meeting" or to finish a political task (*Hopscotch* 425). He says that the trouble all began because he wanted to be an "espectador activo" (*Rayuela* 476) ("active onlooker"; *Hopscotch* 425).

These categories and their interrelations can be seen to break down completely in the discourse of torture in Latin America, a discourse in which the interrogator violates the body in order to get truth. Valenzuela acknowledges this fact in "Cambio de armas" by presenting metaphors based on the body, specifically on the relationship between the mind and the body of the woman, which suggest a new theory of knowledge not encompassed within the received understanding of the term "epistemology." In "Cambio de armas," the relationship between the decentered subject and the object is a surreal environment until, because of a shift in the historical context, Laura is able to remember. Furthermore, the notion of a self-conscious subject is inadequate in the case of Laura since her ability to act is the function of a change that takes place outside of the room where she has been held prisoner. In this way agency and history are inextricably linked in her act. Laura's relationship to history is mediated by, or rather negotiated with, agency.

In her book *Sexual/Textual Politics*, Toril Moi discusses Julia Kristeva's belief that the way out of the prison house of language is to become the speaking subject. This strategy is particularly relevant in the consideration of the Anglo woman reader, who in fundamental ways has been excluded from speech; further, she has been excluded from dialogue with women in Latin America. It is instructive to compare the case of the "banned citizens" in South Africa in the 1980s with the case of many women in the United States. The "banned citizen" was prohibited from speech except to her or his spouse. Many North American women still enact a bizarre version of this type of arrangement with their mates. They speak for the most part only to their husbands, thereby restricting their interaction with the world. It would be necessary for them to speak to more people in order to gain confidence and knowledge; however, this is forbidden. In fact, part of what attracts the husband in the first place is a woman's willingness to accept this arrangement, one which results in a de facto ban on speech outside the domestic sphere.

Hegelian and Hegelian-Marxist Models

In his commentary on Hegel's *Phenomenology* in *Introduction to the Reading of Hegel*, Alexandre Kojève writes:

> What reveals and realizes freedom, according to Hegel, is the fight for pure prestige, carried on without any biological necessity for the sake of recognition alone. But the Fight reveals and realizes freedom only to the extent that it implies the risk to life—that is, the real possibility of dying. . . . The fight for pure prestige, moreover, is a *suicide* (whose outcome depends on chance), as Hegel says in the Lectures at Jena of 1805–1806 (vol. XX, p. 211, the last three lines): "it appears [to each adversary, taken] as external consciousness, that he is going to the *death* of another, but he is going to his own [death]; [it is] a suicide, to the extent that he [voluntarily] exposes himself to danger." . . . The fact that the adversaries remain alive subjects them to the *necessities* of existence; but this necessity passes in the Slave (who rejected the Risk), whereas the Master (who accepted it) remains free: in his work, the Slave undergoes the laws of the siren; but the idle Master, who consumes products already "humanized" by work, prepared for Man, no longer undergoes the constraint of Nature (in principle, of course). It could also be said that the Master is actually humanly dead in the Fight: he no longer *acts*, strictly speaking, since he remains idle; therefore, he lives as if he were dead; that is why he does not evolve anymore in the course of History and is simply annihilated at its end: his existence is a simple "afterlife" (which is limited in time) or a "deferred death." The Slave progressively frees himself through work which *manifests* his freedom by creating through victory the universal and homogeneous State of which he will be the "recognized" Citizen. (248)

Hegelian-Marxist categories may be historically necessary in understanding the problem of the relationship between the master and the slave in political discourse, both in Europe and Latin America, but they are ultimately inadequate in understanding the structure of the relationship between Laura and her captor in "Cambio de armas." Of course, as long as Laura remains content in her bondage, she can never be free, and it is true that she appears to resist the knowledge that would help her to remember, preferring again and again to forget. Thus it is necessary that Laura's act emerge from a conjuncture of history and agency, not from her deliberation as a self-conscious subject.

In *La nausée*, on the other hand, it is Being that constitutes the bridge between self and other, subject and object, human and nature. Being, however, becomes a third rather than a bridge. The alienated relation of Roquentin to nature is apparent in the following passage:

> Impossible de voir les choses de cette façon-là. Des mollesses, des faiblesses, oui. Les arbres flottaient. Un jaillissement vers le ciel? Un affalement plutôt; à chaque instant je m'attendais à voir les troncs se rider comme des verges lasses, se recroqueviller et choir sur le sol en un tas noir et mou avec des plis. *Ils n'avaient pas envie* d'exister, seulement ils ne pouvaient pas s'en empêcher; voilà. Alors ils faisaient toutes leurs petites cuisines, doucement, sans entrain; la sève montait lentement dans les vaisseaux à contre-coeur, et les racines s'enfonçaient lentement dans la terre. Mais ils semblaient à chaque instant sur le point de tout planter là et de s'anéantir. Las et vieux, ils continuaient d'exister, de mauvaise grâce, simplement parce qu'ils étaient trop faibles pour mourir, parce que la mort ne pouvait leur venir que de l'extérieur: il n'y a que les airs de musique pour porter fièrement leur propre mort en soi comme une nécessité interne, seulement ils n'existent pas. Tout existant naît sans raison, se prolonge par faiblesse et meurt par rencontre. Je me laissai aller en arrière et je fermai les paupières. Mais les images, aussitôt alertées, bondirent et vinrent remplir d'existences mes yeux clos: l'existence est un plein que l'homme ne peut quitter. (169)[6]

> [Impossible to see things that way. Weaknesses, frailties, yes. The trees floated. Gushing towards the sky? Or rather collapse: at any instant I expected to see the tree trunks shrivel like weary wands, crumple up, fall on the ground in a soft, folded black heap. They did not want to exist, only they could not help themselves. So they quietly minded their own business; the sap rose up slowly through the structure, half reluctant, and the roots sank slowly into the earth. But at each instant they seemed on the verge of leaving everything there and obliterating themselves. Tired and old, they kept on existing, against the grain, simply because they were too weak to die, because death could only come to them from the outside: strains of music alone can proudly carry their own death within themselves like an internal necessity: only they don't exist. Every existing this is born without reason, prolongs itself out of weakness and dies by chance. I leaned back and closed my eyes. But the images, forewarned, immediately leaped up and filled my closed eyes with existences: existence is a fullness which man can never abandon. (*Nausea* 133)]

Here Roquentin has generalized his own state of consciousness by displacing it onto the trees and to all that exists. His relationship to nature can be contrasted with that of the Slave who frees herself or himself through labor.

Sartre attended Kojève's lectures at the École des Hautes Études in Paris in the 1930s. *La nausée* was written in 1938; the quoted passage of Kojève was delivered as part of the lecture of the academic year 1934–35. Not only *La nausée*, but *Being and Nothingness* as well is indebted to Kojève's lectures. It is clear from the cited passage that Roquentin has diverged from Kojève's Marxist reading of Hegel; instead of identifying the proletariat with the bondsperson, praxis with risking life, and then placing himself on the side of the bondsperson, Roquentin identifies with the lord, and attributes to the trees his own feeling of living as if he were dead. Roquentin recalls with contempt the idiots who speak of willpower and struggle for life.

In fact, it is not the trees, but rather Roquentin who does not want to exist. He is like the Master who is "actually humanly dead in the Fight: he no longer acts, strictly speaking, since he remains idle; therefore, he lives as if he were dead." Why does Roquentin attribute to the trees an inability to either commit suicide or to live? Why does he claim they are too tired to exist? As Hegel says in the passage from the Lectures of Jena, the Fight involves a choice to go to one's own death, which is tantamount to suicide. But the Fight implies a risking of life, whose outcome depends on chance. This is a different kind of chance from that of which Roquentin speaks when he says everything dies by chance. Kojève refers to a chance that comes into play after a decision to act. Why Roquentin would attribute certain of his own characteristics to a tree can only be understood by considering his social position.

Roquentin is an academic, a historian who says of himself: "Moi je vis seul, entièrement seul. Je ne parle à personne, jamais; je ne reçois rien, je ne donne rien" (*La nausée* 18) ("I live alone, entirely alone. I never speak to anyone, never; I receive nothing, I give nothing"; *Nausea* 6). He lives as if he were in a marginalized position in regard to the production of goods and services in the economic system in which he lives. But as a historian doing research, a member of a university faculty, he is in the process of producing a book. We know that the university itself depends on the exchange value of professors who increase their value by publishing and that the exchange of ideas is subject to the laws of the marketplace. But Roquentin perceives himself to be outside of the processes of exchange, superfluous to the carryings-on of the capitalist system in which human activities for the reproduction of daily needs and the sustenance of the system are inscribed. As far as he is concerned, he gives nothing and he takes nothing. He mistakes the irreducibility of his life to the processes of exchange for the mere lack of any personal relationships. Just as Marx notes in *Capital* that Robinson Crusoe was dependent on social labor for his very survival, although he thought himself alone, Roquentin, from the subjective perspective of his island of consciousness, thinks himself alienated from everyone and everything. At a material level, he consumes in order to exist, but he does not partake in the production of the objects of his consumption except in a highly mediated way. At the epistemological level, he fails to understand that his perception of the object before him, even the tree, rests on the human activity and labor of previous generations.

Roquentin's physical activity consists in little else besides going to cafes, sitting in the library, and collecting dividends. Thus, at the end of *La nausée*, he is able to conclude:

> Trente ans! Et 14.400 francs de rente. Des coupons à toucher tous les mois. Je ne suis pourtant pas un vieillard! Qu'on me donne quelque chose à faire, n'importe quoi . . . Il vaudrait mieux que je pense à autre chose, parce que, en ce moment, je suis en train de me jouer la comédie. Je sais très bien que je ne veux rien faire: faire quelque chose, c'est créer de l'existence—et il y a bien assez d'existence comme ça. (216)
>
> [Thirty years! And 14,400 francs in the bank. Coupons to cash every month. Yet I'm not an old man! Let them give me something to do, no matter what . . . I'd better think about something else, because I'm playing a comedy now. I know very well that I don't want to do anything: to do something is to create existence—and there's quite enough existence as it is. (*Nausea* 173)]

Rather than looking at his own social position, he forgets that the object is produced by human activity and takes a detour from the movement toward self-consciousness by ascribing characteristics to the tree rather than risking life. He chooses to remain inside his own consciousness rather than to act. In this avoidance, there is the play of Thanatos against Eros. The unconscious element in this detour to death reveals itself in the displacement of his own anxieties onto the tree. The coupon is a sign of the absent bondsperson. Marx describes fetishism in *Capital* in terms of the confusion between the actual social relations between humans and the illusory or fantastic form that hides the actual relations and in which appears instead a relation between things. The actual human relations that have produced the livelihood of Roquentin remain hidden to him because they have been reduced to the coupon, the only visible sign. Roquentin is paralyzed by guilt that he is the lord and not the bondsperson. Yet he was merely born into his position as the Master; he never earned it by risking life. Like the tree, he will not risk life or commit suicide. As a result, freedom remains unrealized, even though he is the Master.

Valenzuela's story presents, on the other hand, the actual displacement of agency from the self-conscious subject by making plain that the gun, as an object against which she constitutes herself as "subject," depends not on her self-conscious awareness of it, as in Roquentin's tree, but rather on the political activities of many other people. In the context of border subjectivity, Laura's act is not that of a self-conscious individual; rather, it arises under specific historical conditions within which she is inscribed.

In "Cambio de armas," Laura risked her life once in a failed attempt to assassinate the man who would become her torturer. As Hegel writes in *The Phenomenology*, only by risking life does the lord become the lord (228–40). Laura did not attain sovereignty. She picked up the gun and aimed only when her life was not in danger, when her oppressor turned his back to her and left. The double aspects of both positions, lord and bondsperson, have been rewritten as sadist and masochist in the Freudian-Lacanian perspective. The scene in which the torturer brings Laura a present, a whip, in order to enhance the eroticism of their sexual relationship, constitutes Valenzuela's comments on the absurdity of sadomaso-chism as an explanatory model in the context of torture. The double aspects of the lord and bondsperson, rewritten as sadist and masochist, provide a dialectical alternative to the subject-object relation in which the other is seen as alterity, but the model is still unable to recuperate Laura.[7]

In the Hegelian model, Laura would be the bondsperson, the one who has the advantage of a privileged relation to work and therefore to knowledge, but suffers from the inability to gain mastery. In *The Phenomenology*, Hegel writes that the bondsperson "affirms itself as unessential, both by working upon the thing, and . . . by the fact of being dependent on a determinate existence; in either case can this other [the bondsman] get mastery over existence, and succeed in absolutely negating it" (236). On the other hand, while the lord enjoys mastery, he suffers from the unhappy consciousness; this is a result of the alienation of his position obtaining from the impossibility of changing, and thus in a material sense, knowing the world through work. This is what tortures the conscience of Laura's torturer. He knows that Laura has a mission. Like the bondsperson, La Maga has knowledge that Horacio does not have. The narrator tells us of La Maga: "Hay ríos metafísicos, ella los nada como esa golondrina está nadando en el aire" (*Rayuela* 116). ("There are metaphysical rivers, she swims in them like that swallow swimming in the air"; *Hopscotch* 106). This relationship between her mind and her body is different from that of Horacio. Yet, their relationship is one of bondage, in which neither receives the recognition both desire.

In "Cambio de armas," Laura does not recognize Roque until the end, and the life and death struggle described by Hegel remains metaphorical. Horacio wants recognition—that of another lord, Traveler—but this recognition is denied him by Traveler. Horacio does get recognition of his position as lord by La Maga, as Roque does by virtue of Laura's subservience. Still, the agony of Horacio is that recognition does not come from an equal. "But for recognition, proper," writes Hegel, "there is needed the moment that what the master does to himself, he should do to the other also. On that account a form of recognition has arisen that is one-sided and unequal" (236). Thus, since recognition must come from an equal, and this is impossible when the source of all recognition may be occupied by one higher than all others, for example, by the shaman/revolutionary—who escapes this system—then the recognition Horacio gets from La Maga, or that Roquentin gets from the Self-Taught Man, is insufficient. The recognition Horacio wants can only come from Traveler.

Talita mediates the relationship between Horacio and Traveler by crossing the bridge (a border) from one to the other. This crossing is significant, first, because at this time Talita understands the relationship between Horacio and Traveler, and second, because she is being-for-other. Horacio is sure she will miss "como todas las mujeres" ("the way women always do") and that the yerba mate and the nails will go all over the street (*Rayuela* 290; *Hopscotch* 258). He seems less concerned with the possibility that she may fall. As in the rest of the novel, she is an object for the two men; in Irigaray's terms, she is being exchanged by two men. Yet both her lords are satisfied with her—Traveler, because she comes back to him, and Oliveira, because she sacrifices herself for him. Thus, the moment of reconciliation for Horacio is when he sees Traveler with his arm around Talita's waist. His brotherhood relationship with Traveler is greater than any desire for totality. The relationship of La Maga and Horacio, and of Horacio and Traveler to Talita, prevents each from knowing the other. As long as Horacio holds La Maga, metaphorically, in bondage, he can never be free. Given the cul-de-sac in which Horacio is left at the end of *Rayuela*, it is no surprise that Cortázar/the narrator adopted a Marxist stance in his next novel, *Libro de Manuel*.

In both Sartre and Cortázar, in the novels under consideration, desire rests on the definition of the other as absolute alterity. In one passage, Horacio thinks to himself that there may be no otherness, only togetherness. The omnipotent narrator breaks in with a revealing discussion of love, which is called "ceremonia ontologizante" (*Rayuela* 120) ("an ontologizing ceremony"; *Hopscotch* 109). For Horacio, the presence of his beloved is not necessary: his love could do without its object and find nourishment in desire alone.

To the Anglo reader, Latin American literature can be dismissed as "magical" because of the relationship between the United States and Latin America, in which the actual human relations that produce the everyday life of the Southern Californian reader, for example, remain hidden because they have been reduced to mass-media stereotypes, the only visible sign. Thus, the complexity of the Mexico-U.S. border is reduced to an image of a place to go on the weekend. The labor provided by Mexican workers is "forgotten" through the stereotype of "undocumented workers" who must be controlled through arrest. The oppression suffered by political exiles from Central America, Chile, and Argentina is "forgotten" through the same media control of strings of signifiers, since all are subject to the threat of arrest under the sign of the illegal crossing of the border. When asked if Laura were not a metaphor for all politically unconscious women, Valenzuela replied that this was the case, and further, that Argentina had forgotten its own history of the 1970s.

From Freud to Irigaray: Oedipus at the Border

The following analysis deploys Freudian categories from Lacanian and Irigarayan perspectives. I will examine the relationship between Annie and Roquentin; two lexia constituting Cortázar's treatment of the Oedipal relation (chapter 5, which describes the lovemaking of La Maga and Horacio, and chapter 28, which recounts the death of Rocamadour); and finally the relationship between Laura and Roque. In the works of all three authors, the categories of Marxism and psychoanalysis are shown to be inadequate in critical study of the women characters.

Annie cannot be understood by Roquentin. She is defined as absolute alterity. Roquentin's attitude before the other and in relation to her is one of fear and discomfort. When he sees Annie after a period of separation, they merely repeat the ritual that maintains their separation: he says he is happy to see her, they quarrel, and the conversation ends with Annie telling him to get out. The narrator tells us that at one time Annie and Roquentin had loved each other. Yet the obsession of the entire novel is the impossibility of overcoming the confines of the self. Roquentin's attempts to overcome this isolation with Annie fail. What remains unexplained is his reaction to the parting, about which he says he did not suffer, but rather, felt emptied out. Annie is much more articulate about her feelings of icy hatred toward him. Not only has he come to mean "une vertu abstraite" (La nausée 174) ("an abstract virtue"; Nausea 137) for her, but he never tried to understand her "moments parfaits" (La nausée 180) ("perfect moments"; Nausea 143). In fact, it is Roquentin who has treated her as an abstraction. When she complains of his condescension toward her, comparing it to the (La nausée 183) ("kindly distrait manner . . . of little old ladies"; Nausea 145) who used to ask her what she was playing when she was a child, she is complaining precisely about his conception of her as absolute alterity.

Annie is given more space to express herself in La nausée than La Maga is given in Rayuela. She vents her anger and ridicules Roquentin's coldness. His categories can never explain her, any more than the Lacanian psychoanalyst semiotics professor can diagnose the problem of the Argentine revolutionary in Valenzuela's Como en la guerra. Roquentin rejects Annie, Horacio fantasizes about killing La Maga, and Roque tortures Laura: Laura may kill him at the end.

With respect to the discussion of La Maga it is crucial to note that historically, Uruguay emerged as a border region between the two largest South American colonies, Argentina and Brazil. Uruguay is the product of two colonizing cultures, Spain and Brazil. It is a country of two languages. It is culturally and geographically situated within the most extreme opposition in South America: Argentina, with a population that is 98% European, and Brazil, with one of the most culturally diverse populations not only in South America but in the world.

La Maga is from Montevideo, which the Argentines established as their center in Uruguayan territory in 1724. From 1810 to 1828, Uruguay and Argentina were one country, fighting against Brazil. It was only after negotiating with Great Britain that Argentina and Brazil agreed to recognize the independence of Uruguay.

Culturally, there are common referential codes between Uruguay and Argentina, such as the *gaucho*, an equally important figure in both countries.

Thus, the relationship between La Maga and Horacio can be understood as a border relationship. Furthermore, it is a deterritorialized relationship, signified by their having become acquainted in Paris. As a result, the relationship displays many features characteristic of an interference pattern between logocentrism and *la otredad* (the otherness). Horacio wishes to cross over into the nonlinear world of La Maga, and she longs to be accepted into his circle of intellectuals, the Serpent Club. The relationship expressed through their lovemaking is that between an intellectual Argentine man who is the product of phallocentric Western culture—with the agonized contradiction between its homosexual Platonic origins and its contemporary heterosexual norms—and a nonintellectual Uruguayan woman. Thus, La Maga is overdetermined by both of these systems: she cannot be a male lover, yet the conditions of heterosexuality in her relationship to Horacio subjugate her to a silent role.

Their relationship is described by the narrator as a possible desire for death on the part of La Maga. This death would make her entrance into the Serpent Club possible. The referential codes here include Aztec sacrifice and Plato's homosexual world of love and knowledge. The link between sex and death also can be found in Plato's *Symposium*. La Maga wants to learn; the semen that goes into her mouth is compared by the narrator to the dissemination of the Logos. She is also compared to an adolescent male, an evocation of homosexuality that in this context suggests the relation of Socrates to his young male students.

How is gender constructed in the description of Horacio and La Maga: "le chupó la sombra del vientre y de la grupa" (*Rayuela* 44) ("he sucked out the shadow from her womb and her rump"; *Hopscotch* 38)? In the opposition between penetration and sucking, and the logical square in which we could place anal penetration and anal sucking as activities in the realm of male homosexuality, this image takes on rich significance. Sucking the rump also recalls the vulture fantasy detailed in Freud's study of Leonardo da Vinci. In "Leonardo da Vinci and a Memory of His Childhood," Freud analyzes Leonardo's fantasy of sucking a vulture's tail. In that analysis, the tail is both the breast of the mother and the penis, and the fantasy is interpreted as pointing to da Vinci's passive homosexuality. The desire arises from the fear and disgust he experiences when he discovers that his mother does not have a penis; he speculates that she has been wounded or castrated.

Luce Irigaray, in *Speculum of the Other Woman*, raises a pertinent question: "If woman had desires other than 'penis envy,' this could call into question the unity, the uniqueness, the simplicity of the mirror charged with sending the man's image back to him" (51). She writes:

> Man would have to be not too horrified and disgusted by his wife, his mother, as a "castrated" creature. Whence his need to go in for anal,

fetishistic overcathexis of his organ, and flight into real or fantasy homosexuality. (76)

In Freudian terms, La Maga is doubly castrated in *Rayuela*: first, she does not possess a penis; second, her manifestation of her desire for the phallus, which is replaced according to Freudian theory, as Irigaray reminds us, by the wish for a baby, is taken from her as well, when Rocamadour dies (73). In Irigaray's terms, however, this castration, grounded by Freud in nature or autonomy, could "equally well be interpreted as the prohibition that enjoins woman—at least in this history—from every imagining, fancying, re-presenting, symbolizing, etc. (and none of these words is adequate, as all are borrowed from a discourse which aids and abets that prohibition) her own relationship to beginning" (83).

The Serpent Club, which refuses La Maga entrance except through the price of death, refuses as well to tell her of Rocamadour's death. The members of the club do not listen to her; nor do they speak to her; nor do they allow her to speak. As a result of these constraints, she is unable to represent herself. Valenzuela points out that the discussion of penis envy avoids the issue that men envy the ability of women to have children.[8] This may provide some clue to the club's behavior. Did, for example, unconscious envy result in the collective murder of Rocamadour by lack of attention of members of the Serpent Club? It is not immediately clear why killing La Maga would allow her in. The narrator tells the reader that in her death she would rise as the phoenix and join the Serpent Club. As a political metaphor, is it only through the obliteration of otherness that the other can enter the realm of European self?

The ambiguity in the relationship of Horacio and La Maga arises in the contradiction in which they are inscribed: as a Latin American nonintellectual woman, La Maga is excluded from the opportunity to obtain specialized philosophical knowledge. On this point it is interesting to remember that Irigaray points out that the exclusion from philosophical discourse proceeds from Plato's allegory of the cave, which depended on the silence of "men carrying burdens" (257). In spite of this cultural determination, Horacio attempts to cross the bridge by giving La Maga knowledge and allowing her into the club; yet he stops midway in his fantasies. Instead of giving her knowledge, he gives her sex, that knowledge "que sólo el hombre puede dar a la mujer" (*Rayuela* 44) ("which only a man can give to a woman"; *Hopscotch* 38). Instead of killing her, which would have allowed her into the club, he merely fantasizes about her death by strangulation. The place of articulation, the throat, must be twisted in order for the articulation of knowledge to occur. This fantasy of the open mouth, dead, dripping with saliva that might still be mixed with semen: in what sense can this La Maga of Horacio's imaginings be said "to know"? In fact, to give La Maga the power of language would be to threaten his own power. If he were to "kill" her, would he be able "a hacerla de verdad suya" (*Rayuela* 45) ("to make her really his"; *Hop-*

scotch 39)? Does he want to "kill" her because he is afraid of her? Why does the narrator tell us that Horacio "la sintió llorar de felicidad" after they make love this way (*Rayuela* 4) ("felt her crying with happiness"; *Hopscotch* 38)? Why is it that the only way "ella podía conseguir encontrarse con èl" is if he kills her (*Rayuela* 45) ("she could get together with him"; *Hopscotch* 39)?

The narrator explains that Horacio does not love La Maga, and that his desire for her will cease. Were he to love in any significant sense, there would be no end to his desire. But Horacio's desire is limited, while La Maga's is not. La Maga wants to learn; she desires philosophical power, not only the power of the phallus. Love and knowledge are linked: Horacio can love only a man, Traveler, one who possesses the phallus. Women will be only replaceable objects of desire.

Irigaray's provocative comparison of shitting to giving birth also allows us to recover an interesting reading of Cortázar. Irigaray writes:

In this [the sexual economy], woman's job is to tend the seed man "gives" her, to watch over the interest of this "gift" deposited with her and to return it to its own in due course. The penis (stool), the sperm (seed-gift), the child (gift), all make up an anal symbolic from which there is no escape. One wonders, ultimately, if the standard underpinning of the system is the penis? The sperm? Or "gold"? Values waver, falter, and the most productive, the most easily representable as (re)productive seems necessarily to carry the way. But, in fact, all these "equivalents" collect interest on the capital invested in the feces, which would remain the standard of value. As for woman, she will be the receptacle for the sperm (gift) injected by the penis (stool) and she forces the child (feces) out through the vagina (rectum). Thus she is apparently party to anal eroticism. But except for her pregnancy, when she makes matter from within her so as to have more jouissance after her delivery (?), woman's roles seem to require only that she detach herself from the anal "object": the gift-child, just as she is required to give up the "fecal column" after coitus. Repeating, thus, her separation from the feces. But without pleasure. (75)

We can conclude, therefore, that the anus in capitalist society is neither the phallus nor its absence; rather, it is entirely incommensurable with the phallus and seeks to order desire in both heterosexual and homosexual relationships. Phallocentrism, as the logic of Oedipal sexuality, is constituted by the phallus at the center. In this system, it is either possessed by the father, desired by but denied to the other, or desired by and denied to the girl child. It is the fetish, the universal measure, analogous to money in the capitalist economy. The place of the anus is not the social sphere but private sphere. Guy de Hocquenhem, in *Homosexual Desire*, argues that the logic of capitalism performs a syllogism in which money, by definition privately owned in order to circulate, is linked to the anus, the most private part of the individual (82).

The ambiguous nature of the anal intercourse of Horacio and La Maga is that it occurs in a border realm, in the space of resistance to phallocentrism and heterosexuality on the part of Horacio. Although engaged in heterosexual relations, they push to the furthest limit of heterosexuality to subsume eroticism under the logic of the phallus: anal intercourse denies the centrality of both the vagina and the vaginal orgasm for the woman; it denies the centrality of the vagina, the locus of heterosexual interest for the man. It is irreducible to either the arena of the heterosexual or the homosexual.

At the level of La Maga's desire for reproduction, anal intercourse is another deferral of the possibility of a child, and, as Irigaray shows, a parallel structure to the birth process. To the extent that La Maga is used by Horacio as a male "adolescent," or "the most abject prostitute," her desire is being thwarted. Yet she puts up with it without complaint, possibly following the logic of displacement of the process as a substitute for the birth process. What remains undecidable in the passage is the extent to which she sees herself as an object—and since she is not allowed to speak for herself the reader can only speculate; for Horacio, she is both an object and a potential subject. In Freudian terms, La Maga not only desires the child as a substitute for the phallus, but she desires knowledge, the phallus itself. There is a double code here: the code of giving birth and the code of gaining knowledge. In fact, is not playing the role of the male adolescent also playing the male student of philosophy?

Although this is changing, homosexual desire, like the desire of bohemian cafe culture, is synchronic in that no children are produced as a manifestation of continuity; heterosexual desire, in contrast, has been and continues to be diachronic. The desire of La Maga for a child is frustrated with Rocamadour's death. She speaks of him after his death in a compulsion to repeat what has been forced into the synchronic, the present, because of the impossibility of the diachronic.

After the death of Rocamadour, La Maga's whereabouts are discussed by Gregorovius and Horacio. Gregorovius recalls a conversation with La Maga before her disappearance, concerning a wax doll. Horacio had found the doll and stepped on it; the doll had pins stuck in its breasts and one pin stuck in the genitals. Gregorovius insinuates that there may be a link between the illness of Horacio's new lover, Pola, and the doll incident. He then tells Horacio about poisoned portraits. A poisoned portrait is painted with poisoned paints in the light of a "favorable" moon. Gregorovius describes the mysterious death of his grandfather. His mother had attempted to paint the father in the prescribed manner; there were interferences, and the father died three years later. He began to choke due to diphtheria and tried to perform a tracheotomy in front of the mirror by inserting a goose quill or a similar object. This is another example of Cortázar's fascination with strangulation, which is linked in this text to discourse. La Maga has resorted to an alternative method of the management of signifiers: magic.

In *The Psychoanalysis of Children*, Melanie Klein provides a useful context in her description of the Oedipal conflict in the girl. She understands the conflict as stemming from a double resentment against the mother: she has withdrawn the nourishing breast and she has withheld the father's penis as an object of satisfaction (195). Klein writes that "since the girl's destructive impulses against her mother's body are more enduring than the boy's, she will have stronger clandestine and cunning methods of attack, based upon the magic of excrement and other excretions and upon the omnipotence of her thought, in conformity with the hidden and mysterious nature of that world within her mother's body and her own" (205). Klein's explanation is particularly revealing in the light of Irigaray's links between excrement and the child.

According to Klein, dolls become the mother's reconstituted body in the play of older girls. In magical practice in Brazil, the doll is the body of the victim. In this lexicon, the Oedipal relation is presented in the sadistic activity of La Maga: all the pins but one are stuck into the breasts of the doll; one is reserved for the genitals. In Kleinian terms, the loss of Rocamadour and Horacio in conjunction with Horacio's new relationship with Pola results in a murderous jealousy, in which Pola takes the place of the mother. Gregorovius functions as the analyst, underlining the relation between Pola and the doll.

In *The Psychoanalysis of Children*, Klein cites her essay "Infantile Anxiety-Situations Reflected in a Work of Art and in the Creative Impulse" (1929), in which she analyzes an account by Karen Michaelis of a young woman who suddenly begins to paint portraits without prior artistic experience. Klein explains: "Painting female portraits symbolized a sublimated restoration both of her mother's body, which she had attacked in fantasy, and of her own: she had feared retaliation" (219–21, note 4). Given Irigaray's argument that castration is actually a misnomer for the obstacles between women and their own places in history, their own beginnings, then it is possible to see artistic "impotence" on the part of women as a blockage or deterritorialization that needs only a space for release, not "prior artistic experience."

In the case of Gregorovius's mother, the painting magically protects her while she plots to kill her father. In this function, it is like the shaman's mask. The practitioner of magic is protected by being displaced from the scene of the crime. This makes the practitioner of magic similar to a *guerrillero*. The attempt of the father to save himself recalls the first lexia: Horacio fantasized about strangling La Maga's throat so that she could finally speak and join the Serpent Club. The father strangles because of his disease and then attempts to save himself by cutting his throat with a quill. In one case, the throat must be strangled in order that one may die/speak; in the other case, the throat must be cut with a writing utensil in order that one may live. The formation of the self, which occurs at the mirror stage in the Lacanian model, results in the constitution of the self qua self for the man, but of the self to be looked at, for the woman.

La Maga is never able to constitute herself as a subject in *Rayuela*, but she does, nonetheless, present the problematic nature of the concept of the subject, for she is a citizen of a border region and cannot be understood in terms of European philosophical models. Whereas the father witnesses his fragmentation in the mirror as he dies, La Maga, unable to write or speak the discourse of the Lacanian Father, is situated in opposition to the father, the master of both the written word and of discourse. The situation is quite different for Laura in "Cambio de armas." Here, the phallus can no longer be inscribed, for the moment has been regained by Laura, who replaces phallocentric logic with vulvacentric logic. The vagina is linked to the concept in her way of seeing the world. La Maga never constitutes herself as a subject in the terms of Western philosophical thought. Laura acts, but not in terms that can be fully explained by Marxism or psychoanalysis. La Maga is never free, although she risks life. Laura embraces her freedom at the conclusion of "Cambio de armas." Although there are multidimensional or decentered subjects in both *Rayuela* and "Cambio de armas," it is only in "Cambio de armas" that both the subject and the object may be said to be presented from more than one perspective.

The codes of love in *La nausée*, *Rayuela*, and "Cambio de armas" are not identical. The first two define women as absolute alterity. In "Cambio de armas," Roque and Laura are shown to be linked historically through the object, the weapon. The ideal speech situation is implied: a situation is created in which Laura is able both to give and to receive orders.[9] In "Cambio de armas," objects appear unreal and dreamlike; this is due not to any link with surrealism but rather to a multidimensional concept of agency. In this way, Valenzuela rejects the European model of subjectivity together with its traditional psychoanalytic analogues. This rejection overturns the characterization of Latin American literature as magic or surreal, since such a designation ultimately depends on these European categories. In short, Oedipus becomes a border subject.

Cortázar: Surrealism, Technology and Border Comics

Surrealism must be considered in the context of the confrontation of traditional and information-based societies, which involves the impact of the postindustrial upon the preindustrial, and results in techno-pop tangos and AIDS/SIDA cumbias. While surrealism may be a possible referential code in the consideration of the texts under discussion, it is clearly insufficient. Insofar as it leads to inactivity, for example, it opposes the Marxist project, a project that is certainly not rejected by "Cambio de armas." Insofar as it raises the problematic of political action and political inaction, however, it remains essential in understanding Roquentin and Horacio. Plank argues, in *Sartre and Surrealism*, that Roquentin confronts the surrealist problematic and that he is provocatively presented to the reader from the perspective of a writer "on his way to Marxism" (71). Outside of this discussion, but very important, is the fact that technology has radically altered the lives of women in Latin America and continues to do so in the case of the *maquiladoras* in the border region.

In her study *¿Es Julio Cortázar un Surrealista?*, Evelyn Picón Garfield attempts to prove that Cortázar, while not a surrealist if we define the movement as that whose principal characteristic was automatic writing, is a surrealist in his mode of life and thought. She finds that surrealism is how Cortázar finds his way out of the given reality. Unfortunately, she limits her discussion of the two realities that coexist in Cortázar to the surrealist tradition (the magic realist tradition might be mentioned), and thus remains unconvincing. Cortázar's distinction between appearance and essence, waking life and dream, the visible and invisible, stems as much from a phenomenological tradition as from the surrealists. Moreover, the political implications of overcoming the given are understood by Picón Garfield only as Cortázar's stated political beliefs. His opinions are not a sufficient basis for an analysis of either his ideology or the ideological perspective put forward in his work. The ideology of his work may be looked at from several perspectives. Since Picón Garfield has no developed notion of ideology in her book, it is not surprising that she concludes that Cortázar chooses no ideology and that he is committed to the revolution for all humanity that will concern itself with every aspect of life. She implies that such a goal differs from that of socialism. All of Cortázar's work and expressed political view since the writing of *Rayuela* to his support of the Sandinista revolution points to a different direction than that predicted by Picón Garfield.

In his article "Twos and Threes," Robert Brody also attempted to establish a relationship between surrealism and Cortázar (128, note 12). He directs the reader to the works of Alfred Jarry. Jarry explains pataphysics as the science of the particular and the exceptional that describes a world that can and should be envisaged in place of the traditional one. On the basis of this concept alone, it is not difficult to understand Cortázar's appreciation and admiration for the alleged grandfather of surrealism. However, Brody's notion that Latin American reality is "exceptional" must be rejected as ethnocentric.

A very different and more useful analysis of surrealism in terms of border writing is that of Walter Benjamin; for him, surrealism is the "last snapshot of the European intelligentsia."[10] According to Benjamin, the surrealists were the first to experience the bourgeois tradition of "high art" even as it was already becoming information. It is in their willingness to accept the facticity of technology that the surrealists are found by Benjamin to be on common ground. Like the surrealists, border writers have a set of referential codes that is prior to the technological age.

In "The Work of Art in the Age of Mechanical Reproduction," in *Illuminations*, Benjamin argues for the democratizing possibilities of technology in the cultural realm: although the "aura" of the work is lost in its mass reproducibility, the possibility of mass availability is gained. In "Surrealism, the Last Snapshot of the European Intelligentsia," Benjamin poetically evokes the relation between art and technology in his claim that the surrealists "exchange, to a man, the play of human features for the face of an alarm clock that in each minute rings for sixty seconds" (56). When Duchamp retouches a photograph of his work *Nude Descending*, he is both removing it from the realm of "high art" as a unique work and at the same time recovering the brush-strokes that are lost in photography, the traces of his labor, by adding them to the photograph. The result is more than a technique; its cultural resonance could only occur at a certain historical moment, when the memory of the unique work and the experience of photography were both, multidimensionally, present in the mind of the viewer. That historical moment may occur at different times in different countries, as Eugenio Dittborn has explained in relation to Benjamin's impact on the Chilean artists of his generation.[11] Benjamin holds that only the surrealists have understood the "present commands" of *The Communist Manifesto:* "only when in technology body and image so interpenetrate that all revolutionary tension becomes bodily and collective innervation, and all the bodily innervations of the collective become revolutionary discharge" ("Surrealism," 56). Benjamin does not take a critical view of technology itself; he assumes it is necessary.

On the other hand, in "The Question Concerning Technology," Martin Heidegger does attempt to take a critical view of technology (3–35). Along with his student Herbert Marcuse, he finds art to be the only critical space from which to view technology. For Heidegger, art itself is "akin to the essence of technology" and yet fundamentally different from it (35). For Marcuse, art is the one activity that can still defy subsumption under the logic of technology. Whereas Heidegger concedes that art is "akin to the essence of technology," Marcuse clings to "high art" as that which remains *techne* and *episteme*, both of which were names until the time of Plato for knowing in the wide sense (Heidegger, 13). Yet the rupture between *techne* and *episteme* is assumed by the surrealists. Faced with the reduction of experience to information, with *episteme* to *techne*, they privilege language and replace the object with the word:

> Language only seemed itself where sound and image, image and sound, interpenetrated with automatic precision and such felicity that no chink was left for the penny-in-the-slot called "meanings." Image and language take precedence. Saint-Pol Roux, retiring to bed about daybreak, fixes a note on his door: "Poet at work." Breton notes: "Quietly. I want to pass where no one yet has passed, quietly!—After you, dearest language." Language takes precedence. (Benjamin, "Surrealism," 48)

The granting of the precedence of language by the surrealists coincided with a rejection of "meaning," a decentering of the subject and a reconsideration of what the literary work was. Literature became demonstrations, watchwords, documents, bluffs ("Surrealism," 48).

In Cortázar's work the inclusion of newspaper clippings, experiments with narrative structure, and the attempt to exploit mass cultural forms are all manifestations of a trend already present in the work of the surrealists. The decision to write a comic book is Cortázar's clearest statement about the role of the artist in the age of information. This gesture could be linked to the work of the surrealists without failing to respect Valenzuela's warning against labeling Latin American literature as surrealist. In *Fantomas contra los vampiros multinacionales*, Cortázar treats the role of the writer directly: as a member of the Russell Tribunal II, he finishes another session and begins to read a comic book he has purchased, *Fantomas contra los vampiros multinacionales*. We are told that in his comic book great literary works are disappearing from libraries all over the world (the disappearance of "high art"). Libraries burn in Calcutta and Tokyo, and it is announced on television that all the Bibles have disappeared. Famous writers are contacted, including Cortázar himself. Meanwhile, Cortázar receives a call from Susan Sontag, informing him further of the crisis. Fantomas confronts the culprit, Steiner, in Paris, but Sontag is not satisfied; for her, the destruction of the libraries is merely a prologue, and the adventure of Fantomas is mere deception, like the Alliance for Progress and the OEA. Sontag then points out that intellectuals similarly deceive themselves; they greet the loss of a single book with greater moral outrage than they do hunger in Ethiopia. Thus, on one side, Fantomas, in his attempt to save "high art," has fallen into the trap of the multinationals by believing that the confrontation with the culprit, Steiner, is sufficient. On the other side, the intellectual similarly falls into a trap: by privileging art, the intellectual assumes that the loss of high culture can be considered apart from the sociohistorical context in which we live. The intellectual forgets that present conditions produce both starvation and the loss of "high art." This is a dilemma from which the self-conscious subject cannot escape. Once again, the action of the artist must be seen in terms of agency and history, not in terms of the intentions of the individual artist.

In breaking down the distinction between art and life, which technology makes possible, there is the danger of the aestheticization of life. This is the impossible tightrope traversed by Cortázar in *Rayuela*: carefully balanced in the heights of "high art," he writes in a state produced by the agony of knowing that "high art" no longer exists. Moving high above everyday life, he makes the everyday life of his characters art, and simultaneously avoids life. By the time he writes *Fantomas*, he treats the subject from a perspective of humor.

Feminism and Border Writing

The essentialist argument for the existence of a separate feminine nature has been made by women and men, feminists and nonfeminists. Marcuse, in a lecture delivered at Stanford in 1974, said "the link between utopia and reality" consists "in the characteristics of the feminine nature, including receptivity, sensitivity, and nonviolence." Cortázar may have a similar notion of a feminine nature in his description of La Maga. La Maga is said to be immersed in "the metaphysical rivers of desire," which the males in the novel attempt to fathom with logic. The strategy of border writing, however, at least begins to displace traditional philosophical categories, of which, for example, ontology and subjectivity make an inseparable pair. With respect to the categories of border writing, a more interesting approach to La Maga is to consider her as a textual construction of "the feminine" that overlays many fantasies of men about women, particularly Latin American men influenced by jazz, poetry, travel in Europe, and the beat generation.

In this manner, Laura can be considered as a textual construction of two roles of women, the lover and the revolutionary. Would Laura's action be logical in terms of phallocentric Western logic, or would it arise out of a multidimensional interaction between agency and history? In *Rayuela*, La Maga has a privileged role in Cortázar's view of the revolutionary project, which, in this novel, is a spiritual individual revolution of the self, Horacio's self. Gregorovius tries to comfort La Maga after Horacio has left her with these words:

"Entiéndame, quiero decir que busca la luz negra, la llave, y empieza a
darse cuenta de que cosas así no están en la biblioteca. En realidad
usted le ha enseñado eso, y si él se va es porque no se la va a perdonar
jamás." (*Rayuela* 161)

["Understand me, what I'm trying to say is that he is looking for the
black light, the key, and he's beginning to realize you don't find those
things in libraries. You're the one who really taught him that, and if he's
left it's because he's never going to forgive you for it" (*Hopscotch* 144).]

In contrast to Laura, two roles of La Maga are the lover and the housewife/mother. A paramount problem faced by socialist feminism is how to situate the work done by woman in the home in the capitalist system. The difficulty derives, in part, from a dependence on a traditional Marxist vocabulary within which the term "productive labor" refers explicitly to an arena of social interaction. The experience that is supposed to arise out of this social form is charged with informing a consciousness capable of bringing about revolutionary change. It is questionable at best whether or not "housework" can be subsumed under the same concept.

Juliet Mitchell, in *Woman's Estate*, and Sheila Rowbotham, in *Woman's Consciousness, Man's World*, bring crucial issues of the problem to the surface, but reach very different conclusions. Mitchell's structural reading of woman's condition, influenced by Louis Althusser, distinguishes four structures: production, reproduction, sexuality, and the socializing of children. Thus, "housework" is not present in her analysis as separate from the function it performs. The family is brought into the debate by Mitchell, but since she holds that the final determining instance in woman's condition is the economy, she remains inside of the traditional Marxist analysis. For Mitchell, women can only overcome their oppression if they leave their homes, where they are isolated and, as purveyors of the ideology of private property and individualism, conservative. Rowbotham, on the other hand, avoids the surplus value and housework debate altogether by understanding the family structure as a mediator of capitalist ideology. Her analysis allows for both a conservative and an oppositional moment in the home. She expands upon Marcuse's list of feminine qualities to include negative ones as well; in effect, she combines them with Mitchell's analysis of the housewife and mother as backward and conservative. Nearly twenty years later, the debate continues. It is hoped that feminist theorists will take into account the situation of women living in border regions, forced to live apart from their families for long periods of time, and in some cases doing the housework of others as maids, hotel workers, and baby-sitters.

In "Production and the Context of Women's Daily Life," Ulrike Prokop develops socialist feminist theory by directing her attention to the contradictions within women's production in the home and their relationship to commodity production in advanced capitalism (18–33). In her analysis, women in the home, by virtue of their separation from the world of commodity production, satisfy human needs. Although domestic work acts as a safety valve for the alienation produced in other workplaces—and thus to a certain extent strengthens capitalism—it also looks forward to a socialist feminist society of workers' control in which work would be based on the satisfaction of self-determined needs of members of that society.

La Maga satisfied the human needs of the Serpent Club, and particularly of Horacio. While she thinks "es tan violeta ser ignorante" (*Rayuela* 157) ("it's so purple to be ignorant"; *Hopscotch* 142), her very confusion when confronted with intellectual discussions reinforces the sense of superiority of the males with whom she converses (*Rayuela* 157). Prokop's discussion of the relationships between woman and desire can give insight into La Maga. Prokop writes:

> The woman represents desires . . . the imaginary is connected to the everyday world of women. On the one hand, their exclusion from the system of professional competition means decreasing the possibility for cooperative appropriation of reality; on the other hand, a woman tries (in different ways, depending on her particular resources) to make herself an object of the imagination, both for herself and for men. (25)

The La Maga who emerges from the various codes of Uruguay-as-border-country, motherhood, the unexpected, female sexuality from a male perspective is portrayed as vaguely aware of the power to make herself sexually desirable and as a signifier of a world outside that of male intellectuals.

Babs, another woman in *Rayuela*, rejects the roles described by Marcuse, Rowbotham, and Prokop. As an American student, she has attempted to live as an intellectual. Babs is allowed into the Serpent Club, possibly because her boyfriend Ronald is a member and possibly because as a woman from the United States, she is not treated the same as a Latin American woman. Presumably, Babs is a middle-class woman, as is La Maga, but La Maga, as a signifier, refers to a generation in which middle-class women were not encouraged to receive a university education to the same extent as men were. We know that La Maga is not a student and is not educated, although she enjoys novels. Having spent her life around intellectuals and artists, she quickly tires of their discussions and ultimately prefers a life away from them. We see this in her decision to leave Horacio.

Babs and La Maga ultimately share exclusion from the Serpent Club. Babs is finally ostracized because she breaks the code of silence and condemns Horacio openly. This outburst follows the tacit agreement of members of the Club not to inform La Maga of the death of Rocamadour and to allow her to discover his dead body herself. Babs feels remorse and anger, and as a consequence, lashes out at Horacio. Ronald, who has encouraged her to express her fury in bedtime baby talk, cringes when she actually confronts Horacio; he is determined to speak to her about her impropriety later, when they are alone. The speech of Babs is the antithesis of the silence of La Maga: whereas Horacio fantasized about strangling La Maga so that, after death, she might be transformed into one who could speak, the Club expels Babs precisely because she has spoken. But, even though Babs condemns Horacio, she does not then establish a relationship of solidarity with La Maga; she does not speak with her.

What has been absent in both the United States and Latin America, in all social classes, is an intellectual community or culture of women analogous to the Serpent Club. Adolescent women do not discover their sexuality and a need for intellectual discourse in an environment of mutual encouragement as some adolescent men do. This situation is worse in some ways for many women in the United States than for upper-middle-class women in Buenos Aires, insofar as there is a longer tradition of women writers in Latin America than in the United States. Cortázar, however, does not choose to show this cultural difference. Perhaps the development of such traditions will result in the creation of alternative textual treatments of "the feminine."

Literary criticism is always a rewriting; furthermore, it is the kind of rewriting in which the silences in the text are made to speak. We are perfectly justified to ask, therefore, a number of hypothetical but no less pertinent questions. What, for example, would have happened in *Rayuela* if La Maga had spoken, and further, if she and Babs had spoken to each other? Instead, she writes to the dead Rocamadour, in the only passages in the novel in which we have any notion of her subjectivity. Even in the scene in which La Maga and Horacio are making love, the reader is told what the narrator/Horacio thinks; we can only imagine how the scene is experienced by La Maga. She might have spoken of her desires, to learn and to read. She might have told Horacio that anal intercourse was painful, or pleasurable, and described her fantasies; that she was freed, at that moment, from being a woman as defined by vulvacentrism; that the new sensation gave her a sense of control over a part of her body that was usually forgotten and private; that the sensation recalled the erotic experience of defecating, and then perhaps of playing with her feces as a child, keeping what she had made herself to play with and to smear, to control the way she wanted to; that if her mother had not told her where to dispose of her feces, if she had been allowed to keep them instead of always fearing that they would soil her clothes, get her dirty, like boys, if she could have hidden them somewhere and played with them later . . . but her mother always discovered them. She might have felt ashamed to share her anus with him, such a private part of her body. She might have despised him for having anal intercourse with her, knowing that it could never result in pregnancy.

If La Maga had been able to talk to Babs, they might have discussed how the Serpent Club possessed philosophical knowledge, the phallus, and excluded La Maga, just because she was formally uneducated, and La Maga might have expressed her jealousy of Babs. Babs might have admitted that she enjoyed her inclusion in the Club, and that she never noticed La Maga's exclusion until the death of Rocamadour. They might have found themselves attracted to each other. La Maga could have expressed her hatred of her own ignorance and Babs could have taught her philosophy. La Maga could have told Babs what she thought about literature. Babs might have found the friendship with La Maga more satisfying than her membership in the Club and her relationship with Ronald, because there was no competition with La Maga, just the desire to talk together. La Maga might have explained to Babs that she had been allowed into the Club because she was American and that she had received an education from which La Maga had been excluded. Together, they could have formed an intellectual community for women, in which sensuality, friendship, politics, and intellectual interests were combined.

These imaginary, possible chapters in fact begin to be actual chapters in *Libro de Manuel*, in which Ludmilla comments to Susana, after Patricio threatens to "whack" their "asses" if they do not fix mate, "Es realmente un macho" (*LM* 78) ("real macho stuff"; *MM* 76).[12] Francine tells Andrew, "No es culpa nuestra, quiero decir de Ludmilla y de mí. Es una cuestión de sistema, te repito; ni tú ni nosotras podremos quebrarlo, viene de muy atrás y abarca demasiadas cosas" (*LM* 205) ("It's not our fault, I mean Ludmilla's and mine. It's a question of system, I repeat; neither you nor we can break it, it comes from too far back and takes in too many things"; *MM* 207). And Ludmilla articulates her perception of Francine: " . . . fresquita de la universidad y de la haute couture, con su autito rojo y su librería y su libertad" (*LM* 93) ("fresh out of the university and haute couture, with her little red car and her bookshop and her freedom"; *MM* 91). The letter of Leilman Borges Vieira to Aparecida Gomide is an explicitly political communication from one woman to another. In *Libro de Manuel* women teach each other: when Ludmilla does not know who Lamarca is, Susana continues to read the newspaper account of his death, and in the discussion, Ludmilla is educated politically. In contrast to the women in *Rayuela*, the women in *Libro de Manuel* are speaking subjects: they speak to each other and about themselves.

As we saw in the previous discussion, the absence of the world of work outside of housework in *Rayuela* does not mean that the effects of such work are not present in the novel. The logic of fragmentation, a by-product of technology, is present in the form of *Rayuela* itself. The dissolution of the self that occurs in the twentieth century, both inside and outside the text, is explored by Cortázar not in the industrial workplace of the office but in the margins of society: in the cafe, on the street, late at night, in the apartment. Cortázar throws into question the unity of personal consciousness: there is no longer an "I" of a narrator or a protagonist that remains constant in all of its experiences. The narrative voice shifts, slips, and dissolves into a random order of bits of information—the story becomes one of eternally recurring fragments.

Such recurring fragmentation brings to mind this passage in Friedrich Nietzsche's *Will to Power*:

A certain emperor always bore in mind the transitoriness of all things so as not to take them too seriously and to live at peace among them. To me, on the contrary, everything seems far too valuable to be so fleeting: I seek an eternity for everything: ought one to pour the most precious salves and wines into the sea? My consolation is that everything that has been is eternal: the sea will cast it up again. (547–48)

In *Rayuela*, everything will be cast up again, ad infinitum. Cortázar achieves this not by instructing the reader to jump about through the same 155 chapters over and over again in an infinite circle but in one of two ways described in the "Table of Instructions." The first way tells the reader to begin at chapter 1 and continue through chapter 56; in the second way the reader should begin with chapter 73 and follow the instructions in the chart until reaching the eternal return of chapters 131 and 58 and 131 . . . Had Cortázar ended the second way of reading with chapter 73, the first chapter of the second method, he would have "cast up" over and over the same events. His ending is much more effective because of its simplicity: the eternal recurrence of this and that, and this.

As Nietzsche enjoins us to remember:

If the world may be thought of as a certain definite quantity of force and as a certain definite number of centers of force—and every other representation remains indefinite and therefore useless—it follows that, in the great dice game of existence it must pass through a calculable number of combinations. In infinite time, every possible combination would at some time or another be realized, more: it would be realized an infinite number of times. And since other possible combinations would have to take place, and each of these combinations conditions the entire sequence of combinations in the same series, a circular movement of absolutely identical series is thus demonstrated: the world as a circular movement that has already repeated itself infinitely often and plays its game ad infinitum. (549)

The concept of time here is not infinite regress or progress but eternal return. In a world without God or meaning, this concept actually offers a new kind of immortality: all is not lost, and it may all be tossed up again by the sea. Human life is fleeting, but the conception of eternal return holds out the possibility of recuperation of meaning, a Western possibility of the reincarnation of every moment that has ever passed. This concept of time opposes itself to progression.

The concept of time has provided many critics with a focal point for their discussions. Jameson, for example, in "On Magic Realism and Film," distinguishes between postmodernism and magic realism in part on the basis of their respective treatments of time. He notes that, whereas in postmodernism time serves only for the evocation of nostalgia, within magic realism it serves to present historical knowledge. Heidegger discusses Nietzsche's concept of time in *What Is Called Thinking*. He rejects the position that Nietzsche's concept of time is cyclical or that it borrows from a notion that can already be found in Heraclitus's fragments and elsewhere. Although both Heraclitus and Nietzsche write of eternal change and flux, Nietzsche is in fact much closer to Parmenides' notion of time. Parmenides argues that the statement is eternally true. Since there was never a time when it was not true, nor will there ever be such a time, then there is never a "was" or a "will be," there is only a perpetual present.[13] Nietzsche writes: "Revenge is the will's revulsion against time and its 'It was' " (99).[14] Heidegger interprets "time" here to mean that by which the temporal is made temporal, and the temporal as that which must pass away: "Time persists, consists in passing. It is, in that it constantly is not. This is the representational idea of time that characterizes the concept of 'time' which is standard through the metaphysics of the West" (99).

But why should Cortázar resort to this concept of time? For all his avoidance of structure, does it not cause him to fall into the view of time in Claude Lévi-Strauss's *Structural Anthropology*, that history is not necessarily linear, and that its structures repeat themselves? Yet, the poignancy of *Rayuela* results from its ambiguity. In the first reading, the structures do not repeat themselves. Cortázar, therefore, may be opting instead for a kind of undecidability. In "Cambio de armas," on the other hand, Valenzuela gives Laura a second chance to complete her mission. Perhaps it is possible to see here a link between feminism and non-linear narrative structure.[15]

In *El signo y el garabato* Octavio Paz argues that technology destroys the notion of endless time, the world without end. Change no longer is equated with progress, but extinction. This insight of Paz offers a possible understanding of how Cortázar could distill Nietzsche's concept of time in the postwar context and produce the narrative structure of *Rayuela*. Yet even though Cortázar may have a notion of undecidability with regard to the problem of time in narrative structure, he ultimately ontologizes fragmentation.

For the Anglo reader, the political experience to which "Cambio de armas" refers must be filled in; these referential codes must be gotten from newspaper articles, the stories of political exiles, and research. The Derridean dictum to examine philosophical assumptions is important for the Anglo reader. However, one must go further than this in attempting to understand border writing; not only must a critique of subject be made but there must be a willingness to participate in a dialogue in which the notion of the subject as defined in European philosophical discourse is no longer relevant. While Anglo feminists have not discussed the role of the woman in a manner revolutionary enough to provide the rich background of debate that can be found in Latin America, nonetheless, the unfolding of the political metaphors of these texts can be approached initially with only a sketchy view of the Argentina of the 1970s, through an analysis of the relationship between the multidimensional, border, or decentered subject and object as viewed from more than one perspective. The "class interest" and gender interests of the perceiver are of crucial importance in the reception of the text in the United States. The next step is a multidimensional or decentered memory. The process of remembering will depend on the cultural background of the reader. The Anglo reader cannot hope to appropriate the border text. For if art may be described as a creation of short-term referential codes and as a cultural negotiation, then the North American negotiation with the border text will not arise through a willed activity by a self-conscious subject, but instead will emerge in an interference pattern created by agency and history.

Chapter 3
Cortázar:
The Task of the Translator

Deterritorialization and Reterritorialization of the Real

For much of his life, Cortázar was under severe scrutiny by the left, and this fact is by no means superfluous to any adequate reading of his texts. In the case of *Libro de Manuel*, for example, if he sets a trap for the reader by appearing to write a "merely" didactic text, this strategy allows him to plead guilty to the lesser of two counts; meanwhile, he is not even charged for the real deed—the unforgivable act of criticizing revolutionary ideology at its core. Thus, many critics have responded to *Libro de Manuel* the way the police did to the crime in Edgar Allan Poe's "The Purloined Letter," that is, by deciding that the case cannot be solved. It follows that, like the detective Dupin, any "active reader" of this demanding text must resort to unconventional strategies, that is, to border strategies, in an attempt to understand it. Like Dupin, the "active reader" of *Libro de Manuel* must not only know the codes used by the "police" but will have to resort, finally, to an alternative logic, specifically to border logic, in order to solve the "crime." Cortázar's reader must know political and literary referential codes, including debates about didactic literature and experimental fiction if *Libro de Manuel* is not to be dismissed as inferior to his other works. Such a reader cannot take anything for granted; sacred precepts, including the notion that only certain information constitutes a clue, must be laid aside. Everything in the text must be allowed to speak.

Libro de Manuel is not the only text in which Cortázar's narrative strategies resemble those of a mystery novel. In "Apocalipsis de Solentiname," reality and fiction converge: the circumstances of the death of the Salvadoran Roque Dalton remain a mystery in fact, and in the story Cortázar has chosen to look at an event which he could not see in reality.[1]

We can take this as one of many indications that the problem of the absent cause is of great interest to Cortázar. In *Libro de Manuel* he explores this problematic by deliberately omitting the narrative's "main event," a political kidnapping. Likewise, in "Las babas del diablo," he gives us a short story in which closure is never reached and the reader is left without knowing the exact nature of the relationships among the characters.[2] Related to the problematic of the absent cause is our capacity to distinguish fiction from fact. In his *Literary Theory: An Introduction*, Terry Eagleton recalls that in the seventeenth century no strict distinction was made between what we now consider news and fiction (2). Cortázar's blending of current events into his creation challenges our assumption that we can make such a distinction today. By translating the "fact" of Dalton's death into the account by the name of "Apocalipsis de Solentiname," Cortázar, in effect, celebrates his life. To borrow from Jacques Derrida, just as there is "impurity in every language," so there is impurity in every historical fact. In *The Ear of the Other*, Derrida refers to Benjamin's metaphor of "The Shell and the Kernel"; he argues that our desire, in the context of translation, to grasp the intact kernel, may be desire itself: "I would oppose desire to necessity, to *ananke*. The *ananke* is that there is no intact kernel and never had been one. That's what one wants to forget and, furthermore, to forget that one has forgotten it" (115).

There are many layers of translation in "Apocalipsis." Nature has been painted by the *campesinos* in the paintings that Cortázar photographs. The entire story, despite desire for it to be otherwise, is about Cortázar himself and his role as a writer. In the story, he says that he is tired of being asked about the role of the artist, a complaint echoed in the short story "Diario para un cuento" in the collection *Deshoras*. While fantasizing about being Adolfo Bioy Casares and translating a passage of Derrida's *La vérité en peinture*, he realizes that although he had hoped to write about Anabel (the reference is to Poe's poem) he has fallen once again into writing about himself. And to write about himself is to write about translation. ("Diario," 168).

"Apocalipsis" was written in Cuba in April 1976, nearly a year after Dalton's death. It begins with the depiction of an academic conference in Costa Rica at which Cortázar meets Ernesto Cardenal, the leading Nicaraguan poet and the Minister of Culture following the Sandinista revolution. Cardenal founded the religious community of Solentiname in 1965, and in the story, he and Cortázar go to Solentiname together. After they arrive, Cortázar takes some pictures of primitive paintings of outdoor scenes by local peasant artists. Upon his return to Paris, he develops the slides, and when he projects them for viewing, he discovers that, rather than the paintings, he has developed a set of horrifying images from all over Latin America: a boy being shot, a woman being tortured, and in the final image, the murder of Dalton. After stopping the projections, his friend Claudia asks him if he liked the slides. He is unable to face her, fearing that she will see how upset he is. She is completely unaware of his strange experience. He decides not to ask her a question that refers back to a conversation he had with Cardenal about the snapshots, in which Cardenal asked him to imagine that a different image might appear instead of the one photographed; that is, Cortázar decides not to bother asking Claudia if she saw "Napoleon on a horse."

In connection with Cortázar's use of photos in "Apocalipsis," it is useful to recall that in their study of Kafka, Deleuze and Guattari distinguish between portrait photos and musical sound. They equate the first with "a blocked, oppressed or oppressing, neutralized desire with a minimum of connection to childhood memory territory or reterritorialization" (5). Sound, however, is equated with "a desire that straightens up or moves forward, and opens up to new connections, childhood block or animal block, deterritorialization" (5). In Cortázar's work, the two opposing tendencies combine. The move toward defining an absent cause is often associated with a photographic image, whereas the underlying narrative structure is often based on music. In this story, Cortázar carefully balances image and reality: there are eight shots and eight paintings. He frees photography from its essential referentiality, discussed by Roland Barthes in *Camera Lucida*. Reality is subsumed under the imagination and desire of the photographer.

The rendering asunder of a signifier from referent as we see it in "Apocalipsis" has roots in the work of Marcel Duchamp and is continued by surrealists: unusual narrative associations in which objects with a "symbolic function" cause a psychological response, allowing the viewer to become conscious of another more abstract reality. The object, in this case the referent that would have been depicted — under nondeterritorialized conditions — by the photo, is released from its usual function in order to free the poetic function that is "truer" than the original. The "meaning" of Solentiname, in this analysis, is the unsaid and the invisible: the torture and death that appear in the transformed photographs.

By breaking the bond between the photograph and reality, Cortázar enables the viewer to freeze-frame an unknown event and to record it as it might happen or might have happened. He makes the familiar strange by beginning with a process we believe we understand, photography, and then proceeding to tinker with it until it is no longer recognizable. His forced separation of the link between the photograph and reality reminds the reader that the "real" in "Apocalipsis," even as it was recorded by the peasants in their paintings, was already a representation. Thus, Cortázar chooses a familiar object, the photograph, as his signifier for the problem of representation, thereby appropriating this contribution of technology to modern life for the border project. This code signals an essential element of linearity, the single referent; its juxtaposition with a multiplicity of references demands a multidimensional perspective, and reminds the reader that she or he has a position with relation to the frame.

By reversing the normal process, Cortázar also addresses the way in which images shape our understanding of history: by changing the photographic image, a representation or translation, he enacts a change in the real, he reverses causality. Thus the reader is empowered to change reality by retranslating it, by transforming its representation after the fact. This is similar to the deconstruction performed by Luisa Valenzuela in *Cola de lagartija* in which history itself is thrown into question and the event itself is revealed to depend on perspective. A multidimensional perspective is required, which will enable the viewer to observe parallax the various relationships among perspectives.

For the Anglo observer, the relationship between the event and the media became unmistakenly clear during the Vietnam era. Others have also observed the Heisenbergian aspect of images of social reality. In "Film, the Art Form of Late Capitalism," Stanley Aronowitz observes that our knowledge of the Russian Revolution is a translation rather than a firsthand experience of the event and that the translator is Eisenstein: "For us, Eisenstein's *October* is the Russian revolution, not a representation, not a report" (201). Similarly, for many readers in the United States, Cortázar's account of Dalton's death is his death, and not merely a report of it. The same can be said of García Márquez's account of the strike in *Cien años*.

The intrusion of a mass cultural medium, photography, into our experience of reality is analogous to the mediation of the newspaper between ourselves and the event. Experience, as Benjamin said, has been replaced by information. The problem becomes at times crucial in the education of Manuel in *Libro de Manuel*, for even his teachers have forgotten recent history. His curriculum is a series of translated newspaper articles. Just as Valenzuela sometimes deconstructs the effect of the discourse of the other through an exorcism, so Cortázar focuses upon the process and activity of translation as a strategy for reminding us that we do not perceive reality directly. In both cases, these authors are concerned about a lack of historical memory, which, in the absence of direct experience and as a result of our even having forgotten that we did not directly experience the event, can only maintain our state of delusion.

Cortázar is hopeful, however; " . . . una cámara de esas que dejan salir ahí nomás un papelito celeste que poco a poco y maravillosamente y polaroid se va llenando de imágenes paulatinas" is a metaphor for the effect of mass culture on our perception ("Apocalipsis" 97) (" . . . one of those cameras that let the little piece of sky-blue paper pop out right there and little by little and miraculously and Polaroid it fills up little by little with images"; "Apocalypse" 267). Mass culture fills us up with images "little by little," and yet, we can reverse the process. If we view the meaning of life and death in a multidimensional sense, then we can change the fate of Roque Dalton by interacting with his memory at the level of the image.

An early example of Cortázar's refusal of closure in narrative structure as a strategy for eliciting the active participation of the reader in the production of meaning is the short story "Las babas del diablo," upon which the film *Blow-up* was based. Another unsolved mystery, this story leaves the reader within the realm of the hermeneutic code: Who is the boy? Who is the woman with the red hair? Who is the man with the gray hat? Who is Michel? Who is narrating the story? The implication is that there has been some sort of transgression committed, again, as in the murder of Dalton. In both stories, Cortázar chooses to omit the details that would explain what has happened, thus depriving us of an answer. Rather, we must piece together the fragments and repetitions that Cortázar gives us.

Just as in "Apocalipsis," there is a strange occurrence when the photographs are being developed in "Las babas." The narrator is in the darkroom when he discovers that the negative is very good; he decides to blow it up, that is, to make an enlargement. The enlargement is so good that he makes another one. There is a digression to the task of translation in which the narrator is simultaneously engaged, the translation of a work by José Norberto Allende. This juxtaposition underscores the link Cortázar makes between photography and translation. There is a tension between the desire of the photographer to "reterritorialize" and the nonlinear narrative structure of the story, which is decentered or "deterritorialized."

The narrator discovers that " . . . cuando miramos una foto de frente, los ojos repiten exactamente la posición y la visión del objetivo; son esas cosas que se dan por sentadas y que a nadie se le ocurre considerar" ("Las babas" 533) (" . . . when we look at a photo from the front, the eyes reproduce exactly the position and the vision of the lens; it's these things that are taken for granted and it never occurs to anyone to think about them"; "Blow-up" 127). Then, something very strange occurs. He observes that "La foto había sido tomada, el tiempo había corrido; estábamos tan lejos unos de otros, la corrupción seguramente consumada, las lágrimas vertidas, y el resto conjetura y tristeza" (536) ("The photo had been taken, the time had run out, gone; we were so far from one another, the abusive act had certainly already taken place, the tears already shed, and the rest conjecture and sorrow"; "Blow-up" 129). This description of displacement, or deterritorialization, and "conjetura y tristeza," brings to mind Deleuze and Guattari's discussion of nostalgia, a desire for "reterritorialization" (*Kafka*, 77). Suddenly, everything changes: incapable of intervening, the narrator watches as the figures begin to move. Here, Cortázar again brings the reader's attention to the relationship to the object and its representation. On the one hand, once reality has been represented, it is fixed within the form of the representation or, in Deleuze and Guattari's terms, the form of "blocked desire" (*Kafka*, 5). On the other hand, it can be changed; causality can be reversed.

"Las babas" is based not on a linear plot or developed characters but rather on the repetition of certain structures and codes from which the characters emerge. The narrative is a self-conscious narrator. He tells the reader at the beginning of the story: "Nunca se sabrá cómo hay que contar esto, si en primera persona o en segunda, usando la tercera del plural o inventando continuamente formas que no servirán de nada" (520). ("It'll never be known how this has to be told, in the first person or in the second, using the third person plural or continually inventing modes that will serve for nothing"; "Blow-up" 114). He then returns to a strategy of compulsive repetition: clouds are linked to the woman with red hair. The characters are presented in relation to objects, such as clouds, but more fundamental questions about their relationships to one another are left unanswered. Ambiguity exists in the relationship between the boy and the woman. Are they mother and son? Lovers? Is incest occurring between them? The referential codes of morality of the reader cannot be applied until the relationship is clarified, and it never is. The distance between the narrator and the scene is mentioned often: five meters. The narrator does not let the reader forget that there is a gap, a difference, between the event and the subject representing or translating the event.[3] The dichotomy fiction/reality is emphasized in the observation about Michel: "Michel es culpable de literatura, de fabricaciones irreales. Nada le gusta más que imaginar excepciones, individuos fuera de la especie, monstruos no siempre repugnantes" (530) ("Michel is guilty of making literature, of indulging in fabricated unrealities. Nothing pleases him more than to imagine exceptions to the rule, individuals outside the species, not-always-repugnant monsters"; "Blow-up" 124).

As in "Apocalipsis," Cortázar balances image and reality in "Las babas." The essential referentiality of photography is meaningless since we do not know the relationships among the people. The narrator calls the woman and the boy "presos en una pequeña imagen química" (530) ("ignominiously recorded on a small chemical image"; "Blow-up" 124). The objects recorded by the image, in this case, the woman and the boy, are released from their usual function in order to release their poetic function. The "meaning" of the story is in the transformations that occur after the photographs are developed.

By appropriating the codes of photography and music, Cortázar is able to emphasize the constructed nature of any text. He rejects the "seamlessness" of the nineteenth-century text. Plot and character are deemphasized in favor of reference, symbolic, and semic codes. Characters exist as doubles in both "Apocalipsis" and "Las babas." That is, they exist both in the fictional reality of the narrative and as their re-presentation on film. The opposition and interaction between the doubles, their mutual translation into the other, is reconstructed in the experience of reading the text, when the characters emerge as "real" from their production from a chemical process.

Deterritorialization, Music, and Narrative Structure: ## Libro de Manuel

Libro de Manuel, a novel about various levels of conflict between Latin American revolutionaries and repressive regimes, is constructed from fragments.[4] In it,

Cortázar interrogates his own identity as a novelist who worked as a translator for UNESCO. The text is a commentary on its own production and on the process of translation, translation from one language to another, between reader and writer, and between the Joda and Manuel. Like Valenzuela, Cortázar is aware of the contradictory role he plays as a politically committed writer. He left Argentina in 1955, the same year García Márquez left Colombia, and lived in Paris until his death in 1984. He was acutely aware of the ideological as well as directly confrontational activities of Latin American revolutionaries within their own countries and as political exiles. He supported the Cuban and Nicaraguan revolutions and was in contact with political exiles in Paris and elsewhere. Part of his job at UNESCO involved selecting articles from newspapers and translating them. His transformation of newspaper texts into novels parallels his representation of Solentiname with photographs, and may be understood as his attempt to recapture the object that he had to translate for others and to present it to the critical consideration of the reader.

The attempt to recuperate the "meaning" of the event within the novel is undermined by the fate of the novel itself as a commodity in the world literature market. Even so, Cortázar's attempt proceeds from a tradition of artists who have turned to formal experimentation as a means of avoiding absorption by the mass media. Certain problems of narrative structure led Cortázar in *Rayuela* to forms of experimentation similar to the structure used by twentieth-century musical composers. As I have indicated, Deleuze and Guattari link these musical structures to their notion of "deterritorialization."

Karlheinz Stockhausen, for example, writes music in which the performers are given a score from which they construct their own performance or translation. Basic elements are given, but the performer is free to choose the order or sequence of certain parts. The interactive aspects of such formal experimentation, the sort that has its parallel in *Rayuela*, could be considered precursors to the structure of interactive video games. The form that appeared, as we have seen, as an emphasis upon translation in "Las babas" and "Apocalipsis" and as the encouragement of the active participation of the reader in *Rayuela* is continued in *Libro de Manuel*.

The form of *Libro de Manuel* allows the reader to reflect upon the process of translation itself. The reader is thus able to go beyond the limits of Roman Jakobson's categories of translation (intralingual, interlingual, and intersemiotic), categories that Derrida refers to in *The Ear of the Other*. Although there are passages translated directly from other languages into Spanish, examples of his "interlingual" translation, it is their placement in a broader context, the text of the novel and the social text of global politics, that betrays the immensity of Cortázar's translation project, which is nothing less than an investigation of the process of translation itself. Fragments of the news are discussed by members of the Joda, a group of urban revolutionaries. The juxtaposition of the newspaper clippings creates a rhythm that structures the narrative. As they unfold in time, they appear visually produced on the page, and in the discussions of the characters. A kind of visual music is created.[5] For this reason, the structure can be analyzed in musical terms. In this reading, the terms will be taken from the description of a composition by Stockhausen, *Momente*.

Cortázar attempts to historicize the events that have been presented out of context in the newspaper. He focuses the attention of the reader on the displacement between the observer and the observed. The situation demands a reconstruction from the perspective of an outsider, that is, a translation: the position of marginality from which any event we do not witness directly must be re-viewed as that in which the border writer finds herself or himself. Just as the New Critics stayed inside the text, not wishing to go outside it in order to understand it, so modernist writers remain ensconced inside a marginal subjectivity. Border writers such as Cortázar and Valenzuela distinguish themselves from the modernist traditions precisely because they are conscious of this dilemma. Border literature that proceeds from the margins of society can deal with political content in an indirect, deflected narrative, as a juxtaposition of fragments that themselves raise the question about the unified event in history; however, such a perspective is condemned to remain on the outside, unable to record the event and unaware that this is the case. Border texts are directly political, although the narrative structure may be nonlinear.

The main event in a traditional narrative is not present in *Libro de Manuel*. The main event, the kidnapping, must be discovered through the hermeneutic code; it cannot be assumed. Central events are deleted from the narrative because Cortázar's project is one of a radical decentering. The absence of the central event is related to the situation of the writer faced with reports of the event rather than the event itself. Like Foucault in *The Order of Things*, all Cortázar can do is to "squeeze" the event out of fragmentary and partial reports. As a border writer, Cortázar refuses the role of the omniscient narrator who would pretend to have access to the thing itself; instead, he offers a multidimensional view of the text that emerges from a process of translation: (1) the original text is translated into Spanish; (2) the members of the Joda discuss the event to which it refers, that is, they reconstruct what Lacan calls the "real"—and what Deleuze and Guattari call "the political"; and (3) the reader actively inserts herself or himself into the string of signifiers provided by Cortázar's text and engages in an act of reflexivity, a becoming aware of one's own positionality vis-à-vis any event. Cortázar implies that one can never get inside the thing itself, that there is no essence to be distinguished from appearance. Thus his is not an essentialist position, nor is it ultimately a Kantian position: that we cannot know the thing-in-itself. Rather, he offers a model of multidimensional perception: the "real" can be known through reflexive activity in relation to it. Art provides the possibility of gaining access to such reflexive knowledge. The "active reader" thus collaborates with the artist, in this case the writer, and through this activity reality becomes intelligible.

Thus the privileging of the original over the translation is an assumption that Cortázar forces the reader to reexamine. *Libro de Manuel* is both the original and a collection of translations; its very existence deconstructs any opposition between the two terms. The subsumption of the translation under the original is a logical extension of the philosophical problem of form and content. The relationship between form and content may be conceived as occurring at three levels. At the level of analytic logic, there is a correspondence between the two; at the level of dialectical logic, one is negated and preserved in the other; finally, at the level of multivalenced or multidimensional logic, there is a relationship of incommensurability.

A Marxist critique of ideology that would define ideology as content proceeds from a reflection theory of knowledge and, like analytic logic, is concerned with the relationship of correspondence between the original or truth and its form as a "bad" translation or ideology. Sartre's use, for example, of reified laws to investigate the realm of appearance points to his assumption that there must be an analytical moment, later to be subsumed by a dialectical moment. Structuralists who focus upon form in their readings of texts are likewise informed by analytic logic. Their assumption of a shared semiotic system among all discourses allows for this type of analysis. Cortázar's appropriation of the codes of music and photography suggests another approach, one that can allow for a process of interaction between the real and its representation.

Adorno, in *Negative Dialectics*, describes what we can recognize as a deterritorialized form of logic in his discussion of rhetoric. Distinguishing himself from those who regard "the body of language as sinful," he writes:

> Utopia is blocked off by possibility, never by immediate reality; this is why it seems abstract in the midst of extant things. The extinguishable color comes from nonbeing. Thought is its servant, a piece of existence extending—however negatively—to that which is not. The utmost distance would be proximity; philosophy is the prism in which its color is caught. (57)

The multidimensional approach shares with the deconstructive stance of Derrida and the negative dialectical approach of Adorno a reexamination of Hegel. Adorno notes that Hegel's distinction between appearance (translation) and essence (the original) supports his insistence upon the superiority of the dialectical over analytic thought. Although the realm of appearance may be studied with a formal analysis based on representation, only conceptual or dialectical thought may hope to fathom the relationship between the terms. Adorno argues that Hegel ultimately returns to a theory of identity. This third kind of logic, a multivalenced, multidimensional logic, is able to embrace both analytic and dialectical logic. It offers, in the place of the equation of appearance and essence, an ultimate irreducibility.

Sartre's approach to the text, which argues that analytic logic must be the starting point of criticism, to be transcended later by dialectical logic, remains ensconced, therefore, within the tradition of analytic logic and its obverse, dialectical logic. This tradition shares the philosophical assumptions of analogical and homological thought. Arguments by analogy, in which a metaphor connects two elements, privilege content. Homologies, in which attempts are made to show similarities or to establish that given terms may be compared, also stress content. From the point of view of dialectical logic, form and content in both these cases are dialectically linked, and the moment of form rather than the moment of content is stressed. Thus, links may be made between analytic logic and analogical thought and between dialectical logic and homological thought. Such a formulation rests on several assumptions: (1) that analytic logic is subsumed under dialectical logic; (2) that there is a relation of identity between form and content; and (3) that we can speak of totality.

A third kind of logic, holographic or multidimensional logic, throws these assumptions into question. As Adorno argues in *Negative Dialectics*, analytic and dialectical logic are in obverse relation to one another. From a multidimensional perspective there is no necessary identity between form and content; rather, there is a relation of incommensurability. While accepting that the assumption of totality is necessary in order to conceive of fragmentation, Adorno seeks to understand fragmentation rather than to remain within the confines imposed by the notion of totality.

I wish to argue that the notions of the border and the holographic interference pattern, unlike the analogical and the homological, allow for a description of the mediations of a logic of nonidentity. An "identity" that does not exclude differences characterizes the "sameness" of the holographic relation. Thus, form rather than content is emphasized by rejecting the notion of the identity between form and content; in this way, difference, most readily apparent in form—and as noted by Cortázar, in its disruption—may be apprehended.

Cortázar is not the first writer to have been inspired by a literary form nor is he the first artist to have attempted to use one form to deconstruct another. T. S. Eliot's *Four Quartets* is an example of a tightly organized literary form, the quartet, which seems to have fascinated Eliot. More open forms could be represented by the rhapsody and the prelude. *Four Quartets* may have been based on musical compositions, perhaps by Ludwig van Beethoven or even Béla Bartók. An example of the variations of the form can be seen in the work of Beethoven's middle period. He follows the rules of the classical quartet; for example, four movements are arranged as, first, the allegro, second, the scherzo or the theme and variations, third, the andante, and finally, the allegro. He uses the sonata form ABA in the development of dominant and subordinate themes. His late quartets, however, break these rules; from op. 127 to 135, each quartet has one more movement than the preceding one.

In *Four Quartets*, Eliot divides his quartets into four parts or movements. He uses the rhyme scheme of the sonnet form on occasion, as in the second part of "Burnt Norton" in the first stanza. In the second stanza, this formal constraint begins to break down and is abandoned by the third stanza. The sonnet form recurs briefly through the *Four Quartets*, but is not sustained. Of greatest interest are the points where the constraints are abandoned by Eliot, because these points signal the slippage between the form and that which he tries to recuperate as content.

Contemporary composers who have used this eighteenth-century form, the quartet, include Rudolf Kolisch, Alban Berg, Anton Webern, and Arnold Schoenberg. Although the quartet form was preserved in the romantic era after the time of Beethoven, it clearly had become subordinate to the symphony. After Beethoven's sixteen quartets and many chamber works of Franz Schubert, including his fifteen quartets, such leading figures of the romantic era as Felix Mendelssohn, Robert Schumann, Peter Tchaikovsky, and Johannes Brahms composed less than five quartets each. Of the major figures in the late romantic period, Gustav Mahler composed no published quartets; Anton Bruckner published one; and only Anton Dvořák was prolific in this form. One reason why an eighteenth-century form could become central in the twentieth century is that it filled a need that other forms did not. Its transparency allowed Schoenberg to use it in order to showcase his innovations. It became his strategy for the deconstruction of the symphony. In his theory of nonsynchrony presented in "Nonsynchronism and the Obligation to Its Dialectics," Bloch attempts to account for this social phenomenon, in which discarded forms are recycled or in some cases maintained in an altered form. If a form has not been completely exhausted and if it answers needs that the current hegemonic forms do not, it will reappear. In *The Philosophy of the Future*, Bloch describes how that which he calls the "new" can safely reside, unnoticed, in the old.

Cortázar himself admits to using a musical structure in his short story "Clone," one of the stories in the collection *Queremos tanto a Glenda*.[6] In "Note on the Theme of a King and the Vengeance of a Prince," a kind of afterword to "Clone," he writes:

> Cuando llega el momento, escribir como al dictado me es natural; por eso de cuando en cuando me impongo reglas estrictas a manera de variante de algo que terminaría por ser monótono. En este relato la «grilla» consistió en ajustar una narración todavía inexistente al molde de la *Ofrenda Musical* de Juan Sebastián Bach. (122)

> [When the moment arrives it's natural for me to write as if someone were dictating to me; that's why I impose strict rules on myself from time to time as a variant of something that might end up being monotonous. In this tale the "catch" (the Spanish is *grilla*) consisted in adjust-

ing a still nonexistent narrative to the mold of *A Musical Offering* by Johann Sebastian Bach. ("Clone" 55)]

In his appropriation of the structure of Bach's *A Musical Offering*, Cortázar uses the musical forms of the canon, the trio sonata, and the canonical fugue. Similarly, the most interesting aspects of the narrative structure of *Libro de Manuel* are those points at which Cortázar breaks or disrupts any patterns he may have sought to establish, for it is in the interstices of these irreducible differences that the incommensurability between form and content surfaces. Cortázar discusses the imposition of a musical form on his work in the notes on "Clone":

> La regla del juego era amenazadora: ocho instrumentos debían ser figurados por ocho personajes, ocho dibujos sonoros respondiendo, alternando u oponiéndose debían encontrar su correlación en sentimientos, conductas y relaciones de ocho personas. Imaginar un doble literario del London Harpsichord Ensemble me pareció tonto en la medida en que un violinista o un flautista no se pliegan en su vida privada a los temas musicales que ejecutan; pero a la vez la noción de cuerpo, de conjunto, tenía que existir de alguna manera desde el principio, puesto que la poca extensión de un cuento no permitiría integrar eficazmente a ocho personas que no tuvieran relación o contacto previos a la narración. ("Clone" 123)

> [The rules of the game were threatening: eight instruments had to be transfigured into eight characters, eight musical sketches, responding, altenating, or opposing one another, had to find their correlation in the feelings, behavior, and relationships of eight people. Conceiving a literary double of the London Harpsichord Ensemble seemed foolish to me in the degree that a violinist or flautist does not in his private life cleave to the musical themes he performs; but, at the same time, the notion of a body, a group, had to exist in some way from the beginning, since the short scope of a story wouldn't permit the effective integration of eight people who had no relationship or contact previous to the narration. ("Clone" 55–56)]

The relation between literature and music, in the context of such a discussion, would be one neither of homology nor analogy, but of multidimensionality.

The "sameness" of the project of Cortázar and Schoenberg consists in the fact that both avoid the central, the obvious, and the crucial, and instead focus on the "trivial." Referring to "Clone," Cortázar writes:

> . . . vi que el fragmento final tendría que abarcar a todos los personajes *menos a uno*. Y ese uno, desde las primeras páginas ya escritas, había sido la causa todavía incierta de la fisura que se estaba dando en el conjunto, en eso que otro personaje habría de calificar de *clone*. En el mismo segundo la ausencia forzosa de Franca y la historia de Carlo Gesualdo, que había subtendido todo el proceso de la imagina-

ción, fueron la mosca y la araña en la tela. Ya podía seguir, todo estaba consumado desde antes. ("Clone" 125)

[. . . I saw that the final fragment would have to include all of the characters *minus one*. And that one, from the first pages already written, had been the still-uncertain cause of the fissure that was growing in the group, in what another character would describe as a clone. In the same moment Franca's necessary absence and the story of Carlo Gesualdo, which had underlain the whole process of imagination, were the fly and the spider in the web. Now I could go ahead, everything had been consummated since before. ("Clone" 57)]

Both Cortázar and Schoenberg looked to the interstices and narrow passages that divide and unite the melody, harmony and rhythm, narrative structure, central problematic or conflict, and the historical. That is, in terms of their modernist aesthetic, that which cannot be described is the historical event. Only the fragments that surround it may be captured. The unutterable, that which cannot be written, is the origin, the explanation, the key. The difference between the form in the literature of Cortázar and that in the music of Schoenberg is the difference between two forms of discourse, which are not reducible.

Thus, a multidimensional approach seeks to force the limits of their reducibility and to allow for their differences as well as their identity in the interference pattern that records their interaction. And in the "melody" we will construct, based upon the narrative structure of *Libro de Manuel*, we shall hear a crescendo that points to but does not specify a crucial moment in the text: the kidnapping of the VIP. In fact, the suspense builds to silence, since the actual kidnapping is not recorded in the text. Yet, the strong emphasis in *Libro de Manuel* upon political concerns might lead a reader to resort to a Marxist reading. Neo-Marxist readings are also possible, especially when one considers the influence of the May event in France on Cortázar; certain neo-Marxist sentiments are recorded in *Ultimo Round*. Nonetheless, the analysis in terms of musical structure is finally more adequate to border writing.

The narrative structure of *Libro de Manuel* is heard contrapuntally against the sequence of newspaper clippings. Counterpoint also characterizes the technique used within the narrative structure itself. For example, in some chapters even the type size plays a role, with certain phrases appearing in OED-sized type above the regular type. In the following passage, for example, "¿por qué la luna llena?" is printed above the words "importante misión":

De todos modos era tiempo de pensar un poco en eso que estaba esperando en la otra punta, ir poniendo desde ya la cara de veterinario consciente de su importante misión, el problema . . . (*LM* 126–27)

["In any case, it was time to think a little about what was waiting at the other end, to start assuming the air of the veterinarian conscious of his important mission now, the problem . . . " (*MM* 126). Above the words "important mission," in OED type, is the phrase, "why the full moon?"]

Other elements that embellish the nonlinear narrative structure include the reproduction of a letter and a footnote that asserts the authenticity of the letter, although certain "pasajes personales y referencias políticamente comprometedoras para terceros" have been deleted (*LM* 48) ("personal passages have been left out as well as any references that might be politically compromising for third parties; *MM* 44). This is a sort of politicized appropriation of the well-known use of footnotes in fiction by Jorge Luis Borges.

Another example of counterpoint in the typography of *Libro de Manuel* is found in two pages that contain seven lines each of words reproduced in such a way that they are incomplete; the lines appear as a puzzle that may be impossible to solve, since they may have been lifted from a much larger passage:

y se la m
ta la man
ras cómo llo
orcía y me sup
—Hicistes b
al cabo.—Así
derán esas p (*LM* 187)[7]

Within these fragments (*LM* 96, 112; *MM* 94, 111) in search of a context is congealed the problematic in the structure of the entire level: form and content must be seen in their mutual interaction. The concrete poets used the technology of the typewriter to create a new kind of poetry; Cortázar continues this tradition.

The multidimensional logic that underlies Cortázar's system of representation is closer to that of twentieth-century music than to a one-dimensional logical explanation of an event isolated from its context.[8] Two composers to whom Cortázar refers in *Libro de Manuel* and whose structural innovations have influenced him are Schoenberg and Stockhausen. Cortázar's novels are not organized around the principles of the nineteenth-century level: there is not a development of strong characters or linear plot. Randomness and a breaking of rules are the only order. In twentieth-century music, the twelve-tone system of Schoenberg and his followers, and more recently, the combination of Eastern and Western traditions in the music of Stockhausen, juxtapose randomness and order in a manner similar to that found in Cortázar's work.

The rise of mass culture has meant that both "high" literature and classical music have been confronted with their counterparts in the mass media. Cortázar revels in this confrontation, as evidenced by his inclusion of newspaper items and his references to such popular writers as Raymond Chandler. A twentieth-century composer in the "high" art tradition, Darius Milhaud, was influenced by the jazz of such composers as George Gershwin. Gershwin, conversely, was influenced by classical composers such as Maurice Ravel. Cortázar's interest in music, particularly jazz, is present from his first published work; in *Presencia* (1938), a collection of sonnets, he makes references to jazz. Music is an important referential code from which Cortázar's work emerges, a reference code that dissolves the boundaries between "high" art and mass culture.

In the works of some writers, referential codes are more important at the level of content than at the level of form. For example, in *S/Z*, Barthes's discussions of Balzac's referential codes are fascinating but not always necessary to understand the story. In the case of Cortázar's work, his very undermining of Western logic as a central concern makes his choice of music as a referential code crucial in understanding the work. The investigation of the formal aspects of his work using musical paradigms is much less arbitrary than would be, for example, a Greimasian analysis, in which logical squares would serve to force the text into a Procrustean bed whose architect, Aristotle, epitomizes the very system of Western logic.

Cortázar seeks to throw into question. Structuralist thought in France has also left its mark on *Libro de Manuel*, particularly in the diagrams, one of which is accompanied by the warning "N.B.: Como todos los organigramas, éste no se entiende demasiado" (*LM* 162) ("N.B.: Like all organigrams, this one is not too easily understood"; *MM* 165). Certainly, in a country in which students in the late 1970s at the University at Vincennes were gathering in mass meetings to engage in semiotic analyses of government decrees about university reforms, the semiotic referential code must be respected; kidnapping plans laid out in semiotic notation are included by Cortázar for the reader who will have the reference code of semiotics at hand. Cortázar is also ironic in his portrayal of the Joda and the deadly serious planning that goes into their politics of spontaneity. But by examining the reference code of music, Cortázar's form can be juxtaposed against his content in order to see how the problem of language as a shared system and/or as a set of separate discourses presents itself in his work.

The three elements commonly held to be fundamental in music are melody, harmony, and rhythm. The first two are concerned with intervals, and therefore, according to René Leibowitz in *Schoenberg and His School*, space. Rhythm, he believes, as it "articulates sound-forms in time" seems limited to time (3). However, since repetition is a possibility of rhythm, it has the possibility of abolishing time as well. Melody and harmony also have temporal aspects, insofar as both unfold in time. An example of how the rhythm of the game of hopscotch abolishes time is found in *Rayuela*. In the "Table of Instructions," the list of chapter sequence in the second reading ends with a repetition of chapter 131: "-131–58–131."

In the music of Stockhausen, melody, harmony, and rhythm are reformulated as melody, sound, and duration. Stockhausen's music, unlike Schoenberg's, is not confined by the rules of seriality in which each tone of the twelve must occur in the tone line before a new tone line may begin. Stockhausen does not proceed from the structural innovations of Schoenberg in which a series of tones—he does not restrict himself to twelve—forms the basis of the composition and all the sound forms must consist of "successive or simultaneous presentations of the complete row, a fragment of it, or several forms of it" (Leibowitz, 102). The different forms are: (1) the original; (2) its retrograde form, which is produced in the reading of the original form from the last note to the first; (3) its inverted form, which involves reversing the directions (ascending or descending) of the intervals; and (4) the retrograde inversion. At least a spiritual kinship, if nothing more, is present between the second nonlinear way to read *Rayuela*, described in the "Table of Instructions," and Schoenberg's system. Of course, *Rayuela* is not based on any sort of twelve-element system. It is not accidental, however, that the reader is urged to read fifty-four chapters in order, even as these are interspersed with other out-of-sequence chapters, thereby integrating a random element into a partially linear system. The seeming contradiction between order and randomness in the chapter sequence "73–1–2–116–3–84–4–71–5–81–74–6–7–8––93" also appears in *Libro de Manuel*, although in different forms. In the structure of *Libro de Manuel*, whether or not it is conscious as in "Clone," Cortázar may be said to have something in common with Schoenberg. *Libro de Manuel* is filled with references to Stockhausen's *Prozession* as well as to other twentieth-century composers such as Varese. The following reading of *Libro de Manuel* will be based on another work by Stockhausen, not mentioned by Cortázar in the book itself. *Momente*, was composed in 1961–62, and, like *Rayuela*, it is not a closed work "with unequivocally fixed beginning, unfolding, and end, but a multi-faceted variable composition of independent events."[9]

Momente is based upon three moments: (1) *M* (melody—monodic, or heterophonic); (2) *K* (sound); and (3) *D* (rhythm). In addition to these main moments, there are also *i* (non-formal) and three reflexive moments, *m*, *k*, and *d*. Combinations such as *Mm* would signify a reflexive moment in which *m* would be the feedback mechanism, the possibility of reflecting back or commenting upon *M*.[10] That is, *m* could be a musical space opened to allow for metacommentary about the melody *M*. In the reading of *Libro de Manuel*, only *M*, *K*, and *D* moments will be emphasized. Further work might show that the relationships among *M*, *K*, and *D* moments to the *m*, *k*, and *d* moments would be reflexive. For example, in the steel band music of the Caribbean, harmonics are created that operate on another level in addition to the rhythm, sound, and melody. These harmonics are a kind of feedback. In rock and roll music, feedback is literally the electronic feedback produced when an electric guitar is held toward an amplifier, as Jimi Hendrix showed the world.

Presence and the Border Narrator

The narrative structure in *Libro de Manuel*, in which the central event, the kidnapping of the VIP by the Joda, is omitted, bears a resemblance to the acts of urban revolutionaries described in the newspapers. The reason why hostages are taken is often obscure to the hostages and the citizens of the countries from which the hostages are taken, because the cause of the kidnapping is absent. In other words, the causes of political events are missing from everyday life; the events themselves, ensconced in a myriad of causes that are repressed in the discourse of everyday life, are likewise omitted from Cortázar's border narratives. In this way Cortázar comments on the distance of most people from political activities known in the mass media as "terrorism" and, at the same time, on the lack of reflexivity on the part of the so-called terrorists themselves. The Joda, a group of revolutionaries, is presented as imitating mass-media images of revolutionary activity without realizing that this is indeed what they are doing.

As has been argued earlier, historical perspective is based on media images. By presenting the reader with a view of "terrorism" from the other side, in its mundane details, Cortázar deconstructs the media view of terrorism: that terrorists are monstrous others. Cortázar's very structure crosses the border of alterity. His translation of the everyday life of "terrorists," and the omission of the political actions that distinguish "terrorists" from humans—bombings, kidnapping, etc.—allows Cortázar as a writer to express critical support for political commitment while at the same time calling for reflexivity on the part of revolutionaries and for greater political awareness on the part of the nonpoliticized populace. He is able to be at once respectful to and irreverent toward all sides.

By refusing to write about the act, the kidnapping, as it occurs, in its historical specificity, Cortázar is making a statement about history and revolutionary activity, that is, theory and praxis: revolutionary activity may be neither predicted nor determined. The relationship between the theory of the group or party and its praxis is a fractured one. Indeterminacy and undecidability more accurately describe the coming into being of political activity. Such a perspective, which is multidimensional, looks to the unexpected as a source of political activity. Even as Cortázar creates an urban revolutionary group in *Libro de Manuel*, he simultaneously subjects it to a critique about its ability to control the revolutionary future. The previous analysis based on musical form allows this critique to emerge.

The three kinds of literary "sounds" in *Libro de Manuel* are based on the confrontation between the urban revolutionaries and the repressive leaders of the state. These can be designated as M, or ideological confrontation; K, or negotiations with the state and between states and superpowers; and D, or direct confrontation. Examples of direct confrontation are kidnapping, bombings, bank robberies, and shoot-outs with the military and the police. Ideological confrontation, a much broader rubric, is defined here as confrontation in the cultural and social arena: human rights, liberation theology, advertisements in the mass media, astrology, and sports. An example is a report about a nineteen-year-old who committed suicide because he was forced to have his hair cut. Negotiations with the state occur in the demands for the release of political prisoners. Some items are difficult to classify because they overlap the boundaries of the divisions drawn among urban revolutionaries, Latin American state powers, and superpowers/ Western European countries. For example, the purchase of planes from France by the Argentine government to fight subversives in Bolivia is determined to be a k, or negotiation, because it involves a mediated confrontation between *guerrilleros* and the state.

The accompanying diagram borrows the notion of the interval from the language of music. Arrows point toward the victim of the action in order to show the direction of the aggression: "prof←police" is to be read as "an act of aggression against a professor by the police." The interval takes on the characteristics of a vector. It is constituted by the distance between the revolutionary column, on the far left, and the superpowers, on the far right. The column under the heading "Latin American countries" should be understood as the state apparatus of the country: the police, the mayoralities, the embassies, and so on. Those groups whose members have a contradictory class status, such as students, youths, and gays, are indicated in brackets because they are not represented by either the revolutionary groups discussed by Cortázar or by the state. The gay liberation movement in Argentina began in the mid-1970s and does not appear in *Libro de Manuel*. The first column has the heading "Moments" and uses the musical code of M, K, D, m, k, and d.

In determining which moments are ideological and which are directly confrontational, there is no intention to privilege or devalue either. Some items may appear to be placed arbitrarily; for example, political prisoners and torture are both given an M classification, ideological confrontation, rather than a D classification, direct confrontation. Human rights, which include political prisoners' rights and the ultimate abuse of human rights, torture, fall within the category of ideology. The primary function of torture is ideological; hence, the M classification. The numbers of political prisoners at any given time, recorded by Amnesty International, is seen as a record of a moment of reflexivity.

The "instruments" employed by Cortázar in *Libro de Manuel* are newspaper clippings, narration, dialogue, testimonies of torture victims, letters, poetry, diagrams, varying sizes of type, and telegrams. If we rewrite the "Moment" column horizontally, we can hear the "performance," which includes only the score of the newspaper clippings: M–M–M–M–M–D–D–M–M–m–M–D–M–K–D–D–D–D–D–M–M–M–M–D–D–M–M–d–D–M–M–M–M–M–M–k–M–K–M–M. The repetition of five D classifications can be heard immediately. Not surprisingly, the passage in which this occurs (*LM* 184–86, *MM* 186–88) coincides with the building of suspense before the kidnapping of the VIP (the plan for the kidnapping is de-

"Moment"	Guerrillas Latin American countries	Superpowers and developed Western European Nations	Incident
M	Professor ◄── Police		Police beat professor
M	Student ──► Mayor's Office		Student attack on public property
M	Professor ◄── Police		Police attack professor
M	Bishops ◄── Government		Bishops censure government
M	Youth ──► Parents		19-year-old commits suicide over haircut
D	Guerrillas ──► Embassy		Guerrillas attack Swiss Embassy
D	Guerrillas ──► Embassy		Brazilian leftists kidnap German ambassador
M	[Horoscope predicts coup]		Horoscope predicts coup
M	Youth ──► State		Youths riot, escape from institute
[m]	Political Prisoners ──► State		Number of political prisoners in the world
M	"Extremists" ──► State		Four extremists tortured
M	Student ──► State ──── State offical (U.S.A.)		Student attack on flag
D	Guerrillas ──► State		German students protest McNamara
K	[Falkland Islands] ──── State ──── State (International agreement)		Sovereignty to Falkland Islands
D	Guerrillas ──► State		Five guerrillas escape
D	Guerrillas ──► The Rich		Guerrillas rob Almeida
D	Guerrillas ──────► U.S. Embassy		American ambassador kidnapped
D	Popular Struggles ──► State		Popular struggle
D	Guerrillas ──► State ──── U.S.A.		Arms robbery in Uruguary

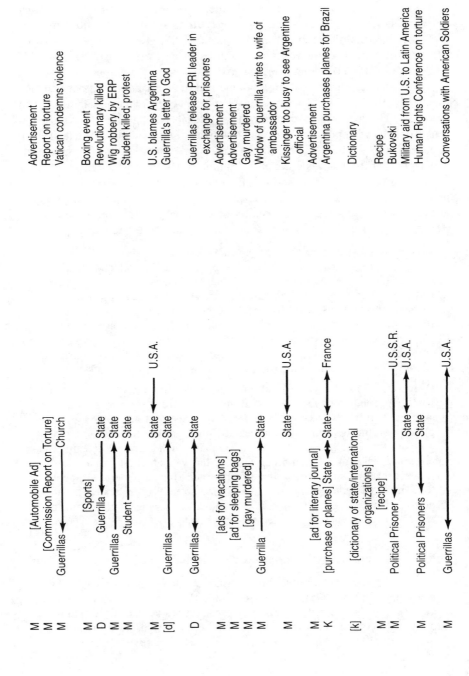

scribed on *LM* 176–77, *MM* 178–79). Furthermore, the two critical events in any narrative about *guerrillero* activity are, first, the moment of the action, and second, the moment of the arrest and/or death of the *guerrilleros*. In *Libro de Manuel*, the moment of the action is substituted by a description of the scene (*LM* 252–60, *MM* 255–63), a long interlude, and the subsequent reference to the action in the past tense. The reader must assume that the kidnapping has been carried out by *LM* 295, *MM* 296. Thus, the most important event in the novel is described obliquely. The reader is not permitted to witness it. As an event, it can be represented only by what precedes it and in the activity of its planning. The actual event is undecidable and unpredictable. Cortázar's representation of the event is itself a metaphor for the elusive nature of revolutionary activity. Although possibilities of political action may be described, the one that will actually occur cannot be predicted with certainty. In musical terms, we can "hear it coming," but we never actually "see" it. Instead, a description of the luncheon in a restaurant on the Champs-Élysées and an apology by the narrator are all the reader is given:

> Lo que le hubiera gustado al que te dije poder contar las cosas desde el temor y el temblor de la papada del Vip en el auto de Roland, desde la cara de la Vipa cuando la bajaron en una explanada por el lado de Pontoise, lugar absurdo si los había para trasladarse del Parc Monceau a Verrières pero que Lucien Verneuil, copiloto y pistola en panza tremante del Vip, estimaba más bien útil para despistar a la policía lanzada ya a una búsqueda general aunque por el momento poco coherente. Lástima pero no le salía, a la hora de asumir palabra en mano los acontecimientos como manda la buena narrativa . . . (*LM* 294)

> [What the one I told you would have liked was to have been able to tell what happened from the fear and trembling of the Vip's jowls in Roland's car, from the face of the Vipess when they let her out on an esplanade on the Pontoise side, an absurd place if ever there was one to go from the Parc Monceau to Verriéres but which Lucien Verneuil, copilot and pistol in the trembling belly of the Vip, thought would be rather useful to throw the police off the track since a general although for a moment rather incoherent search had already been launched. A pity but it wouldn't come out, at the moment of taking up the word to tell about the events as is called for in a good narrative . . . (*MM* 295)]

Cortázar continues his satire of the code of "action-packed" narrative structure:

> . . . la barriga, de la vistosa mueca que le ladeaba a la izquierda el maquillaje Dorothy Gray número ocho a la Vipa convulsionada por uno de esos cólicos que reíte de los megatones en el Pacífico, de Roland piloteando con su fangiofría a milímetro de luces rojas y ya un silbato que les dibujaba la espina dorsal hasta el coxis y si te descuidás un

poco más abajo, de todo eso lo único que le salía al que te dije era una impresión general de despelote por encima o por debajo . . . (294)

[. . . your belly, the gaudy grimace on the part of the Vipess as her Dorothy Gray number eight makeup turned to the left as she was convulsed by a colic that put Pacific megatons to shame, Roland piloting like Barney Coldfield a quarter of an inch away from the red taillights and already a whistle that shook their spines down to the coccyx and if you weren't a little more careful below that, out of all that the only thing that came to the one I told you was a general impression of total confusion above or below. (*MM* 295)]

To which historical referential codes should the reader of *Libro de Manuel* refer? Among the many important historical events of 1969–73, culled from both liberal and revisionist historians, are the May events of 1969, the *Cordobazo*, the general strike in June 1969, labor union conflicts in January 1970, the kidnapping-assassination of Pedro Aramburu in June 1970, the coup that ousted Juan Carlos Organía and set up Roberto Levingston, the assassination of Alonso (a leading Peronist labor leader), nine general strikes in Córdoba in early 1971, a coup that replaced Levingston with Alejandro Lanusse, and events in September 1973 that resulted in the forced call for elections in 1973–74.[11] In other parts of the world during these years, the United States invaded Cambodia in 1970, the Padilla affair occurred in Cuba in 1971, and there was *guerrillero* activity in Uruguay, Argentina, Brazil, Bolivia, and many other countries. In Argentina, in May and April of 1970, a Paraguayan consul and two Soviet diplomats were kidnapped, and there were organized bank robberies and attacks on police and military guard posts. In Uruguay, on New Year's Day, 1969 arms were recaptured from the police. On June 1, Nelson Rockefeller visited Montevideo and was greeted with fire-bombings of U.S. buildings, strikes, violent demonstrations, and the takeover of a radio station. In September 1969, Pellegrini, a banker and publisher, was kidnapped in support of eight thousand striking bank workers. In April 1970, the chief of the Secret Police, Hector Moran Chaquero, was machine-gunned to death, and in August, the U.S. "adviser" to the Uruguayan police on antiguerrilla warfare, Dan Mitrione, was kidnapped and killed when the government refused to exchange him for political prisoners. This event was the subject of a documentary by filmmaker Constantin Costa-Gavras.

Cortázar's history creates a new group of resisters in the gaps between the news and his presentation or "performance" of the musical score constituted by the newspaper clippings of the period. Whereas E. P. Thompson's *The Making of the English Working Class* presupposed the existence of a unified working class whose development can be traced through the fragments of folksongs and historical documents of the everyday life of the common people, the border history presented by *Libro de Manuel* presupposes a mere grouping of forces, and one that is in no way unified by class distinctions. This group, the Joda, is presented through the fragments of news items, narration, dialogue, poetry, charts, letters, and telegrams. Cortázar is concerned with a variety of oppressed groups: revolutionaries, political prisoners, students, youth, Maoists, gays, politically committed professors. His propensity for selecting news items about revolutionaries suggests that he finds them the most prepared to fight back.

To what extent does Cortázar succeed in getting inside historical events? Although the historical events of 1969-73 that were enumerated here are not directly mentioned in *Libro de Manuel*, there are references to events in Córdoba and Rosario as well as in other parts of Argentina and Uruguay in the testimony of the victims of torture included at the end of the book. One of the victims, Tirso Yáñez, relates that he was questioned in connection with the escape of a *guerrillero* from a prison in Córdoba, an action of the Ejército Revolucionario Popular, the ERP (*LM* 375, *MM* 377). It is significant that the news clippings make no direct reference to the *Cordobazo* of 1970. Instead, events occurring in Paris are included: a professor is attacked by the police; a sociology student at the Sorbonne is released after having been charged with violence against the police, willful violence with premeditation, violence against property and degradation of a public monument; a twenty-year-old is attacked by the police. The discussion of members of the Joda includes Fernando's analysis of the situation in Paris: at least such people were not killed as they would have been in Guatemala or Mexico. Patricio adds, "O en Córdoba y Buenos Aires" (*LM* 45) ("Or in Córdoba and Buenos Aires"; *MM* 40). Aramburu's kidnapping is not mentioned but that of a German ambassador by Brazilian leftists is. The coup is recorded in an ad that claims it had been predicted in an astrology journal, *Horoscope*. The reference to astrology calls up another reference code, the bizarre connections between politics and the occult: Roberto Arlt, Hitler, López Rega. Cortázar's interest in astrology is evident in a section of *Libro de Manuel* on the full moon. The lack of respect shown to the flag results in a prison sentence of two months to two years for one Argentine, another example of the disparity between the treatment of citizens in the Third World in comparison to the First World. The "assaults on police headquarters, banks and commercial centers" in August 1970, mentioned by James Scobie in his book *Argentina* (265), are enumerated by Cortázar in his selection, which includes such activities in other countries as well: fifteen *guerrilleros* occupy a city near Córdoba; one thousand German students protest McNamara's visit; five prisoners are freed by *guerrilleros* in Córdoba; and a banker is robbed in an action led by the "Cid" in Brazil. The dates are not always given, but these events appear to have occurred in July and August of 1970. The financial crisis of the meat producers and packing houses appears in *Libro de Manuel* in an article based on an analysis in the *New York Times* that holds Argentina responsible for raising world prices of leather. The assassination of Dan Mitrione by the Tupamaros is included in *Libro de Manuel*, but no mention is made of the nine strikes in Córdoba in the first half of 1971 or of the coup that replaced Levingston with Lanusse.

The year of 1971 that is presented to Manuel in his book includes Kissinger's treatment of Quijano, France's sale of $49 million worth of planes to Argentina, and the condemnation of Bukovski by the Soviet Union. What may be concluded from a consideration of the omissions in the book that is to be Manuel's political and historical education? Why, for example, are no workers mentioned? No strikes? Why are such items as an ad for *Horoscope*, a dictionary of sale organizations, a boxing event, and the murder of a gay male in the sordid story "Crimen de homosexuales" included rather than more important events? Cortázar's method, the welding together of social debris, recalls Benjamin's analysis of the impossibility of literature achieving the construction of totality. The writer can never do more than achieve a partial, edited perspective.

In *Charles Baudelaire*, Benjamin asserts that "the poets find the refuse of a society on their street and derive their heroic subject from this very refuse"; his affection for Baudelaire's figure of the poem "Le vin de chiffoniers" points to his testament to fragmentation (79). Like the figure in the poem, Cortázar has gathered "the day's refuse in the capital city" (79). He has turned to the daily newspaper and to "everything that the big city threw away, everything it lost, everything it despised, everything it crushed underfoot" (79). He catalogued and collected the recipe for fried sandwiches, the love affair/murder of two gay men, the boxing event, the suicide of the youth who was forced to have his hair cut, and the letters to God and to his wife written by the revolutionary who starved to death in the jungle in Bolivia. Cortázar "collates the annals of intemperance, the capharnum (stockpile) of waste" (79). Like a miser guarding a treasure, he saves the "refuse which will assume the shape of useful or gratifying objects" for Manuel, perhaps a bit of protection for a child who inevitably must be delivered up to the "jaws of the goddess of industry" (79).

One could as easily argue that Cortázar is not the *bricoleur* of whom Lévi-Strauss writes; rather, perhaps he has succeeded in constructing a totality out of what Jameson calls, in *Marxism and Form*, the "events and raw materials of daily existence" (170). Perhaps, as the early Lukács claimed literature was able to do, Cortázar has captured the concrete through his formal experimentation. This presupposes, however, that *Libro de Manuel* is a novel, an assumption that would have to be examined.

In any case a multidimensional praxis, based on an understanding of history in which the historical event is an absence, is given a name by Cortázar the narrator: "*contestatión* new style." Part of the new-style *contestatión* is expressed in the term itself, which is bilingual. The appeal of the Joda and its "*contestatión* new style" to its own members and to the readers of *Libro de Manuel* is that it subverts everyday life. Yet, inevitably, the bizarre political activities of the group, such as smuggling counterfeit money in the turquoise penguin affair, the kidnapping, and the final confrontation with the police, all lead to nothing more than Lonstein's return to the job of washing dead bodies in the mortuary, that is, the boring repetition of everyday life.

The seeming impossibility of breaking out of the practico-inert, Sartre's term in *Critique of Dialectical Reason* for congealed human labor that appears to us as reified, coexists with the "performance" of confrontations on all levels present in the score created from the juxtaposition of newspaper clippings. This apparent contradiction between the allure of revolution and the horror of the mundane opens a space for Cortázar's treatment of desire and the grotesque. Passion, sexuality, excitement, and the new are presented in opposition to listlessness, celibacy, boredom, and the old. The eroticism of torture is condemned in the sexuality of the torturer, but Cortázar merely describes Lonstein's necrophilia, that is, his propensity for masturbating during his job. A literary reference in this passage is to the work *Soap* by French twentieth-century writer F. Ponge. Narcissism is a theme that underlies the entire novel and is linked to the inability of the characters to achieve reflexivity.

Cortázar uses the testimonies of torture victims and the opinions of Lonstein on masturbation as a contrapuntal device in order to create a wider framework within which to consider sexuality and politics. On one level, *Libro de Manuel* is a book with a political, didactic aim, as critics have been eager to point out. On another level, it subverts any simple political viewpoint by deconstructing the opposition oppressor-oppressed. Both torturer and victim are shown to operate within a repressive system of desire. The reader of this polemical perspective can only interrogate her or his assumptions about sexuality, narcissism, sadism, masochism, history, politics, and language.

Cortázar explores the process of translation and the processing of desire through the discourse of sexuality, history, and politics. The history that constitutes Manuel's book, translated from newspaper clippings, is made up of what Benjamin calls, in "The Task of the Translator," "fragments of a vessel which are glued together" and which "must match one another in the smallest details, although they need not be like one another" (78). Like Benjamin's translator, Cortázar is cognizant of the way in which culture mediates translation such that "instead of resembling the meaning of the original [the translator] must lovingly and in detail incorporate the original's mode of signification" (78). In other words, there can be no strict division between original and translation. There never was an original that was not already tainted by a process of translation; there never was an original revolutionary organization that was not already seduced by fantasies of its own capture and torture by its enemy. A system of unconscious desire and a concomitant refusal of reflexivity characterize both sides in *Libro de Manuel*.

Cortázar is aware that he is not free from the border situation of translation. Concerning his own status as a writer, he cites Merleau-Ponty:

una frase de Maurice Merleau-Ponty vino a justificar en mi propio terreno, el de la significación, la forma meramental receptiva y abierta a cualquier sorpesa en que yo seguía escribiendo un libro del que no sabía casi nada. «El número y la riqueza de las significaciones de que dispone el hombre», dice Merleau-Ponty a propósito de Mauss y de Lévi-Strauss, «exceden siempre el círculo de los objetos definidos que merecen el nombre de significados» y a continuación, como si me ofreciera un cigarrillo: «La función simbólica debe adelantarse siempre a su objeto y solo encuentra lo real cuando se la adelanta en lo imaginario . . . » (*Ultimo Round* 263)

[a sentence of Maurice Merleau-Ponty finally justified in my own terrain of signification the simple way, open and receptive to whatever surprise, in which I pursued writing a book about which I knew almost nothing. "The number and wealth of signifieds that one has available," says Merleau-Ponty, a propos of Mauss and Lévi-Strauss, "always exceeds the circle of defined objects that deserve the name of signifieds" and he continues as if offering me a cigarette: "The symbolic function must always move beyond its object and it only meets the real when it moves forward into the imaginary . . ."]

In this reading of Merleau-Ponty, Cortázar describes his own writing process, which is not completely controlled by his rational, logical intentions. The text will always suggest meanings that go beyond his intentions. It will complete itself in the imaginary of the reader. The epistemological implications of Cortázar's view lead to an interactive, multidimensional perspective. A political praxis informed by this perspective would define theory and praxis as linked by a mutual process of continuous translation rather than a relationship of absolute identity or absolute alterity. This is a multidimensional ordering, alone adequate to the border text, which cannot be subsumed under either analytic or dialectical logic.

The contribution, then, of *Libro de Manuel* to the current debates in the areas of the new historicism, political activity, and translation is its faithfulness to the *mai* 68 slogan, "Sean realistas: pidan to imposible" (*Ultimo Round* 98) ("Be realists: demand the impossible"). Cortázar lived to see the success of the Sandinista revolution in 1979, and, along with that of Cardenal and García Márquez, his literature has played an important ideological role in giving cultural legitimacy to the Sandinista cause among international supporters.

It is perhaps this very engagement that comes to expression in *Libro de Manuel* by undermining the characterisitcs of the nineteenth-century novel; plot and suspense have been deemphasized in order to focus upon the reference, symbolic, and semic codes from which characters emerge. Its decentered structure omits crucial events that would have been essential in a traditional novel; instead, Cortázar chooses to privilege the trivial. In *Libro de Manuel*, the temporal unfolds in a poetic "play of signification," a kind of visual music. The narrative structure of the work allows Cortázar to examine the dichotomy event/nonevent. The moment of kidnapping is less important than the long preparation, the description of which constitutes much of the book. Even this preparation does not constitute suspense, insofar as it does not lead to any sort of resolution; rather, it is Cortázar's metacommentary about the hermeneutic code itself. The nineteenth-century novel, with its well-developed characters and linear narrative structure, is closer in certain aspects to *Rayuela* and García Márquez's *Cien años de soledad*. This may account for why these works have been more widely accepted than *Libro de Manuel*. The discussion of politics that has surrounded *Libro de Manuel* has obscured its formal experimentation, but readers and critics may have had more difficulty with the form than they might have imagined.

As border writing, *Libro de Manuel* replaces traditional characters, usually organized in the nineteenth-century novel according to social structures such as the family and class, with members of a group, the Joda. Plot development is replaced by fragmentation; a linear narrative is replaced by a collage of moments. The newspaper articles collected for Manuel's book are presented in chronological order, as are the activities of the Joda. The presentation of the moments appears jumbled, however, because of the "trivial" content.

This kind of history written by Cortázar in *Libro de Manuel* is informed by a notion of nonsynchrony. Although it presents newspaper articles about *guerrilleros*, the fictional urban revolutionary group the Joda, and its actions, these actions are presented from the perspective of an outsider. Cortázar translates rather than represents the actions. He implies that the revolutionary group does not represent the masses nor is it a substitute for the people. It is merely one of many possible catalysts for social change. Such a view of history relies heavily on the experience of the *mai* events in France in 1968. The inability of the writer or artist to get inside the political event she or he represents or translates in art is isomorphic with the marginal role of the artist in politics. The modernist perspective condemns itself to the outsider perspective. Border writing seeks not only to include the viewer in an active way, but to engage oneself as a writer. Cortázar is situated in the midst of this dilemma. To get inside the event would mean to write either an autobiographical or traditional linear narrative. Events would be clearly defined from the perspective of actors or subjects. The often noted absence of strong or memorable characters in Cortázar's work, with a few exceptions such as La Maga and Horacio, is a manifestation of his mistrust of the stable, identifiable, centered subject in his novels. His characters, including the border narrator in *Libro de Manuel*, "el que te dije," are strangely disembodied and fleeting. Only Lonstein distinguishes himself as memorable. That he is privileged by Cortázar is evident in the conclusion of the book: Lonstein returns to the job of washing bodies. The job inserts continuity into the life of this character, or so Cortázar implies; revolutionary activity does not. The experience of Nicaragua is sobering: after a successful revolution, revolutionaries who had been fighting had to return to the everyday problems of food distribution and economic planning.

If Cortázar may be said to make a choice between continuity and everyday life on the one hand and discontinuity and revolutionary activity on the other, he clearly chooses the latter. He selects the form of music as a structure not only because it keeps him from becoming monotonous, as he tells the reader in "Clone," but also because it allows for a kind of experimentation that the illusion of representation of the event offered by the traditional linear narrative structure does not. The premise of this chapter has been that the literary form and other forms of art such as photography, painting, and music are all separate discourses, not reducible one to another, and yet all share a common quality: all can be translated. The "melody" that was constructed included a crescendo accompanied by an absence; the kidnapping of the VIP occurred in a hiatus of silence. The reflexive moments in *Momente*, constituted by combinations in which there was a reflexive mechanism, were rarely present. Their absence points to a lack of reflexivity on the part of revolutionary groups. If, in fact, reflexive moments in *Libro de Manuel* were to be constituted by the reflexivity of the members of the Joda, then the absence of such moments may be accounted for as signifying Cortázar's critique. The Joda is presented as lacking reflexivity. The character with the most reflexivity is Lonstein. Herein resides Cortázar's attitude about activity at the margins.

Ariel Dorfman has observed that while the previous generation of Latin American writers wished to leave their countries of origin and live in Europe, the contemporary Latin American writer, often in exile, longs to be able to live in Latin America.[12] Cortázar has had the opportunity to see two successful revolutions in Latin America: the Cuban revolution and the Sandinista revolution in Nicaragua. He has seen friends of his such as Ernesto Cardenal play double roles as writers and political leaders. What Cortázar did not find in the Argentine political organization satirized in the Joda was historical memory, the reflection upon the past. This was the case even as the group constructed the book for Manuel. Through his sexual fantasies, Lonstein presented a certain kind of reflection, but it was limited to his fantasies. Continuity, if it existed at all, remained in a tenuous relationship to political praxis.

Finally, it must be the border writer who will translate reality and make it intelligible. The border writer, as an artist, can overcome the dilemma of being faced with reports of events rather than events themselves, and then somehow writing a translation of these events. The border writer as translator understands that art is not a representation of reality that lies beyond itself, but rather a nonlinear movement among the fragments that constitute it.

Chapter 4
That Which Resists:
The Code of the Real in
Luisa Valenzuela's *Como en la guerra*

The Multidimensional Perspective and the Juxtaposition of Codes

Como en la guerra (*He Who Searches*) is the title of a short novel, or a long short story, written by Luisa Valenzuela in 1977. It is also a metaphor that underlies the six most obvious referential codes that structure the narrative: (1) the traditional tale; (2) the hermeneutic code; (3) the Freudian-Lacanian psychoanalytic code; (4) the code of Marxism and politics in Latin America; (5) the code of feminism and (6) the code of the real.[1] In terms of the multidimensional or holographic model, these referential codes are double in that they force a division of readers into two groups, those who are aware of the codes and those who are not. The codes also overlap, such that politically conscious readers may guess that the protagonist is a political activist while political Lacanian readers will fall into the trap of analyzing Valenzuela's tongue-in-cheek Lacanianisms. Feminists will note Valenzuela's irony, while Marxists may not. Some readers will be more familiar with the traditional tale than others and will be surprised by the so-called "magic realist" elements in the story. Readers of Roland Barthes and spy novels will recognize the importance of suspense in the novel—the hermeneutic code. Readers who have experienced some form of therapy will know something about the psychoanalytic code. Only readers who are able to negate their assumptions about all of these codes until they can hold both strands of the double code simultaneously will be able to "see" the text in its full dimensionality. This can be imagined by remembering the experience of wearing 3-D glasses. The image is printed twice, in two colors of ink. The glasses make it possible to see both at once, to perceive depth. The code of the multidimensional or holographic real is that which remains after the reader has examined his or her assumptions.

The "border" metaphor, "como en la guerra," in the context of feminism, Marxism, and psychoanalysis, juxtaposes traditional and technological cultures, which in the context of Latin America are at war with one another. In this aspect, Valenzuela's story is similar to García Márquez's *Cien años de soledad*; her characters do not all live in the same "now." Her juxtaposition of codes allows her to focus on nonsynchronic elements.[2]

The traditional tale, as analyzed by Vladimir Propp in his book *Morphology of the Folktale*, depends on the unified subject, the hero. In the traditional tale, the hero is male, which makes this code a target of Valenzuela's critical eye. Valenzuela's "characters" are split and/or merge into one another: the semiotician refers to himself as "we"; the patient he studies has a twin sister and dreams her lover Alfredo Navoni's dreams as if they were her own. Nevertheless, Valenzuela does follow certain aspects of the code of the traditional tale. In her story, the search, the hunt for the holy grail of the traditional narrative, becomes the search for the absent object of desire, often discussed by Lacan and René Girard, and, ultimately, the self.

The hermeneutic code is important in *Como en la guerra* because of the many traps Valenzuela sets for the reader. In Valenzuela's story, the hermeneutic code conceals and reveals the identity of both "she," the patient under study by the semiotician, and of the semiotician himself, who does not find his true identity until he has sacrificed himself in an act of political commitment.

The psychoanalytic code, with its references to Freud and Lacan, carries the reader to an absurd and horrifying logical extreme when the sexual fantasy of wanting the penis beaten becomes the reality of genital torture with cattle prods. This dramatic example of nonsynchrony serves to politicize the reader who may have only considered sadomasochist imagery in the hermetic environment of First World fascination with "decadence," fashion, or personal preference. The code of the real can be defined, using the Lacanian model, as that which resists symbolization. In *Como en la guerra*, it is presented as problematic but central. The character referred to as "she" embodies this code insofar as she is a revolutionary; however, the life of the political activist is deconstructed: betrayal is revealed to lurk behind revolutionary heroism. Thus, the metaphor "como en la guerra" provides no simple explanation, but rather is itself a metaphor for the interaction of conflicting systems of codes.

In her decision to emphasize the relationships of conflicting codes rather than plot, character, and other characteristics of the bourgeois linear narratives of realist writers and some modernist writers, Valenzuela might be called a postmodernist writer. The logic of her textual strategy—X no longer equals X—prevents her from being able to create unified characters in good conscience: the inner reality of the individual cannot be made equivalent to the reality of torture;

the woman revolutionary who has gone underground cannot be reduced to the patient in therapy treated by the semiotician/analyst. The cultural cohesion of a stable society which still allowed Jean-Paul Sartre to equate existential angst and everyday life in *La nausée* is no longer possible in Argentina, where a bourgeois fascination with French culture is daily eroded by inflation and where the social fabric has until recently been rent by fear. At the time of this writing, economic fears continue.

The reader of *Como en la guerra* will not be able to understand it without considering the current political situation in Argentina. The problem of the literature of the generation prior to Valenzuela's, which includes Cortázar, is the problem of the passive/active reader and the narrator as voyeur. As I have argued in the discussion of *Libro de Manuel*, Cortázar was aware of the modernist writer's situation as an observer of political struggle. Valenzuela throws her narrator, the semiotician, into the midst of experience. At the beginning, on page zero, he is being tortured. Whereas a text such as *Libro de Manuel* refers to politics in its content, political references are not critical in understanding the narrative structure or the form of *Como en la guerra*. The brilliance of Valenzuela's strategy is that the reader must come up against the wall of the multidimensional real, or even the plot will not make sense. This strategy is as important an aspect of the text as any political ideology, such as vaguely sympathetic feelings for revolutionaries, a feminism that extends to sympathy for the semiotician's wife, or an interest in semiotics and Lacanian theory.

Propp's categories, briefly summarized, include an initial situation in which the hero is introduced, an absenting of himself by the hero, an interdiction, a violation of the interdiction, and the introduction of the villain. The villain seeks information about the victim, attempts to deceive the victim, and then does something harmful. A lack is made known, the hero leaves home, the hero is led to the location of the object of the search. The hero fights the villain, the villain is defeated, the object of the search is achieved, and the hero returns, victorious.

In *Como en la guerra*, these steps are followed religiously. The hero, a professor of semiotics and a psychoanalyst, goes to work every day in order to analyze his patient. The interdiction, spoken by his wife, is not heeded: "Be careful at night." The wife, who is the villain in the story, worries about her husband but says nothing. While she continues to do research and type for him, she is suspicious of his activities and waits for opportunities to sabotage him; for example, she puts perfume on his clothing before he goes to work.

At this juncture, two codes converge. The semiotician meets an obstacle, following the code of the traditional tale; however, the obstacle is presented through the psychoanalytic code. The patient, "she," does not fit the psychoanalytic model, an assumption of which is the isolated individual rather than the politically committed social individual. Returning to the code of the tale, a lack is made known: the hero, the semiotician, wants his desired object, who has left town, and goes in search of her. This behavior is inappropriate in terms of the psychoanalytic code. His departure also signals the beginning of his search for himself. Although psychoanalysts do go to other psychoanalysts for analysis as part of their own training, Valenzuela is ironic here with this analyst who does not know who he is: he leaves Spain and takes off for Latin America to search for his patient. He, like his patient, is now deterritorialized.[3]

Many border elements appear at this point: the analyst finds himself in the jungle, where he meets Indians and revolutionaries. The code of the tale reemerges: he is given a powerful agent, mushrooms. In the context of traditional Indian culture in the jungle, mushrooms are not unusual. In the life of the analyst, however, they are a sign of a complete rupture with the rational world. The story ends in an unidentified war-torn Latin American city. The semiotician finds himself in a line, waiting, and then suddenly is thrust into battle by his companions. He is given the task, by an unidentified woman, of placing dynamite in specified places. He accomplishes his task and blows up his target. The object of his search is achieved: in the explosion, he has a vision of his patient/beloved: "she."

There is a second conclusion, page zero, the close-up, that introduces the hermeneutic code. This sequence is a description of the fate of the semiotician after he has been captured by the police and is being tortured. In a classical narrative, the hero defeats the villain; in this sequence, the police officer blows the semiotician to bits. Roland Barthes, in S/Z, explains that the hermeneutic code distinguishes, suggests, formulates, holds in suspense, and finally discloses the enigma. The identity of "she" is obscured by what the semiotician first tells the reader: she is the object of his study, she is Argentine, and she is a prostitute. After a few meetings, which double as therapy sessions and sexual encounters, we read that "she" wants to kill the semiotician, but no reason is given. Others in the story have opinions about her identity: she is thought to be a witch who may torture animals, who never eats food, and who may eat men's genitals. Valenzuela is ironic here; the reader aware of the feminist referential code is able to recognize the negative images of the witch as a "man-hater." The feminist code is also present in the pimp's report about her: she organizes prostitutes to fight for their rights, thereby distracting them from their work.

Ultimately, it is within the terms of the code of the multidimensional real that the identity of "she" is revealed. She is a political exile in Barcelona, the reader is told, whose lover, Alfredo Navoni, was a revolutionary. When he went underground, he forgot her. She now dreams his dreams, those that he dreamt during his imprisonment in Formosa after an unsuccessful mission. The omnipotent narrator further explains that "she" had a twin sister, who was also a revolutionary, and that "she" suspects Navoni of having turned her and her sister in to the police. The semiotician never asks her name, and "she" never mentions it.

The Multidimensional "Real"

Even using his Lacanian categories, the professor of semiotics is unable to understand the nature of his patient's problems. At the moment he decides to follow her to Latin America, he abandons his research. The search acquaints him with a new code, the code of the real: political symbolization. Returning to the hermeneutic code, we see that in the disclosure of the enigma, he not only has a vision of her, but he finds himself.

Although the limitations of the psychoanalytic code are mercilessly paraded before the reader by Valenzuela, this code propels the narrative into the realm postmodernism shares with non-Eurocentric experimentation. Valenzuela accepts the view that there is no unified subject of self-consciousness, both a Lacanian position and a tenet of the postmodernist narrative. Rather, the subject emerges from the interaction between conscious and unconscious elements and the social order.

In the Lacanian process of the construction of the subject, the child at birth is like an "hommelette": this pun means both "little man" and "broken egg." In *Como en la guerra*, the semiotician records a childhood memory of his patient in which "she," at the age of two, went to the refrigerator, opened the door, took out eggs, and dropped them to the floor. This pleasurable activity was repeated, in different forms, throughout her life. In the next step of the Lacanian theory, the conscious subject emerges from the relationship between the subject's own body and the constraints of the social order manifested as language. At this point, the child experiences a complete union with the outside world. This world begins to fall apart with the comings and goings of the mother.

In both *Como en la guerra* and *Cola de lagartija* (*The Lizard's Tail*), Valenzuela highlights the image of the mirror. In *Como en la guerra*, she rewrites what Lacan calls the mirror stage. As the child's world begins to fall apart, in Freud's model, the next stage of the development of the subject is the mirror stage, in which the child sees himself or herself disappear and reappear in the mirror. Lacan emphasizes the shift from the fragmented view to the view of the whole body. According to Lacan, the subject is actually constituted as a double, since it comes into being as a reflection. Valenzuela uses the twin sister as a signifier of the mirror stage in *Como en la guerra*. She rewrites the mirror stage such that the sister takes the role of the mother. When the sisters are separated, following the Freudian structure of the separation of mother and child, there is the structural possibility in the narrative that they have been betrayed by Navoni. Continuing her reformulation of the Freudian, Lacanian, and Oedipal origins of the subject, Valenzuela has the substitute father, Navoni, take the substitute mother, the sister, from the unnamed heroine. This preserves the incest taboo and allows the father figure, Navoni, to assert his power in The-Name-of-the-Father. The narrative structure is ambiguous in that it does not clarify whether or not Navoni betrayed the sisters to the police, or, in a parody of Lacanian terminology, the Law.

Valenzuela structures the narrative so that it must be read as an interference pattern between two codes: a strict Lacanian reading will not work, and the irony will be lost with a simple political reading. In her political recasting of Lacanian categories, it is through the "father," Navoni, that the doubled "child," the two sisters, enters the symbolic order, that is, that the "child" is possibly betrayed. To rewrite entry into the symbolic order as betrayal is to use the Lacanian model to make a critique of the Argentina of the years of the "dirty war."[4]

Evidence that Valenzuela is critical of psychoanalysis may be found in her choice of revolutionaries as the only characters who dare to overthrow the Oedipal order. In the episode involving Fatty in *Como en la guerra*, Valenzuela parodies Freud's totemic meal, in which the band of sons commemorates the mythic killing of the primal father. In the totemic meal postulated by Freud, taboos are broken: there is the destruction of the totem figure and incest is allowed. The father who had kept all the women to himself is killed and eaten. In *Como en la guerra*, the semiotician meets a group of men and women keeping a vigil for the death of a revolutionary. This parallels the commemoration of the death of the primal father. The group tells the semiotician about Fatty: in a ritualistic totemic meal, Fatty was covered with food by the group and eaten. By rewriting the totemic meal as the eating of a woman, the mother figure Fatty, Valenzuela has forced a provocative juxtaposition: the destruction of that which is desired.

Another example of Valenzuela's use of the nonunified subject in *Como en la guerra* is the way in which characters have shared personal dreams. Reading Navoni in the Lacanian if parodying terms of the-name-of-the-father, "she" is delivered to the law, the symbolic order, by dreaming Navoni's dreams as if they were her own. Her Wolf Man dream foreshadows the totemic meal in which Fatty is eaten. In Freud's case study of the Wolf Man, the seduction by his sister resulted in the Wolf Man's passive fantasy, which was transformed into the masochistic desire to be beaten, specifically, on the penis. This fear disguised itself as the fear of the wolf. The desire to be beaten on the penis, regardless of unconscious desires, is ludicrous in the context of genital torture in Argentina.

Valenzuela has rewritten Freud's Wolf Man case in *Como en la guerra*. In Navoni's dream, a man eats a wolf, becomes a Wolf Man, and then eats a dog and ducks. Lacan discusses the Wolf Man case in the essay "Tuche and Automaton." He considers Freud's question, "What is the real that lies behind the fantasy?" He decides that it is the seduction by the sister, a view that brings him close, for a moment, to Deleuze and Guattari's view of the sister as she who allows Gregor Samsa to become deterritorialized. For Lacan, the real is the encounter. In *Como en la guerra* the semiotician's encounter occurs when he is thrown into battle. Unlike the situation of Cortázar's narrator in *Libro de Manuel*, for whom the real is a moment missed or an absence, the semiotician confronts political torture. Valenzuela forces the reader to consider Freud's question at two levels. First, what is the real that lies behind the semiotician's passive fantasies, which he has expressed in his transvestism revealed in the visits with his patient at the beginning of *Como en la guerra*? Second, what is the real that lies behind the masochistic desire to be beaten in the context of political torture?

In Valenzuela's rewrite of the Wolf Man case, the man fights the wolf, kills him, and eats him. In *Como en la guerra*, the semiotician successfully places the dynamite in the specified location. Even when tortured, he refuses to reveal the name of the heroine, "she." At the level of narrative structure, the code of Marxism and politics in Latin America is hegemonic in relation to the psychoanalytic code.

In Valenzuela's superimposition of six referential codes, the codes of the traditional tale, suspense, the psychoanalytic, political commitment, feminism, and the multidimensional real, it is the psychoanalytic that is not only highlighted but reserved for satire. The semiotician denies his unconscious desires when he has an affair with the patient without ever looking at his actions critically. He is oblivious to her actual situation, to the fact that she is a revolutionary in exile. One insight of Lacanian analysis that is not rejected by Valenzuela in this work is the decentered or nonunified subject. As the tale unfolds, the semiotician's actions betray the inadequacies of his theories. Through his introduction into political activity, an alternative discourse to the symbolic order, he gains a greater understanding of himself. He does not articulate this understanding in language, however; the reader is shown the change through his behavior.

Although Valenzuela uses the code of political commitment to reveal the inadequacies of the code of psychoanalysis, the life of the political activist does not escape her critique. Navoni is portrayed as someone who may have betrayed the two sisters. Valenzuela presents this code as an equally treacherous path away from the real. In her use of this textual strategy, she recalls Theodor Adorno's discussion of the relationship between truth and rhetoric in *Negative Dialectics*, where he defines truth and rhetoric as inextricably linked.

Although Lacan's theories are subjected to the greatest amount of parody in *Como en la guerra*, the final irony may be that one of his categories can lead the reader to a political reading of the text. In his essay on the real, "Tuche and Automaton," Lacan refers to a dream recounted by Freud, in which a father attends his dying son. After the son dies, the exhausted father retires to a nearby room in the house, leaving someone else to watch the body. As he leaves, he lights a candle near the bed. While he is away, the candle falls over and sets fire to the bed in which the child's body lies. The father is awakened by a dream in which his son reproaches him, saying, "Father, can't you see I'm burning?" Freud gives what Lacan considers a rather unconvincing explanation: the father felt guilty and the dreamwork made a montage of fever and some other bit of conversation. Lacan's reading is much more sensitive. He tells us that the grief-stricken father was unable to maintain his vigil. Lacan defines the real as that repetition, the son's insistent question, that divides sleep from waking.

In the interference pattern created by the conflicting codes of *Como en la guerra*, the children of Valenzuela's generation—the disappeared, the writers in exile—ask their "fathers": "Can't you see I'm burning?" With the exception of the mothers who demonstrate every Thursday in the Plaza de Mayo in Buenos Aires with photographs of their children who have "disappeared," did not the Argentine middle class sleep in the wake of their children's deaths?

Chapter 5
Valenzuela:
The Imaginary Body

Toward a Metaphoricity of the Grotesque

Cola de lagartija is a feminist, postmodernist, meta-allegorical narrative—in short, a border work—in which Valenzuela uses elements of the grotesque in order to perform an exorcism; she will exorcise the demons that have destroyed the country from within.[1] Rather than ridding the country of subversives, however, she rids the consciousness of her reader of identification with the repressive regimes that have countenanced the torture and the disappearances of the 1970s. Valenzuela's shamanistic cure uses signs and symbols that provide meaningful equivalents to the "dirty war" of the 1970s in which the fear of the "other," the *subversivo*, manifested itself in the ultimate refusal to tolerate otherness altogether and led to the creation of a political euphemism to obscure a new reality of everyday life, the *desaparecido*.

Reading Luisa Valenzuela's *Cola de lagartija* without being aware of contemporary Argentine politics, therefore, is like watching a Fellini film without having been to Italy: it seems so exaggerated until one spends an evening in the Piazza Navoni in Rome, where beautiful transvestites promenade the latest creations in French and Italian fashion, and it becomes clear that Fellini is merely making documentaries. Similarly, the outrageously grotesque imagery of *Cola de lagartija* is no more bizarre than the figures whose stories it tells, including Eva Perón, Isabel Perón (Perón's wife at the time of his death), and José López Rega, Isabel Perón's Minister of Social Well-Being. Even historian Gary Wynia, in *Argentina and the Post-War Era*, is forced to resort to medieval imagery in an attempt to describe the situation in Argentina after Perón's death in July 1974:

> One irreverent Argentine observer has described the last days of Perón as something resembling a kingdom from the Middle Ages, where a wise old king, who had been a famous swordsman in his youth, was surrounded by a kind queen, a court sorcerer, wicked viziers, fauning courtiers, and a multitude of buffoons. Like the monarchs of old, he was uncritically loved by his subjects, who cared little for many in his entourage. But once he died, it was the sorcerer, viziers, and courtiers who fought over his throne by manipulating and deceiving the kind queen. (222)

As Wynia points out, Perón was unwilling to institutionalize a line of succession, for this would require him to violate his strategy of maintaining his support by constantly "shifting his favor among competing factions" (223). Even if he were simply a fascist dictator, a historical understanding of his rise to power would be of interest. But his relationship to *peronismo*, that movement in Argentina that contains both the right and the left, both the problems and the solutions, makes the story of this one figure large enough to be an allegory for the future of Argentina.

The multidimensionality of this historicity, perhaps the central feature of border writing, gains in contour when we realize that López Rega functions in *Cola de lagartija* not just as government official but as sorcerer, indeed, the Sorcerer. So too must we remember that Eva Perón functions not just as the wife of Juan Perón, but as a holy figure. J. M. Taylor writes of her in *Eva Perón, the Myths of a Woman*:

> . . . both her enemies and her followers . . . saw not only a woman. They saw a corpse. The repeated emphasis on the different versions of her death and in the constant concern with the fate of her remains were inescapable. The fact that Eva's body had not been buried was an important and disturbing issue for exploited parallels with Christian hagiography. (147)

Taylor explains how the significance of the issue of her "intact" body could become for Argentina a national concern: "Her intact body parallels the identical symbol of sanctity and triumph over death of other saints and martyrs" (147) This sanctity provides Valenzuela with many opportunities for irreverent treatment.

The unsanctified body of *Cola de lagartija*, we may safely say, is itself divided into three parts. The first section opens with the apocalyptic prophecy: "Correrá un río de sangre . . . y Vendrán Veinte Años de Paz" (*CL* 9) ("A river of blood will flow . . . and the Twenty Years of Peace will Come"; (*LT* i). This prophecy perhaps derives from General Rosas, who ruled Argentina from 1929 to

1952, for a similar saying was attributed to him: twenty drops of blood shed at the right time can save twenty thousand drops later. The first hundred pages of *Cola de lagartija* is narrated by the Sorcerer, with occasional interruptions by unidentified characters in the capital. The Sorcerer's activities, which include the torture of Indian women, are described in the language of the *feuilleton*. His saw-men are called "virtuosos de ese instrumento tan delicado que es el serrucho" (*CL* 48) ("virtuosos on that ever so delicate instrument that is the saw"; *LT* 38). They open pathways for him in the marshland where he lives. He refers to his practice of killing people as "sacrificios rituales" (*CL* 49) ("sacred sacrifices"; *LT* 39). The Sorcerer resorts to kidnapping a blonde woman at a cafe and amputating her finger as part of a scheme to determine whether or not the corpse he believes to be that of Eva Perón is in fact Eva Perón. He has the finger of the alleged Perón cut off the corpse and the blonde woman's finger attached in its place.

The second part of *Cola de lagartija* is narrated by Luisa and elaborates her intention to be a politically committed writer. It also contains an examination of the compromised position in which she finds herself. Her ambivalence about her role as novelist finally leads her to make the decision to stop writing altogether, for she fears that even to write about the Sorcerer is to increase his power.

In the third and final part of the narrative, the Sorcerer celebrates the building of his monument to himself, his pyramid, and makes final preparations for the birth of his son, the most grotesque of Valenzuela's images. The Sorcerer has three testicles, one of which is his sister Estrella. He consummates his marriage to her by injecting this testicle with sperm. Thus, in a total rejection of Oedipal propriety, he impregnates himself/his sister and declares that he is the "madrepadrehijo" (*CL* 277) ("motherfatherchild"; *LT* 256), one of many indications that Valenzuela relies on the metaphoricity of the grotesque, a term inextricably linked with "body."

In his study *Writing and the Body*, Gabriel Josipovici explores the relationship between writing and body: "writing . . . suggests a process . . . writing and speaking—unlike 'art' and 'literature'—are at the crossroads of the mental and the physical, the orders of culture and nature" (1). Although Josipovici discusses writing and the body in terms of Borges's "The Garden of the Forking Paths" and Laurence Sterne's *Tristram Shandy*, his readings of these texts are relevant nevertheless to our discussion of Valenzuela's *Cola de lagartija*. Like *Tristram Shandy*, *Cola de lagartija* exists only as "a series of failures, of negations: it is not a straight line, it does not tell a story properly, it is not, perhaps, finally, either a novel or not a novel" (7–8). In light of Josipovici's remark, we can note that the conclusion of *Cola de lagartija* is inconclusive; there is a decided failure of closure.

Josipovici's consideration of the nature/culture distinction of Lévi-Strauss leads him to reject it in the realm of art:

The classic novel implies that the making of the novel and the making of the hero are one and the same . . . Robinson Crusoe, Tom Jones, Humphry Clinker, Clarissa . . . any such distinction such as Lévi-Strauss' simply will not hold either where works of art and not objects of use are being considered. For a book is in one sense produced biologically, in the same way as a laugh or a scream has biological roots. But a book is also, of course, like an axe, the issue not of biology but of a system of representations. But could not the same be said of human beings? Sterne's book is not "about books" while those of other novelists are "about people." Because it takes people seriously, *Tristram Shandy* takes books seriously. Both Tristram himself and the novel, *Tristram Shandy*, hover uneasily between the two orders, of nature and culture. (10)

The same could be said of Luisa herself and the novel, *Cola de lagartija*. López Rega, for example, exists as the character in the text, the Sorcerer, and as "a system of representations." At a certain point, Luisa decides to stop writing rather than to give the Sorcerer more power; the writing of the novel about the Sorcerer, which began as a "cure," has worsened the illness instead of remedying it. Like *Tristram Shandy*, *Cola de lagartija* focuses almost exclusively on the birth process; however, in Valenzuela's text, it is the son of the protagonist, the future of *peronismo* and of Argentina, whose "birth" we await. *Cola de lagartija*, again to some degree following Sterne, differs from the classic novel in its emphasis on conception, pregnancy, and childbirth, that is, the unfinished nature of the body.

In *Rabelais and His World*, Mikhail Bakhtin discusses the repression of the various phases of death and decay in modern life: "The Renaissance saw the body in quite a different light than the Middle Ages in a different aspect of its life and a different relation to the exterior nonbodily world" (29). We know that Freud has linked repression with a failure of translation. Thus, Bakhtin can be understood to be discussing here the failure of translation of the various phases of death and decay into the discourse of modern life. The Sorcerer's relationship to the nonbodily world is grotesque as it is presented by Valenzuela, and recalls this passage from Bakhtin:

As conceived by these canons, the body was first of all a strictly completed, finished product. Furthermore, it was isolated, alone, fenced off from all other bodies. All signs of its unfinished character, of its growth and proliferation were eliminated: its protuberances and offshoots were removed, its convexities (signs of new sprouts and buds) smoothed out, its apertures closed. The ever unfinished nature of the body was hidden, kept secret: conception, pregnancy, childbirth, death throes, were almost never shown. (29)

Nonetheless, *Cola de lagartija*, like *Tristram Shandy*, presents the protagonist as growing and changing. Estrella, for example, is an offshoot or protuberance of the Sorcerer. Conception, pregnancy, and childbirth are phases of life that Valenzuela chooses to emphasize rather than to omit. Bodies in *Cola de lagartija* are not "fenced off from other bodies": the finger of the live woman is substituted for the finger of the Dead Woman's corpse. Valenzuela, like Sterne, concentrates on the marginal, the excluded, the unsaid, as a strategy for translating the character of the Sorcerer and the problem of *peronismo*.

The complexities of *peronismo* are described by Wynia in terms that will be shared by those who have studied the phenomenon: "whether it was authoritarian, democratic, corporatist, populist, liberal, or conservative is still a matter of dispute" (223). The year 1975, the year of the victory of the conservative Peronist faction, led by Minister of Social Well-Being José López Rega, ended in what Wynia calls "political and economic chaos" (223). Valenzuela examines *peronismo* through her portrayal of the structures of everyday life that link all Argentines, right- and left-wing *peronistas*, generals and civilians, fascists and *guerrilleros*. By exploring the contradictions and everyday life, Valenzuela mobilizes all the resources of the border text to give the reader a more multidimensional view of the Sorcerer than if she presented him in his adult life as a closed, "completed, finished product."

In this strategy, the postmodernist and the grotesque converge into the form of the border text. Valenzuela deploys what Bakhtin, in *Rabelais*, calls "the inner processes of absorbing and ejecting" (42). She presents the historical figure of López Rega, for example, not as other, as monster, but rather within the context of *peronismo* and in its "relation to the ancestral body of the people" (42). While the grotesque qualities of *Cola de lagartija* may, under a regime of border reading, be understood to "instruct," they violate the corollary of this neoclassicist dictum in that they never "delight." For, as befits a work of border literature, the novel does not fit what Bakhtin refers to as the "framework of the 'aesthetics of the beautiful' as conceived by the Renaissance" (29). Under this still effective precept of taste, Cortázar's *Libro de Manuel*, similarly, has been found less aesthetically pleasing than *Rayuela*. Of the three principal border writers, Cortázar, Valenzuela, and García Márquez, only the latter has managed both to please and to instruct and at the same time preserve the elements of the grotesque adequate to border literature, an achievement that doubtless accounts for the ease of reception enjoyed by García Márquez in foreign markets. While all three writers may be seen to consider the problem of the "other," and particularly the "other" as monstrous, Valenzuela alone presents us with the possibility that we ourselves have given birth to the monster of fascism, and her proof of paternity consists in the traces we repress.

But why should the grotesque be found so unacceptable? The answer to this decidedly nonrhetorical question is found in the consequences attendant to the suppression of the grotesque. By way of beginning with an answer, we might well consider how Bakhtin has historicized the genre as a whole and linked it to the double:

> Grotesque imagery (that is, the method of construction of its images) is an extremely ancient type; we find it in the mythology and in the archaic of all peoples, among them, of course, the Greeks and Romans of the preclassic period. During the classic period the grotesque did not die but was expelled from the sphere of official art to live and develop in certain "low" nonclassic areas: plastic comic art, mostly on a small scale . . . Kerch terra-cottas, comic masks, Sileni, figurines of demons of fertility, and the popular statuettes of the little monster Tersitus. Humorous vase decorations present the images of grotesque "doublets" (the comic Hercules and Odysseus), scenes from comedies, and symbols of fertility. Finally, in the wider range of humorous literature, related in one form or the other to festivals of carnival type, we have the "satyric" drama, the ancient Attic comedy, the mimes, and others. During the period of late antiquity grotesque imagery attained its flowering and renewal; it embraced nearly all areas of art and literature. (30–31)

As we will see, Valenzuela's inclusion of grotesque elements in *Cola de lagartija*, when considered in the context of the "cure," suggests that, indeed, the repression of those aspects of life that are found distasteful by bourgeois decorum and Renaissance humanism maintains the state of disease. Of central relevance to this concern of *Cola de lagartija* is Bakhtin's description in *Rabelais* of grotesque ornaments: "The borderlines that divide the kingdom of nature in the usual picture of the world [are] boldly infringed. Neither [is] there the usual static presentation of reality . . . no longer the movement of finished . . . " (32). Valenzuela likewise violates the canons of Renaissance beauty in that her figures too seem interwoven, as if giving birth to each other.

In opposition to the grotesque, interestingly enough, is the Sorcerer, for he loathes the weak, the imperfect, and the unfinished. He hates the witch Machi, who is old, and the Egret, his aide-de-camp, whom he considers weak. The only unfinished process in his life, the birth of his son, must be directly under his control. He wishes to perceive reality only in a "perfect" form as a reflection of himself. He says, "¡Qué bien me siento hoy rodeado de mí mismo! Qué libre—qué completo" (*CL* 249) ("How well I feel today, surrounded by myself! How free—how complete; *LT* 231). Even the mirrors of the town of Capivari must be confiscated so that his image will be complete. He despises any form of "otherness," and it is no surprise that he hates women.

Valenzuela: Feminist Shaman in Exile

Valenzuela writes *Cola de lagartija* as an Argentine feminist in exile in Mexico, and the text is psychoanalysis. The narrative structure of *Cola de lagartija* is emblematic of border literature as well in that it is not controlled by one voice but rather emerges from the double narration of Luisa and the Sorcerer, both of whom are writing novels. Valenzuela has worked with this kind of double relationship in earlier works, including *Como en la guerra*. This rich texture arising from a multiplicity of codes allows Valenzuela to examine the construction of allegorical form. She selects several codes, including the Lacanian, the political, the semiotic, and the feminist, and she reveals how the ruptures and gaps in each are filled in by the others. Her references to Aztec practices of sacrifice evoke yet another code, one which has been described by René Girard as a "system of victimage."[2] As we have seen, the framing device of the novel is the grotesque body, including all phases of life—conception, birth, growth, aging, death, and decay. The politically informed reader is able to identify not only Isabel Perón's Minister of Social Well-Being José López Rega as the Sorcerer, but other generals and political leaders as well, but such knowledge is not essential. The work is, as befits its status as a border text, more about the results of an interaction of codes than about individual signifiers within those codes.

In *Cola de lagartija* Valenzuela transforms the sick body of Argentina into a symbolic landscape upon which she performs what can only be described as an exorcism: she creates an allegory in which the Argentine psyche can view the pain that its body can no longer tolerate. Yet, as her two unidentified observers in the capital make explicit, this cure is based on the practice of deconstruction: "Debemos . . . desarticular la textualidad inscripta en el discurso paraoficial" (*CL* 44) ("We should . . . deconstruct the textuality inscribed in the para-official discourse"; *LT* 4). The deconstruction of one of the codes, fascism, has, of course, many precursors, perhaps the most pertinent of which can be found in the works of the Frankfurt School theorists Theodor Adorno and Max Horkheimer. They too had sought to examine the political and the psychoanalytic in terms of each other. Valenzuela follows much the same strategy.

Still, the code of feminism underlies all of Valenzuela's work. In *Cola de lagartija*, residents of the rural community of Capivari are questioned about Luisa and her "subversive" companions. They respond to a question about Luisa with a remark that underscores Valenzuela's penchant for irony: ¿Una escritora? No se haga el gracioso, si las mujeres no saben escribir" (*CL* 279) ("A woman writer? Don't be funny, women don't know how to write"; *LT* 259). But the ironical does not exhaust Valenzuela's response to feminism. In the short story "El verbo matar," included in the collection *Cosas raras pasan aquí*, her treatment of this theme takes a direct turn toward analytical critique.[3] She writes of two young sisters who kill a man with "long bushy hair and gleaming eyes"—a man, an other, whom they imagine to be a rapist and a murderer. They watch him from a distance and fantasize about how violent he is. Finally, on the pretext that they are going to hunt rabbits, they ask their father for his rifle; but instead of game, they shoot the unknown man.

It is no accident that Valenzuela's description of these young girls is strikingly similar to French feminist writer Antoinette Fouque's description of bourgeois feminists, of whom Fouque has written:

> Women cannot allow themselves to deal with political problems while
> at the same time blotting out the unconscious. If they do, they become,
> at best, feminists capable of attacking patriarchy on an ideological level
> but not on a symbolic level. An example? *The Last Tango in Paris*. A
> liberated young woman kills a poor psychotic with her father's revolver.
> That's the typical feminist! Bourgeoise, in revolt, wearing boots. She
> commits a heinous crime in the name of the father and with absolute
> impunity. (Marks and de Courtivron, *New French Feminisms*, 117)

Like Foque, Valenzuela's relationship to feminism does not prevent her from maintaining a critical stance toward it: the political point of "El verbo matar" is that the little girls have resorted to fascist behavior because of their fear of the other, an unknown man who has done them no harm. Valenzuela focuses her attention here on the interaction between men and women, suggesting that if the world is to cure itself of its fascism, this will be through a dialogue between Marxism and feminism. The point here is not whether Valenzuela intends to set forth didactically her opinion about how to solve the problems of fascism. Rather, it is that the structure of her narrative does not privilege either the codes of Marxism or of feminism but instead juxtaposes these codes in a continual mutual interrogation.

French feminist critic Maria-Antoinetta Macciocchi has raised this juxtaposition of codes to the status of a political strategy:

> I believe . . . that thanks to the uncertain and timid design of *an other*
> relationship between men and women, we are in the presence of the
> opening of a *new continent* in history. If all the feminist movements, if
> all revolutionaries understand this, one day there will be no more fas-
> cism. (*New French Feminisms*, 239)

In *Cola de lagartija*, Luisa the narrator subjects her own relationship with the revolutionary Alfredo Navoni to the scrutiny of the reader. As a woman and a writer, she seeks to situate herself within a series of superimposed contexts: the contemporary Argentine political situation, the realm of the Sorcerer, and the semiotic relationships that constitute the production of meaning.

French feminist critic Hélène Cixous evokes the heterosexual couple in the following terms:

Where is she?

Activity/passivity,
Sun/Moon,
Culture/Nature,
Day/Night,

Father/Mother,
Head/heart,
Intelligible/sensitive,
Logos/Pathos.

Form, convex, step, advance, seed, progress.
Matter, concave, ground—which supports the step, receptacle.
Man

Woman

Always the same metaphor: we follow it, it transports us, in all of its forms, wherever a discourse is organized. The same thread, or double tress leads us, whether we are reading or speaking, through literature, philosophy, criticism, centuries of representation, of reflection.

Thought has always worked by opposition,
Speech/Writing
High/Low

By dual, *hierarchized* oppositions. Superior/Inferior. Myths, legends, books. Philosophical systems. Wherever an ordering intervenes, a law organizes the thinkable by (dual, irreconcilable; or mitigable, dialectical) oppositions. And all the couples of oppositions are *couples*. Does this mean something? Is the fact that logocentrism subjects thought—all of the concepts, the codes, the values—to a two-term system, related to "the" couple man/woman? (*New French Feminisms*, 90–91)

The coupling of terms, or binary oppositions, characterizes the various codes from which the characters of *Cola de lagartija* emerge as well as Luisa's relationship with Navoni. Navoni's revolutionary commitment is juxtaposed against their relationship. Valenzuela treats Argentina as a social text that must be deconstructed: its sick body is transformed into a symbolic landscape upon which Valenzuela will perform the exorcism. The disease, as indicated earlier, is caused by repression, and in particular the repression of what may be called "the political conscious."

In his discussion of history and narrative in *The Political Unconscious*, Jameson quotes Marx and Engels from *The Communist Manifesto*: "The history of all hitherto existing society is the history of class struggles" (20). For Valenzuela, the history of Argentina must include the stories of oppressor and oppressed, told both in the linear rational narrative and retold with the addition of those perspectives and elements that have been repressed. This observation on Valenzuela's texts recalls this passage from Jameson's work:

> It is in detecting the traces of that uninterrupted narrative, in restoring to the surface of the text the repressed and buried reality of this fundamental history, that the doctrine of a political unconscious finds its function and necessity. (20)

The disease of fascism, in this analysis, is caused by repression, taken in both its political and psychoanalytic definitions.

In addition to its political form, Freud has given us a description of psychoanalytic repression, that is, repression of the conscious by the unconscious. In "Instincts and Their Vicissitudes," Freud discusses one of the effects of this repression, the transformation of an instinct into its opposite, showing the relationship between repression and the polarities of subject/object and active/passive. In his essay "Lacan, Poe and Narrative Repression," Robert Con Davis makes the point that Freud's essay reveals these polarities to be "linguistic 'positions' within a discourse" (985). In Davis's analysis, Freud opposes a notion of a centered subject and replaces it with the image of a visual drive "repositioned through the operation of metaphor" (985).

Valenzuela juxtaposes the characters of Luisa and the Sorcerer not only in order to reveal that they emerge as polarities from the codes they speak and are spoken by, but to indicate as well that these polarities are positioned squarely within political discourse. The conscious political code of Luisa as a progressive writer is shown to be, in fact, that which repressed the political unconscious signified by the Sorcerer. Luisa says, "Las sutiles hebras de la trampa inconsciente. Que yo creo saber hilar y que hilo tan poco o nada, casi nada. La puntita apenas" (*CL* 150) ("The subtle threads of the unconscious plot that I think I know how to weave but which I'm weaving little or nothing of. The fringe, that's all"; *LT* 135). The old black man/magician she and Navoni have recruited in their struggle tells her, "¿Te has estado metiendo donde no te corresponde? ¿Has estado hurgando en el misterio? Tan oscura te veo" (*CL* 151) ("Have you been sticking your nose where you shouldn't? Are you poking around in mysteries? I see you so dark"; *LT* 136). He tells her to get rid of her devils, which she calls "unos diablitos inofensivos, simpaticones" (*CL* 152) ("small, inoffensive, most pleasant; *LT* 136). He disagrees:

> Nunca tocar los objetos del mal. No acercarse a ellos. Debes desprenderte, hija mía, de todo lo que signifique brujerías y mira que tienes muchos cachivaches. Desprenderte de todos, ya te diré como. (*CL* 152)

Never touch objects of evil. Don't approach them. You have to break away from everything that means witchcraft, and see, my child, you have all kinds of knickknacks. Get rid of them all, I'll tell you how. (*LT* 136–37)

Valenzuela's irony here is that a revolutionary like Navoni must resort to help from a *brujo* and a progressive like Luisa must give up her devils. In all cases, the distinctions between good/evil and conscious/unconscious are blurred.

An important example of Valenzuela's use of polarities is in her transformation of Argentina into an imaginary body by creating a character, the Sorcerer, whose fantastic birth and life are inseparable from this imaginary body of Argentina. In this she is, perhaps, inspired by the actual landscape and geography of Argentina — the *pampas* — as well as by a countryside that is an "absence" in the text, namely, that of Mexico City. The capital of Mexico, unlike the capital of Argentina, Buenos Aires, was built on marshland near a lake, as was the home of the Sorcerer. It is also the location of the pyramids, and in *Como en la guerra* Valenzuela describes the jungle in Mexico in terms that resemble the home of the Sorcerer:

El ojo central de la selva — la laguna — es negro de una intensidad casi petrolífera por las plantas en descomposición y en el fondo invisible de esa negrura viven todos los peligros infrahumanos . . . (164)

[The central eye of the jungle — the lagoon — is black with an almost oil-like intensity because of the rotting plants, and in the inhuman depths of this blackness live all the infrahuman dangers . . . (*He Who Searches* 201)]

A major cultural difference between Mexico and Argentina is that the indigenous population of Argentina was destroyed, leaving Argentina with a 98 percent European population. This is not the case in Mexico, where there is a large mixed population. The references to Mexico throughout *Cola de lagartija* in the form of pyramids and Aztec culture instance a cultural signifier whose signified is the obliteration of otherness. "Otherness" is to be understood here as the unconscious, the non-European culture, subversives, and, in the philosophical sense, the self-other relationship.

Another binary opposition concerning the Sorcerer is the fact that his castle is a field of anthills. As a symbol, the anthill implies the binary opposition builder/destroyer, and the referential code here is National Reconstruction, Isabel Perón's plan to "rebuild" the country by destroying "subversives." The destructive nature of the Sorcerer makes its appearance early in his life: he enjoys sitting on and destroying anthills. That his destructive urges should be linked to this part of his anatomy is a theme developed throughout the book.

The Sorcerer, the hero, comes into the world in a manner befitting a hero: he is an abandoned child. Like Oedipus, he is raised by a man and a woman who are not his biological parents, Doña Rosa and Don Ciriaco. He has an odd and incestuous relationship with his sister, to whom he gives birth. Actually, he has three testicles: his sister, Estrella, is a third testicle. Before his own birth, he meets the spirit of Eva Perón, who tells him he must return to the earth in the form of a man. At age two, he is banned from the anthills and condemned to live on an island in the marshland.

The centrality of the marshland and its multivalent reference is attested to by two unidentified characters in the capital, who discuss this region in the following terms:

> Creo que debemos tomar eso de los Esteros como una metáfora. Debemos analizar punto por punto los elementos que nos han sido brindados y desarticular la textualidad inscripta en el discurso paraoficial. Debemos tratar de elaborar nuestras coordenadas sobre la base de la dicotomía de esta posición del gobierno. Se trata de un perfecto juego especular con un superyó represor en superficie (el gobierno) y su contracara represora bajo tierra (el brujo). Esta figura nos traba el movimiento, no ofrece ni la más mínima libertad intersticial. Es el "doble bind" de Bateson. (*CL* 44–45)

> [I think we should consider that business of the marshland as a real metaphor. We should analyze the elements that have been offered us point by point and deconstruct the textuality inscribed in the para-official discourse. We should try to structure our basic coordinates on the dichotomy of that government position. It's a perfect specular play: with a repressive inverted image underground (the Sorcerer). This double figure hampers our movement, denies us even the slightest interstitial freedom. It's Bateson's "double bind." (*LT* 35)]

The metaphor of the marshland can thus be understood to join two opposites, for it comprises both land and water. Valenzuela's choice of this metaphor as a signifier of the unconscious allows her to explore the relationship between the conscious and the unconscious in a concrete image. As the quote suggests, she deploys the Derridean concept of the deconstruction of textuality in which the process of deconstruction begins by considering a binary opposition. First, the privileged term such as "good" in the opposition "good/evil" is replaced by its paired opposite. Then, the interaction between the two terms through their common elements is revealed. According to this analysis, the metaphor of the marshland can be understood as a deconstruction of the opposition land/water.

There is also an explicit reference to Gregory Bateson here, and it may well point us to his *Steps Toward an Ecology of the Mind*. This text posits that the only solution for the schizophrenic whose childhood has trapped him or her in the "double bind" is to engage in metacommentary. He defines the "double bind" as involv-

ing two or more persons, repetition, and primary negative injunction: "Do not
. . . or I will punish you; Do . . . or I will punish you" (206). This is a no-win
situation. Thus, the childhood of fascism, its period of formation, must be recon-
sidered. Valenzuela uses Bateson's term, which emerges from his analysis of the
family and schizophrenia, to describe the political situation in Argentina.

Like the schizophrenic child, the frightened Argentine citizen seeks to avoid
punishment, or being "disappeared," rather than to pursue reward, which might
be formulated in this comparison as political engagement in order to bring
democracy to the country. The mother of the schizophrenic becomes anxious and
withdraws if the child responds to her as a loving child—the very existence of the
child arouses anxiety. The mother will not allow herself to express the anxiety:
her overt behavior is loving. She demands that the child be good. According to
Bateson, the mother's ambivalence, in the absence of father, can produce a
schizophrenic child. If a person finds herself in a situation in which no matter
what she does, winning is impossible, schizophrenic tendencies may develop. Although Bateson was concerned with individuals and families rather than countries, there are certain similarities between family structures he found to be prone
to schizophrenia and the social structures of Argentina.

Border Writing as Cure

Valenzuela structures the entire text of *Cola de lagartija* as a series of parallels,
mirror images, and binary oppositions. Both the Sorcerer and Luisa are writing
novels. Navoni practices one form of magic with Caboclo de Mar, the witch who
agrees to work with the revolutionaries against the Sorcerer, while the Sorcerer
practices his form of magic in the Kingdom of the Black Lagoon. The govern-
mental position exists, as the unidentified observers tell us, in "a perfect specular
play in relation to the Sorcerer" (35). The same unidentified inhabitant of the capital describes the effect of the Sorcerer on his followers as "despertando el miedo
supersticioso y a la vez una vaga promesa de salvación por la magia, congelán-
dolo, de esta forma, en el dominio do lo imaginario" (*CL* 45) ("awakening in them
superstitious fear and at the same time the vague promise of salvation by magic;
freeing them in that way in the realm of the imaginary"; (*LT* 36). This passage
contains a reference essential to its interpretation. The morass of symbols in
which the Argentine follower of the Sorcerer is trapped can be described in Lacanian terms, that is, in terms of the symbolic, the imaginary, and the real.

The relationship between "the subject on the one hand, and the signifiers,
speech, language, on the other constitutes the symbolic realm"; this may be contrasted with the relationship between the ego and its images, or the imaginary
realm (Lacan, *The Language of the Self*, ix). The imaginary is defined as the
realm that is inhabited by images, be they conscious or unconscious, real or im-

agined. The symbolic is the "determining border of the subject" (ix). It originated in Lévi-Strauss's formulation of the structures of kinship and Jakobson's notion of the binary oppositions that underlie semiotic relationships in linguistics. The real, on the other hand, is a term whose definition has evolved throughout Lacan's work. It may be said that it "resists symbolization" and is lacking in the symbolic order.

Fredric Jameson's interpretation of the Lacanian "real" emphasizes its historical aspect. As he writes in *The Political Unconscious*:

> . . . history is *not* a text, not a narrative, master or otherwise, but that
> as an absent cause, it is inaccessible to us except in textual form, and
> that our approach to it and to the Real itself necessarily passes through
> its prior textualization, its narrativization in the political. (35)

In the previously cited discussion of the marshland and its capacity to act on the observers—and on the Argentine populace as a whole—as a double bind, Valenzuela's unidentified speakers come close to Jameson's definition of the "real," and they are clearly attempting to frame the deconstruction of "the textuality inscribed in the para-official discourse." The process of that deconstruction could lead to a knowledge of the "real," or at least to the ability to distinguish it from the fears and promises in the realm of the imaginary. The Sorcerer has power only through the desire of the other. The discourse of magic plays the role here of Lacan's Law of the Father or the other. "Other" is to be distinguished from *"objet Petit a,"* or the object under consideration in the Freudian subject relation. Luisa collects devils, or objects, but does not believe that they are harmful to her because she does not consciously accept the black magic with which they are associated by believers in witchcraft. Caboclo de Mar has to explain to her that even to touch these objects is to be subjected to the dictates of the symbolic realm, to enter as a subject into the string of signifiers whose relationships are predetermined.

The imaginary is the realm in which we position ourselves and are positioned in the strings of signifiers whose relations are determined by the symbolic. The unidentified inhabitant of the capital is arguing that the Sorcerer is able to gain control of his followers by appealing to their repressed, vestigial beliefs in magic. Rational, modern, industrial society in Argentina does not answer the needs of the country's citizens. "Progress" has brought about, among other things, an increase in the inflation rate to the widely reported figure of over 400 percent in the 1970s. The Sorcerer is able to promise salvation from this unpleasant reality, in which middle-class privileges are being eroded, "in the realm of the imaginary."

Opposed to the Sorcerer's practice of magic is Valenzuela's shamanistic cure, the writing of a novel that provides alternative images and an alternative set of linguistic relationships to counter the hold of the symbolic and imaginary realms already staked out and occupied by the Sorcerer. In *Structural Anthropology*,

Lévi-Strauss draws a parallel between shamanistic practices and psychoanalysis. The cure of the shaman is a result of

> making explicit a situation originally existing on the emotional level and in rendering to the mind pains which the body refuses to tolerate . . . through symbols, that is, through meaningful equivalents of things meant which belong to another order of reality. (192, 196)

In the "deconstruct[ion] of the para-official discourse," the discourse of the Sorcerer, the latent content becomes manifest content. Valenzuela achieves this by revealing the Sorcerer's role in the production of ideology at the level of propaganda. Perón and his Secretary of the Press discuss foreign news reports:

> No nos vamos a sentar en el banquillo de los acusados de nadie, y debemos actuar inmediatamente para evitar hacerle el juego a esa acción psicológica que la subversión busca. Nuevamente la prensa extranjera está publicando infundios sobre nuestro amado país. Mire usted estos recortes, observe, no más. Dicen que en las últimas semanas hemos hecho desaparecer a más de 200 personas, que torturamos a bebés delante de sus padres para que los padres confiesen, que golpeamos a las embarazadas hasta hacerlas abortar. La ruitina de siempre, qué noticia. Por fortuna hemos impartido órdenes para que estos diarios vendidos a la sinarquía internacional no entren al país. Cuanto menos material impreso circule por acá, mejor. Pero igual nos están creando un mala imagen en el extranjero. Y eso es intolerable. Nuestra imagen debe ser limpiada a toda costa. (*CL* 125–26)

> [We have to act immediately to avoid playing into the hands of the subversives. The foreign press is printing lies about our beloved country again. Look at these clippings, just take a look. They say that over the past few weeks we've made more than two hundred people disappear, that we torture babies in front of their parents to make the parents confess, that we beat pregnant women until they miscarry. The usual routine, what else is new! Fortunately, we've given orders to bar these foreign newspapers, which have sold out to an international conspiracy. The less printed matter that circulates here, the better. But just the same, we're getting a bad image abroad. And that can't be tolerated. Our image has to be clean at all costs. (*LT* 111–12)

The Sorcerer then spends five hours with the Press Secretary drawing up a press release to convince Argentines that the allegations in the foreign press have no basis in reality:

> Para cumplir con el Proceso de Reconstrucción Nacional debemos sostener un gobierno fuerte y no meramento recitado, un gobierno sólido y no inerme y deficiente. Debe ser fuerte porque no sabemos cuándo esta agresión va a terminar. (*CL* 127)

[In order to complete the process of National Reconstruction, we must support a strong government . . . what we demand is responsibility in the media and in the people who direct them, so as not to give rise to psychological insecurity, which is exactly what the subversives are seeking. (*LT* 112–13)]

Of course, Valenzuela is ironic here as she has just shown that the Sorcerer is manipulating his followers by appealing to their psychological insecurity.

Although the latent content of Argentina politics exists primarily on an emotional level—specifically, in the psychological insecurity of the middle class—it is pointed out by Valenzuela in its subtextual form which informs the text of the press release. In this way, Valenzuela is able to reveal the inherent logical contradictions visible in the manifest level, and thereby to effect part of the shaman's cure, "making explicit a situation originally existing on the emotional level" (Lévi-Strauss, 192). The press release is based on an illusion of the strength of the government. It asks citizens to accept the illusion without question and to support media censorship so that the illusion will not be revealed.

The next part of the cure is "rendering acceptable to the mind pains which the body refuses to tolerate" (192). Considered as the body of Argentine society as a whole, this collective body refuses to tolerate the pain, the economic and political crises, that has made even middle-class life problematic, but which it is condemned to continue to suffer because of its refusal to face and to accept its problems at the level of the collective mind. The fear of facing these problems is displaced to an intolerance of the other. Valenzuela's cure consists of writing a novel that provides "meaningful equivalents" (Lévi-Strauss, 196), in this case, an allegory, in order to translate one level of reality into another.

Shoshana Felman, in "To Open the Question," calls literature the "unconscious of psychoanalysis" (10). By providing Argentina with "a language, a means by which unexpressed, and otherwise unexpressible, psychic states can be immediately expressed," Valenzuela is able to enact her cure. Once Argentines can recognize and understand the pain to which their collective body is submitted, the healing can begin and the violence can end. At another level, the healing occurs in all readers, so that non-Argentine readers will also situate themselves in the system of relationships that has resulted in the social wound.

In "Introduction: Lacan and Narration," Davis writes that in order to know the unconscious, one must view it as

a sequence of opportunities for linguistic substitutions and (re)combination. The potential for continuity and unity in such sequences makes possible the 'gaps' or 'lapses' that indicate the 'other' scene of signification, the repressed scene of writing not part of manifest narrations but which (like a buoy, or a series of buoys) holds it up and enables it to exist at all. (853)

Symbols, or metaphors, the end product in the production of meaning, must be created by Argentines themselves. They must occupy and self-manage the location at which meaning is produced, the border region between the political unconscious and the political conscious. They must gain control over this production process such that even if the "real" remains elusive, as individuals they will have access to new images, and as subjects, they will effect changes at the level of signifiers, speech, and language.

This entire process is parodied by Valenzuela, to whom nothing is sacred. The finger of a blonde woman in a cafe is substituted by the Sorcerer for the finger of the corpse of the Dead Woman, Eva Perón. This action allows Valenzuela to maintain her ironic stance as she juxtaposes the codes of psychoanalysis, literary and political allegory, and Argentine history in her own playful version of Felman's observation that literature is "the unconscious of psychoanalysis."

Valenzuela's exorcism takes place through a process of collective remembering, a remembering of the existence of the "other" scene of signification. The final stage of the healing coincides with Luisa the narrator's decision to stop writing her novel about the Sorcerer because the mere activity of writing about him increased his power. The Sorcerer senses the change and says he experiences "el delicioso vacío de la memoria" (*CL* 254) ("the delightful emptiness of memory"; *LT* 235). The Sorcerer gives himself over to nonmemory so that those who are trying to tell his story cannot harm him. He feels as if "alguien hubiese dejado de escribirme" (*CL* 254) ("someone has stopped writing about me"; *LT* 235). Yet even as the Sorcerer erases his present memory, Valenzuela revives behind him "an ancient memory":

> Una memoria muy antigua revive detrás de su memoria presente que se le a borrando. Baila para desprenderse de pasados lastres y también porque sabe que en el futuro no bailará más, por un buen tiempo al menos, hasta que nazca el hijo que lo llevará al gran baile del mundo, a la conquista. (*CL* 263)

> [An ancient memory is revived behind his memory that is being erased. He dances to rid himself of past rubble and because he knows that in the future he will dance no more for a good while at least, until the birth of the son who will carry her to the great dance of the world to conquest. (*LT* 244)]

A parallel memory, referred to by the Sorcerer as "the other memory," the realm of the Dead Woman, still holds a place for the Sorcerer: "En el otro mundo, en la otra memoria, no nos ha olvidado" (*CL* 111) ("In the other world, in the other memory, she hasn't forgotten us"; *LT* 97).

The collective memory, according to Luisa, is a possible source of power for the Sorcerer, for "La memoria colectiva también registra un intento de resurrección que nunca pudo establecerse a ciencia cierta si ocurrió realmente, pero cuya descripción redunda en beneficio de la leyenda del Brujo" (*CL* 115) ("The collective memory also registers an attempt at resurrection—never established with absolute certainty—which redounds to the benefit of the legend of the Sorcerer" *LT* 101). The problem presented by Valenzuela here is how to recuperate the past for democracy rather than fascism. Walter Benjamin and Henri Lefebvre both discuss the role of the ritual in this regard. In *Illuminations*, Benjamin writes:

> When there is experience in the strict sense of the word, certain contents of the individual past combine with material of the collective past. The rituals with their ceremonies, their festivals . . . kept producing the amalgamation of these two elements of memory over and over again. They triggered recollection at certain times and remained handles of memory for a lifetime. (159)

Lefebvre discusses the same concept in the context of "permanent cultural revolution":

> The Festival rediscovered and magnified by overcoming the conflict between everyday life and festivity and enabling these terms to harmonize in and through urban society, such is the final clause of the revolutionary plan. (206)

The aim of Valenzuela's exorcism is to rediscover the Festival, and the narrator Luisa organizes the Umbanda Festival as a counterceremony to the Sorcerer's inauguration.

I have discussed Bateson's notion of the "double bind" in relation to the metaphor of the marshland and suggested that certain social structures of Argentina placed the Argentine in a situation similar to that of the schizophrenic. This situation is concretized with respect to Argentina by Wynia in *Argentina in the Post-War Era*:

> By now it should be obvious that there is no easy escape from the vicious circle of economic crisis, political conflict, and policy failure in which export-dependent, industrializing nations like Argentina find themselves. . . . Economic policy and political strategy cannot be separated in practice, especially in societies whose citizens refuse to stand by idly and watch as others try to impose their narrow-minded solutions on them. Recognition of this fact will not by itself end the vicious circle, but it may at least provide a more positive point of departure for those bold leaders who are willing to risk the involvement of their fellow citizens in their campaign for economic development and national self-esteem. (260)

The negative injunction in Argentina was the Social Contract adopted by the Campora administration in 1973. This formal agreement among labor, industry, and government pledged each party to compliance with a price freeze and a two-year suspension of negotiated wage contracts. This put everyone in a "double bind"; the unions had to keep the rank and file in line by preventing wildcat strikes and had to keep local unions from renegotiating contracts. Farmers and cattlemen had to be convinced that they should support price and commodity controls. By 1975, the Social Contract had collapsed and Isabel Perón's "ambivalence" toward the major union, the CGT, reached its highest expression. She agreed to participate in an International Monetary Fund stabilization program, which meant a massive devaluation of the peso. Wynia explains the difference between this sort of leadership and Juan Perón's:

> In contrast [to] Juan Perón, who in 1952 could draw on labor loyalty to secure working class cooperation with his stabilization effort, the best that Isabel Perón could do was to threaten CGT leaders that if they did not cooperate with the plan proposed by the government they had helped elect, they would soon face a more severe one imposed by a military that stood ready to overthrow the government if the IMF plan failed. (227)

It is clear that the structure of the double bind replicates itself continually in this period of Argentine history. Still, the concept of the double bind can be understood in Lacanian terms as well. Davis, in "Lacan, Poe and Narrative Repression," explains Freud's notion of the Gaze:

> Freud creates a surreal theater of masochists, sadists, significant looks, voyeurs, and exhibitions, and eventually he shows visual experience to be governed by an unconscious mechanism that is inscribed through a process of looking and being seen. Freud theatricalizes this mechanism in various ways as a linguistic process and as a series of shifts and substitutions among the subject and object, active and passive positions he sets forth. (985)

Mexican writer Margo Glantz explains the image of "armas" ("weapons") in Valenzuela's *Cambio de armas* in terms of the look or gaze: "Las armas están en la mirada, en la mirada desorbitada que busca con desesperación un reflejo . . . " ("The weapons are in this case in the expression of the face which searches desperately for a reflection . . . "). In *Cola de lagartija* the shifts and substitutions among subjects and objects occur along the string of the signifiers swamp, marshland, mirror, pregnancy/self-fertilization, testicles, pyramid, blood. Lacan's contribution to the study of this system of observing and being observed is to recognize that "seeing's true aim cannot be visual in any immediate sense: seeing is but a function in a largely unconscious discourse that can be glimpsed in what Lacan calls, extending Freud's discussion, the 'Gaze' — the functioning of the whole of shifts" (Davis, 987).

In "Instincts and Their Vicissitudes," Freud describes three scenes of seeing. In the first, "looking" is a gesture whose purpose is to establish control, possession, or mastery of the object (Davis, 985). In *Cola de lagartija*, this coincides with Luisa's monitoring of the activities of the Sorcerer in the process of writing her novel about him. After this initial look takes place, there is a reversal, a seemingly impossible shift from the subject's viewpoint to an object's. In the act of watching the Sorcerer, Luisa becomes the object of the gaze. He invites her to his masked ball, the inauguration of the pyramid. A similar process is described in Cortázar's short story "Axolotl," in which the observer literally becomes the salamander he is observing and finds himself in the aquarium looking out at a human. As Luisa studies the Sorcerer, she discovers similarities, and a blurring of the distinction between them occurs: (l) they are both writing novels about his life; (2) her identity is being shaped to some extent by the Sorcerer as he invades her kingdom (*LT* 126) "La memoria colectiva también registra un intento de resurrección que nunca pudo establecerse a ciencia cierta si ocurrió realmente, pero cuya descripción redunda en beneficio de la leyenda del Brujo" (*CL* 115); (3) her activities form a mimetic relationship with his, as in the case of her counterceremony of the Umbanda people (130); (4) she writes of a "sympathy toward the monster," referring to the Sorcerer (197). In this initial look, Davis explains that

> the subject surrenders visual mastery as it then enters the field of vision as an object in a different position. In reality, the "single" act of looking has created two positions, that of looking and of being seen. Simultaneously, to be understood, one position at a time must be "repressed" or cancelled. (985)

In our earlier discussion of the symbolic and the imaginary realms, the symbolic was said to structure and define through binary oppositions the relationship between the subject and signifiers, language, speech, and the other. Here, we see that the binary opposition is looking/being seen.

In the second scene described by Freud in "Instincts and Their Vicissitudes," "totally masterful (and sadistic) activity" is replaced by surrender, a stage described by Davis in terms of a taking over of the position that has been vacated:

> After this surrender comes the introduction of a new position—a new viewer—who watches one who takes the position left vacant by the subject who looked initially and "to whom one displays oneself in order to be looked at by him." (986)

In *Cola de lagartija*, Navoni moves into the position of voyeur vacated by Luisa. The object position, filled by the Sorcerer, "looks back at the (former) subject"—that is, Luisa. At the point that the Sorcerer invites Luisa to his inauguration ball, we see the mirror stage of development, "in which subject and object are held, as if on the brink of dissolution, in an imaginary and ideal equivalence —as if perfect doubles of each other" (986). Valenzuela's irony surfaces again in the words of the Sorcerer, his own mirror image: "I am . . . I" (*LT* 256).

In Freud's final scene, "the looker is made passive, fully an object for another watcher . . . subjectivity is abandoned altogether and is replaced by an object exclusively for another's scrutiny" (986). The conclusion of *Cola de lagartija* quickly encapsulates the entire process again and simultaneously constitutes the third scene: Luisa and Navoni observe the flow of blood descending from the pyramid. Luisa identifies it (and with it) as the ancient prophecy fulfilled (her desire for peace). Navoni replaces her as the observer and concludes:

> Lo dudo mucho. Las tiranías ya no vienen como antes. Ahora tienen piezas de repuesto. Un presidente cae y otro ya está listo para reemplazarlo. Generales no nos faltan. Además, este hilo no puede ser el tan mentado río de sangre, porque entonces en lugar de veinte años nos tocarían apenas veinte minutitos de paz. (*CL* 302)

> [I really doubt it. Tyrannies are not what they used to be. Now they have replacement parts. One president falls and another is ready to take over. There's no shortage of generals. And this little thread is certainly not the river of blood so often mentioned. If it were so, we would get not twenty years, but under twenty minutes of peace. (*LT* 280)]

Of course, Valenzuela has created the entire text, so the chain of the Gaze continues: Luisa observes the process, and we, as readers, observe her observing . . .

To attempt a cure at all is to embrace the double bind. The outcome is uncertain as can be seen in Derrida's discussion, in *Dissemination*, of the *pharmakos*; the translation of the term as remedy is inaccurate, for "it can worsen the ill instead of remedy it" (97). Valenzuela's exorcism is performed on the body of Argentina: this body is also a text, a social text. Because of the open narrative structure of the border text, however, whether or not the cure is effective is left to the reader.

Although Valenzuela's underlying perspective is feminist, the feminist code is merely one of the many referential codes that appear in *Cola de lagartija*. It is in fact a meta-allegorical novel, a work that consciously explores the relationships among various codes. The psychoanalytic code includes references to Gregory Bateson and Lacan. It has resonances as well with the Frankfurt School's analysis of the fascist personality. The political code is presented most clearly in the character of Alfredo Navoni, in the unidentified Argentines in the capital, and in the fascist discourse of the Sorcerer. The victims of fascism evoke the code of sacrifice, studied in depth by Girard. The only hope for extricating oneself from the obfuscations created by all of these codes, suggests Valenzuela, is a deconstruction of their metaphors, that is, by employing yet another code, that of semiotics. Although her project as an author is the exorcism/deconstruction of the social body/text of Argentina, the codes of exorcism and semiotics also function as reference codes within the text.

The Refusal of Marginalization: Birth of a Fascist according to Bram Dikjstra

In *Idols of Perversity* Bram Dikjstra describes how Leopold von Sacher-Masoch, the author of *Venus in Furs*, "felt his world progressively turning into a congregation of aliens. It was a world in which his hero, Severin, must measure his own insignificance by the subsumption of his Aryan presence into a world of Semites and peasants, 'Mazovians in homespun linen and greasy-haired Jews' ([*Venus in Furs*] 58). Severin yearns to be recognized in an act of supreme humiliation, not by the woman he manipulates into acts of aggression—who is inferior to him 'in brains and bodily strength'—but by a real male, a superman, a godlike master, a true representation of the class of executioners whose mousy menial he is." Wanda can become the man's conduit to the superman (373).

Dikjstra can be seen to link masochism with the refusal of deterritorialization:

The masochism, then, of the late nineteenth-century male, and his manipulation of the image of woman as an all-destroying, rampaging animal was an expression of his attempt to come to terms with the implications of his own marginalization, his removal from the true seats of power in his society. (374)

Deleuze and Guattari take a different but not entirely incompatible view:

Kafka . . . could have something in common with the real cartography of masochism and with Sacher-Masoch . . . the pact with the devil, a masochistic "contrast" that opposes the conjugal contract and works to wish it away; the admiration for, and necessity of, vampirish letters . . . the becoming-animal, for example, in Masoch, the becoming-bear or fur . . . the interest in maids and whores. . . . Masoch, who had a Bohemian origin, was also connected to the same minorities of the Austrian empire as Kafka, a Czech Jew. The fascination of Masoch for the Jews in Poland, in Hungary. (66)

Although producing a seeming contradiction, linking deterritorialization with masochism, Deleuze and Guattari defend themselves:

It is all the more interesting to compare masochists and Kafkians, noting their differences, noting their unequal utilizations of the name, but also noting the similarities of their respective projects. (66)

Valenzuela follows a similar strategy in comparing Luisa and the Sorcerer.

A model of a multidimensional attitude toward otherness, as opposed to a sadistic or masochistic attitude, emerges from the work of Horkheimer and Adorno in the essay "Means and Ends" in *Dialectic of Enlightenment*. This essay provides an alternative to the three steps we have discussed in Freud's model of perception in "Instincts and Their Vicissitudes." In Horkheimer and Adorno's model of perception of the object by a democratic subject, the subject (not in the Lacanian sense we have been using, but in the traditional philosophical relationship between subject and object) "has the external world in its own consciousness and yet recognizes it as something other; therefore, reflection, the life of reason, takes place as conscious projection" (182). The subject is able to return to the object what it has received from it, and becomes richer rather than poorer. The subject reflects the object and reflects upon itself, retaining the ability to differentiate between them. It hears the Enlightenment, in which, argue Adorno and Horkheimer, domination is an end in itself. A multidimensional logic would include domination as moment in a process rather than as an end in itself (189–90).

The model of a multidimensional perception differs from the Freudian model, in which to look is to insert oneself into an endless chain of sadists and masochists, those who dominate and those who are dominated. The intellectual apparatus of the democratic subject is not used against other humans, as it is in the diseased individual described by Horkheimer and Adorno. The intellectual apparatus of that subject is "like the blind hostile organ of animal pre-history as which—in terms of the human species—it has never ceased to fight the rest of nature" (190). An example of such a subject is the Sorcerer:

> Estos tipos del gobierno se amamantan de mí, me quieren sorber el seso para de poder ocupar mi sitial privilegiado. ¿Creen acaso que no me ha dado cuenta? Seguro estoy de que me vigilan, que estudian cada uno de mis pasos y hasta mis más íntimos suspiros (mi emanación vital, mi prana). Por eso miso a veces monto ciertos espectáculos en su honor— me lo monto a mi Edecán, sin ir más lejos, para que entiendan bien por dónde me los paso—pero por otro lado suelo tomar mis precauciones ye a y este vademécum, por ejemplo, lo estoy escribiendo con tinta invisible para que ningún espía pueda microfotografiarlo. (*CL* 134–35)

> [These government guys are suckling from me, they want to gobble up my brains so they can fill my privileged seat of honor. Do they think I haven't noticed it? I'm quite sure they're watching me, studying my every step and even my tiniest signs (my vital emanation, my prana). But I take my precautions and for example, I'm writing this vade mecum in invisible ink so no spy can microfilm it. (*LT* 120)]

The border texts under consideration, particularly *Cola de lagartija*, allow the reader to engage in reflection; indeed, they insist on it. Valenzuela's characters realize that "the textuality inscribed in the para-official discourse" must be deconstructed. The discourse of the Sorcerer is para-official insofar as he is the leader of the conservative faction of the Peronist party and an advisor to Isabel Perón, her Minister of Social Well-Being.

The fascist or paranoid subject, that is, the Sorcerer, perceives the world only as it corresponds to his own purposes. This diseased individual "seems to need no living being, yet demands that all serve him" (190–91). The Sorcerer is both male and female; subject and object. According to Adorno and Horkheimer, the fascist or paranoid's

> will permeates the universe and everything must relate to him. . . . As the perfect madman or absolutely rational individual, he destroyed his opponents by individual acts of terror or by the carefully conceived strategy of extermination (191).

This description certainly applies to the behavior of the Sorcerer:

> Con temblores de dicha voy completando mi obra hasta lograr el dominio del mundo. Dominar el mundo es la única voluptuosidad posible, el gran orgasmo cósmico. La feliciada que se siente al destruir a otros, el goce de la tortura, todo multiplicado al infinito. (CL 298)
>
> [With a cheerful tremor I'll go in with my gestation and one day we will rule the world. To rule the world is the only possible voluptuousness. The great cosmic orgasm. The joy one feels in destroying others and the pleasures of torture multiplied to infinity. (LT 277)]

He delights in fantasies of destruction:

> Venganza, toda mi sangre clama por venganza. Me han estado haciendo brujerías, les voy a tirar encima todas las fuerzas de mi fuerza, los voy a aniquilar, los voy a hacer trizas yo solito, no voy a cruzar la frontera en busca de ayuda, y solo con todo mi poder los voy a triturar, a desintegrar. He impartido órdenes para que los busquen hasta debajo de las piedras. Es gente peligrosa, saben manejar los poderes de la mente y para evitarlo hay un solo remedio: destruir la mente. (CL 86)
>
> [Revenge. All my blood calls out for revenge. They've been practicing witchcraft against me. I will throw the forces of my force upon them. I will annihilate them, I will tear them to shreds, I alone . . . with all my power, will make mincemeat of them . . . They're dangerous people, they know how to manipulate the powers of the mind, and there's only one way to avoid that: destroy the mind. (LT 74)]

Valenzuela often describes the Sorcerer in terms of evil. Adorno and Horkheimer have described evil in the following terms: "It is said that divine power attracts creation, satanic power likewise draws everything into its own impotence . . . The products of false projection, the stereotype is of thought and reality, are therefore products of evil" (190). In the festival of the Capivarians, the Sorcerer is represented in the image Valenzuela describes as somewhere between "terrifying and ridiculous" (58):

> Lo envuelve todo él también su manto de abajo, que tiene pintadas calaveras y huesos. Y arriba le visten su chalequito, y éste está pintado

con miembros humanos despedazados: todo él está pintado de cráneos, orejas, corazones, intestinos, tóraces, tetas, manos, pies. (*CL* 174)

[He is wrapped in a robe painted with skull and bones. On the torso he wears a vest painted with disjointed human members – all of it covered over with craniums, ears, hearts, intestines, thoraxes, teats, hands, feet. (*LT* 157)]

The Sorcerer makes everything in his own image, another characteristic of the paranoid elucidated by Horkheimer and Adorno:

Since the paranoic perceives the world about him only as it corresponds to his blind purposes, he can only repeat his own self which is alienated into an abstract mania . . . . It is as though the serpent which said to the first men "you will be as God" had redeemed its promise in the paranoic. He makes everything in his own image. (185)

Even when he reproduces himself, the Sorcerer's paranoia leads him to choose immaculate conception: "Ahora seré mi propio hijo como una vez fui mi propio padre. Ya sin ayuda de mujer alguna . . . " (*CL* 277) "Now I shall be my own son, as I was my own father. And without the help of any woman . . . "

The discourse of the Sorcerer is based on a series of oppositions in which cruelty and sadism are dominant. An example is his relationship with his aide-de-camp, which is both sadomasochistic and homosexual within the context of denial and repression:

-¡Me measte!
-¡Le gustó, mi amo! (*CL* 64)

["You pissed on me!"
"You liked it, master." (*LT* 54)]

The Sorcerer takes mushrooms for "illumination" – his form of reaching light or understanding. His perception of reality is enhanced by the drug, or, in his words, by "simple phallic association" (*LT* 56) "Por simple asociación de ideas que tanto hacen a la magia contigua supo que la verdad la encontraría en los hongos"; *CL* 66). Valenzuela's irony is informed by the French feminist critique of phallocentrism, the subsumption of all meaning under the power of the phallus. Mushrooms provide the solution to his problems: his relationship to them is one of "simpatía, simbiosis, mimetismo" (*CL* 68) ("sympathy, symbiosis and mimesis"; *LT* 57) Mushrooms are the physical mediation between the Sorcerer and object. They affect his perception which in turn affects the meaning the object holds for him. The mushrooms grow in a grotto in which he performs a ritual before a stalagmite, which he refers to as "la Virgen de Sal" (*CL* 70) ("the Virgin of Salt"; *LT* 59). Salt has magical properties and in the form of a stalagmite, phallic associations. All of this, of course, gives Luisa the narrator the opportunity to juxtapose codes, in this case, the reference codes of psychoanalysis and magic.

In *Dialectic of Enlightenment*, Horkheimer and Adorno write:

> In magic there is specific repression. What happens to the enemy's spear, hair or name, also happens to the individual; the sacrificial animal is massacred instead of the individual; the sacrificial animal is massacred instead of the god. (192)

The narrator Luisa refers to the swamp as "el lugar de una convención, de un símbolo" (*CL* 57) ("a symbolic location"; *LT* 48). It is the location at which we, as active readers, must make our stand. In the "swamp" of the unconscious, the Sorcerer is able to get a lock of our hair, so to speak. He can represent us by capturing what we have discarded, images from our own unconscious. He gains his power through our repression of our own "swamp." The Sorcerer's birthplace is the marshland, our marshland, and we give birth to him. It is both fetid and transparent; it appears to be crystalline, but in reality it is a swamp. Bakhtin's view that we repress decay, echoed by Henri Lefebvre in his discussion of the society of the spectacle which has replaced the society of the Festival of the spectacle, provides a context for considering the signifier of the marshland, where the Sorcerer lives underground and sails about on an island. The narrator Luisa asks the reader: "¿Pueden acaso ustedes encontrar una mejor representación que ésa del inconsciente humano?" (*CL* 57) ("Could you find a better representation than this of the human unconscious?"; *LT* 48).

Cola de lagartija is based on a series of parallels and imitations. The action code for all characters is one of mimetic behavior. Girard defines mimetic behavior as something that occurs once basic needs have been met in the human. At that time, he writes in *Violence and the Sacred*: "The subject looks to that other person [who seems to possess being] to inform him of what he should desire in order to acquire that being [which he lacks]" (146). There is a convergence here with Lacan, who also grounds his systems in what he calls "lack."

Girard finds that Bateson's notion of the "double bind" needs to be broadened in its definition:

> Far from being restricted to a limited number of pathological cases, as American theoreticians suggest, the double bind—a contradictory double imperative, or rather a whole network of contradictory imperatives—is an extremely common phenomenon. In fact, it is so common that it might be said to form the basis of all human relationships." (147)

Girard explains that desire "fills man with despair and turns him into the slave of an involuntary tyrant" because one cannot respond to that universal human injunction, "Imitate me!" without almost immediately encountering an inexplicable counterorder: "Don't imitate me" (which really means, "Do not appropriate *my* object") (147).

Mimetic behavior in *Cola de lagartija* is often humorous. The mushroom witch Machi tells the Sorcerer, "usted es apenas un vil reflejo mío" (*CL* 73) ("you're nothing but a vile reflection of me"; *LT* 63). Navoni practices one form of magic with Caboclo de Mar, the witch who agrees to work with the revolutionaries against the Sorcerer, while the Sorcerer practices his magic in the Kingdom of the Black Lagoon. However, mimesis becomes more serious when Luisa the narrator finds herself in the "double bind." Luisa is invited to the inauguration of the pyramid. This duplicitous and compromised relationship with the Sorcerer is a signifier of the relationship of the writer to politics. Luisa identifies with him to a certain extent since without him she would have no novel. However, she is accused of having awakened him by writing her book (*CL* 179, *LT* 162). He is a subterranean version of her (*CL* 183, *LT* 166). Her revolutionary task, as defined by Navoni, is to kill him: "Mirá, sólo quisiera que en tu novela biográfica o en tu biografía novelada o lo que sea, lo matés al brujo" (*CL* 206) ("All I want for you is to kill the witchdoc in your biographical novel; *LT* 187). This puts Valenzuela as the actual author of *Cola de lagartija* and Luisa as the author of the biography in an impossible situation. She destroys her novel/political biography and therefore herself as writer. When Luisa decides to stop writing, abandoning her belief that "la literatura va a salvarnos" (*CL* 200) ("literature can save us"; *LT* 181), she resolves the dilemma through a Derridean solution, a placing of herself *sous rature*. She erases herself and the Sorcerer, but she has written the book to let us see that this is what has occurred.

An important form of mimetic behavior, according to Girard, is revenge. The theme of revenge recurs throughout *Cola de lagartija* and is consistent with the Sorcerer's paranoic character. According to Girard, revenge perpetuates a system of victimage, that is, a chain of violent acts followed by more violent acts. If we consider this system in semiotic and Lacanian terms, we could see that linear narrative and the symbolic order are rooted in this fundamental violence. *Cola de lagartija* raises a question about the modern notion of violence. What is the difference between the Aztec sacrifices of twenty thousand men a day and the current situation of the *desaparecidos* in Argentina? How is the violence perpetuated by the Gaze? The pyramid, where the sacrifices take place, is double:

A pyramid that's double-faced and single-faced at the same time, unique. Unity symbolizes and divides me. Like my pyramid, which will be Aztec . . . . During the inauguration of the Great Temple of Tenochtitlán, Aztec priests sacrificed twenty thousand men in a single day. They had them four columns of five thousand, each marking a cardinal point, and crack-crack, they went along pulling out their hearts one by one as they climbed up. Like an assembly line . . . imagine what a sublime spectacle. (*LT* 75, 106–7)

To equate the sacrifice of twenty thousand humans to a "sublime spectacle" is to perceive a historical event with the perspective we have described as paranoic. What sort of semiotic system allows the Sorcerer to find meaning in such an event? The system of sacrifice in traditional societies is what Girard calls the "victimage principle." He recalls that the Jews were blamed for the plague in the Middle Ages. The rationale for this behavior is survival; in order to survive, the community must sacrifice some of its own members; On the question of Aztec sacrifice and cruelty, Jacques Soustelle has written:

> At the height of their career the Romans shed more blood in their circuses and for their amusement than ever the Aztecs did before their idols. The Spaniards so sincerely moved by the cruelty of the native priests, never the less massacred, burnt, mutilated, and tortured with a perfectly clear conscience. Human sacrifice among the Mexicans was inscribed neither by cruelty nor by hatred. It was their response, and the only response that they could conceive, to the instability of a continually threatened world. Blood was necessary to save this world . . . the victim was . . . a messenger who was sent to the gods. (12)

Blood is necessary in order for the Sorcerer to save his reality, his world. The image of the "spectacle" must not obscure a deeper refusal to see: in the context of Argentina, middle-class Argentines were willing to sacrifice some of their population in order to preserve their class privileges and the order of their world.

The generation of Valenzuela's parents became passively engaged in the sacrifice of the *desaparecidos*: they watched the deaths of their own children. Valenzuela's cure is the opposite or mirror image of the government's. Rather than removing otherness from sight, she would have us face it. The belief that ridding a society of part of its population could "cure" it recalls our earlier discussion of the *pharmakon*, which can be understood as both a "remedy" and something that can worsen the disease. Girard, in *Violence and the Sacred*, refers to Derrida's discussion of the *pharmakon*. Derrida concentrates on the contradictory meanings of the term — poison and remedy — and argues that reciprocity links the terms. Girard uses Derrida's analysis to support his own notion of the "generative operation." Briefly, he explains this as the fact that "men cannot confront the naked truth of their own violence without the risk of abandoning themselves to it entirely" (*Violence and the Sacred*, 82). Girard believes that the process of finding a surrogate victim is the way in which humans keep the truth of their violence from themselves: "The cure must depend on the identification and expulsion of the individual whose presence pollutes the community" (83). This resembles Freud's view that the voyeur avoids the truth of himself, avoids being seen, by looking at others.

Davis, in "Lacan, Poe and Narrative Repression," discusses a similar strategy in Poe's "The Tell-Tale Heart." In this story, a gambler insists he has no problem

with the old man with whom he lives except for the man's "evil eye." He murders
the old man in order to avoid the gaze of this eye. Davis explains that the gambler
commits murder in order to avoid being seen by the old man's eye, but he makes
himself an object of prosecution as criminal. Davis's explanation of this contradictory behavior is that the gambler prefers death to a passive role in life, the
role of being watched. This contradictory situation is the "double bind." In terms
of Bateson's description of the schizophrenia-producing family structure, the
military acts as the parent and the Argentine middle class as the schizophrenic
child. By making the subversives (who are a reminder of Girard's "naked truth
of their own violence") disappear, the middle class does not have to confront its
own violence. The subversive functions as the surrogate victim. This makes the
way for the military easier: Argentines are told that the *subversivos* have disappeared and that this is necessary for the security of the country, just as the mother
of the schizophrenic child who might like to stay up later tells her child, "Go to
bed, you're very tired and I want you to get your sleep" (Bateson, 214). The
schizophrenic population becomes less and less able to know what its own needs
are, even as it watches the murders of its own children. The one group of Argentines that has refused to submit either to the logic of the surrogate victim or to
the schizophrenic relationship of the double bind vis-á-vis the military is the
group of mothers who are still demanding to know what happened to their children, the Mothers of the Plaza de Mayo. Still acting according to Bateson's
model, the military continues to tell them, "Go home. Forget about your sons and
daughters. Go on with your lives."

Earlier we considered the meaning of the pyramid in relation to the metaphor
of landscape and exorcism. The pyramid can also be used to discern a semiotics
that emerges from Valenzuela's text. There are conflicting semiotic systems in
Cola de lagartija, Luisa's and the Sorcerer's. Just as the pyramid is neither urban
nor rural, but a mediation between the two, so the Sorcerer's movement is neither
in the capital nor in the provinces, but in the Black Lagoon. The pyramid, his
choice of a monument for himself, is a signifier of civilization and barbarism. As
Derrida notes in his essay on Hegel's semiotics, "The Pit and the Pyramid," the
pyramid encloses both a void and a pit. Space separates objects: according to
Pythagoras, the function of the void is to keep things apart or to distinguish the
nature of things. Within the reference code of semiotics, a code familiar to Valenzuela regardless of whether or not she is familiar with Derrida's essay, the
pyramid is linked to *differance* in both of the terms "to differ" and "to defer." A
multidimensional perspective is able to recognize *differance* in the play of signification, while the paranoic personality is involved in a continual struggle for the
control of meaning. Luisa ridicules the Sorcerer's attempt to define the pyramid
and to maintain the boundaries of his identity by forcing the Capivarians to turn
their mirrors in so that the "miracle" of his identity will not leave his hand. At

first, the Sorcerer uses the mirrors to cover the inside of the pyramid, but then he covers them up with white cloth:

> La carpa albísima separa la vieja imagen más o menos viril de le Bruj, por siempre depositada en los espejos, de esta su nueva figura que se va deleitando en mutaciones y empieza a reclamar su dádiva. (*CL* 273)

> [The white tent separates the old, more or less virile image of the Sorcerer, deposited forever in the mirrors, from this new figure that takes delight in mutations and is beginning to demand its gift. (*LT* 254)]

In "The Pit and the Pyramid," Derrida reads Hegel's semiology as if it were a machine that produced language. This machine can be thought of as a circular movement through a double pyramid (See the accompanying diagram).[4]

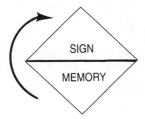

In this pyramid something is returned from memory (stored perceptions that are actually representations) and made present as a meaningful sign. Involved in each reinscription in sign production is loss. This loss results from the nonidentity between the universal and the particular noted by Nietzsche in "Truth and Lie in Extra-Moral Sense." He uses the example of the leaf, in which particulars of individual examples are lost in the abstraction that occurs each time the universal term "leaf" is used in the production of meaning. More and more elements become unrecuperable in the production of each sign. The fundamental problem of language, according to Derrida, lies in its metonymic nature. In the one-dimensional epistemology of the paranoic, the unconscious, or "memory" in the double pyramid, is repressed; it returns in the forms of violence and revenge that we have discussed. In the multidimensional epistemology, unconscious desire is less repressed; there is less of a generalized urge to destruction.

At the same time that traces are left in the production of meaning, much of the object itself is unrecuperated by the sign. Nietzsche discusses this in terms of the repression of nonidentity:

> Every concept originates by the equation of the dissimilar. Just as no leaf is ever exactly the same as any other, certainly the concept "leaf" is formed by arbitrarily dropping those individual differences, by forgetting the distinguishing factors . . . (249)

A border semiotics would allow the subject to break free from Lacan's Law of the Father by not equating what is unequal. It would remember that no particular event ever equals another; it would recognize individual differences by deconstructing "arbitrary abstraction." In terms of narrative structure, it would avoid linear narration.

The link between linear narrative structure and sadism has been explored by de Lauretis in *Alice Doesn't*; she notes, for example, that Lotman links the structure of "the entry into a closed space and emergence from it" to a pattern of mythical narrative "strongly suggestive of the one Mulvey ascribes to sadism":

> Inasmuch as closed space *can be interpreted* as "a cave," "the grave," "a house," "woman" (and correspondingly, be allotted the features of darkness, warmth, dampness), entry into it is *interpreted* on various levels as "death," "conception," "return home" and so on. (118)

Lacan writes of the grave in *Ecrits*:

> The first symbol in which we recognize humanity in its vestigial traces is the sepulture, and the intermediary of death can be recognized in every relation through which man is born into the life of his history. (104)

Taken together with Freud's argument in *Beyond the Pleasure Principle*, that death is the ultimate purpose of life, a semiotics is suggested: based on this system of meaning, might not a detour, of chains of signifiers, toward death, as the ultimate signifier, allow the inclusion of all phases of life—conception, birth, youth, aging, death, burial of the corpse, and decay of the corpse? Would such a semiotics, a multidimensional, negative semiotics, be capable of deconstructing the discourse of the Sorcerer?

The political unconscious and the multidimensional semiotics we are describing could create a language machine in which imagery of the political unconscious would be incorporated, rather than repressed, into a system of the Festival in which it found its meaning. Such a system would produce meaning as an interference pattern, or as Jameson writes in *The Political Unconscious*: "The authentic function of the cultural text is then staged rather as an interference between levels, as a subversion of one level by another" (56).

Viewed as a surreal landscape painting, *Cola de lagartija* depicts a cross section of the earth: molten subterranean layers of unconscious imagery emerge on the surface as semiotics volcanoes, and tiny mountains, or more precisely, anthills. All of this culminates in the image of the pyramid. Why does Valenzuela choose to compare Argentina to anthills and pyramids? The violence of contemporary Argentina is linked to the culture of the Aztec, which included ritual sacrifice. We have determined that the marshland is an appropriate metaphor for the political unconscious. By building near the marshland, Valenzuela is able to link violence to the discussion of the unconscious.

Jameson, in *The Political Unconscious*, writes that the "essential mystery of the cultural past . . . can only recover its 'original urgency' if retold with the unity of a single great collective story" (19). In terms of Valenzuela's narrative structure, considered as a multidimensional, border narrative, the political unconscious is the repressed or unsaid aspect of the reference code. The "real" can only be known indirectly, as an interference pattern created from its traces. Jameson remarks of the method particular to this knowing that

> it is in detecting the traces of that narrative [the collective story], in restoring to the surface of the text the repressed and buried reality of its fundamental history, that the doctrine of a political unconscious finds its function and is necessary. (20)

In the story of the struggle for democracy in Latin America, which is part of a larger story, the story of that struggle in the world, it is necessary to detect traces by looking at contemporary Latin American politics historically, which, as Jameson reminds us, is only available in textual form. We may read it by deconstructing the social text of everyday life. It is not the recuperation of the meaning of the past as a linear narrative, but as the layered, interacting fragments of multidimensional memory exhibited by the border text.

What then, is the cure that Valenzuela's exorcism has attempted? She has attempted to reverse the "Gaze." The fear of being seen—a fear so deep that a majority of middle-class Argentines chose to look away as the police took their children—is replaced by a strategy for facing the fear, a will to deconstruct the language of representation, mimesis, and violence. The gaze that can look back without fear is the multidimensional, the border perspective. The active reader is the new Orpheus, who can look into the Hell of the double, the "horrifying vision," recognize in it herself or himself, and stare back at it.

Chapter 6
Contemporary Border Writing and Reading: From Aztlán to Nicaragua

It has been said that literature is the space in which feminist debates take place in Latin America. I would like to expand upon this idea by adding theory to this space for dialogue. As a displaced woman born in San Francisco, raised between San Francisco and San Diego, and now living in the Mexico-U.S. border region, I am particularly interested in Alice Jardine's criticism of Deleuze and Guattari's model of deterritorialized literature and the question of the feminine border "subject." The women of my generation, too young to be participants in the Free Speech movement but who experienced the anti-war movement, have had to face a painful realization: there is a profound gap of communication among Chicanas, Mexicanas, and Anglo-Americanas. With the passage of the Simpson-Rodino Bill, the continuing violation of human rights may capture the attention of Anglo-Americans in the region.[1] They may find this difficult time to be an opportunity to engage in dialogue with Chicanas and Mexicanas, as opposed to a time to merely continue being critical of Latino culture from the outside.[2] If the anti-war movement of the Vietnam era was a frustrating political experience for many feminists, the movement of anti-intervention in Central America may have proved to be a much more positive experience. Nicaragua and the Mexico-U.S. border region offer two contexts in which women can be active participants in international debates. In "Woman in Limbo: Deleuze and His Br(others)," Alice Jardine is critical of the notion of "deterritorialization." Because I believe that Anglo and French women will have the most to learn from a multicultural dialogue, precisely because many of them are not geographically dislocated, I am concerned that they not tell deterritorialized women which models to reject or accept without seriously considering the consequences of their recommendations. I believe that with some revisions, Deleuze and Guattari's model is closer to a border feminist viewpoint, such as that of Chicana poet Gloria Anzaldúa, than is Jardine's critique of their model, and that their model will help to generate a dialogue among members of border cultures.

Deterritorialization and Women in Border Writing

Jardine's critique is based in part on her concern with the feminine subject. In response to Deleuze and Guattari's call for all of us, women and men, to "become woman," that is, "to resist the dominant mode of representation represented by any majority," Jardine writes: "woman is never a subject but a limit" (54). However, in *Borderlands, la Frontera, The New Mestiza*, Gloria Anzaldúa formulates the question of border identity in a broader context, one that may allow for Deleuze and Guattari's model:

> The U.S.-Mexico border is *una herida abierta* where the Third World grates against the first and bleeds. And before a scab forms it hemorrhages again, the lifeblood of two worlds merging to form a third country—a border culture. Borders are set up to define the places that are safe and unsafe, to distinguish us from them. A borderland is a vague and undetermined place created by the emotional residue of an unnatural boundary. It is in a constant state of transition. The prohibited and forbidden are its inhabitants. (3)

In order to test Jardine's critique, that Deleuze and Guattari's model allows men but not women to flee from their entrapment, I would like to consider the revised model and then consider the revised model in two contexts. In the first, the U.S.-Mexico border region, the role of women is undergoing change and the female/male dichotomy may not have the same significance that it has in the rest of the United States or in Europe. This may also be true in the second context, Nicaragua.

In very different ways, Nicaragua and the Mexico-U.S. frontier are both border cultures. Nicaragua is perceived by many North Americans as the Latin border between the United States and the Soviet Union, although recent events in Eastern Europe are already changing this perception. Both regions are also linguistically multivalenced. Although the major language in Nicaragua is Spanish, Nicaraguans of the Atlantic coast also speak English. These Nicaraguans include the Blacks of Bluefields and other areas, as well as the Miskito, Suma, and Rama Indians. In the Mexico-U.S. border region, English is the official language of *California ocupada*, despite the fact that Los Angeles has the largest Spanish-speaking population outside of Mexico City. In Mexico, there is also a movement to keep Spanish untainted by English. Some Chicanas and Chicanos, but not all, are bilingual. Not all Mexicans living in the U.S.-Mexico border region speak English; relatively few Anglos living in the region speak Spanish. In Nicaragua, the situation is reversed; the English speakers are bilingual.

In order to test the border model, I have chosen to consider texts that deal with desire directly: love poems and poems that include images of women. The main reason for these choices is that I want to focus on the interaction between two dominant referential codes: love and revolution (or what Deleuze and Guattari would call "the political"). I want to focus on one specific distinction made by Deleuze and Guattari in *Kafka*: blocked desire (desire trapped in nostalgia; linked to the portrait-photograph) vs. unblocked desire (desire freed by deterritorialization; linked to music/sound). The first question I will pose is, can Jardine's critique of Deleuze and Guattari's model also be applied to a revised version of that model, the border model?

In "Narrative Surplus: The 'Blow-up' as Metarepresentation and Ideology," Deborah Linderman argues that in both Cortázar's story ("Las babas del diablo") and Antonioni's film (*Blow-up*), "the single locus of subjectivity . . . is the photographer" (100). In terms of the border model, this single locus of subjectivity can be distinguished from "the collective voice of enunciation" in the border text. The latter does not refer back to a single subject. The photograph in "Las babas," taken by a single photographer, differs from the holographic plate, which records the interference pattern, in that the latter emerges from two vantage points rather than the single viewpoint of a photographer. Just as a holographic plate can be broken, and a piece will hold the entire image, so a "piece" of border "subjectivity" can be randomly selected from the border social text and it will contain a recording of the interference pattern between the two dominant cultural modes, the Anglo and the Latino. Linderman concludes her article with the assertion that the narrative "surplus" in Cortázar's text serves to hold the subject in place rather than to contain deconstructive elements (114). The term "surplus" refers to the various repetitions that force an emphasis on certain links among signifiers. If we conceive of the border as a multidimensional or holographic text created from the interference pattern formed by two dominant cultural codes, we will find that no links among any two signifiers can all hold. All signifiers and their binary oppositions *al otro lado* will continually struggle for dominance and be dismantled. The second question I will address in this chapter is whether or not the poetry of postrevolutionary Nicaragua and border writing of the Mexico-U.S. border region, the "collective voice of enunciation," is continually "deterritorialized" and whether or not there is narrative "excess," that is, deconstructive elements.

I want to consider this question of the "locus of subjectivity" along with Laura Mulvey's query, "What is the relationship between nonlinearity and sadism?" Mulvey explores this question in her well-known essay "Visual Pleasure and Narrative Cinema." Is it possible, as many film critics have suggested, that an alternative or nonsadistic method of filmmaking would be nonlinear, and that "deterritorialization" could provide a metaphorical opportunity for women to flee from the entrapment of film conventions? If we extend this to border writing, could it be said that Jardine's critique is not applicable to the border model?

The political task suggested by both Jardine's critique and Deleuze and Guattari's model is to restructure the unfolding of desire. Before such a restructuring can be imagined, it is important to remember some of the historical reasons for certain geopolitical phenomena. Two political situations in which the United States has produced deterritorialization for at least 140 years in one case (the Mexican-American War) and over 120 years (Nicaragua, first U.S. invasion) also happen to be centers of deterritorialized cultural production. The Sandinista revolution of 1979 resulted in the establishment of poetry workshops in Nicaragua, including a genre not normally associated with revolutionary situations: the love poem. The U.S.-Mexico border region has also produced a significant amount of poetry, some of which has appeared in the Chicano magazine *Maize*, and more recently, in *The Broken Line/La Línea Quebrada*. The latter is linked to border regions around the world, and also to revolutionary contexts, because of its relationship with Cesar Espinosa's mail-art collective, Post-Arte.[3]

It is logical then, that both the Chicano movement and the Sandinista government have made cultural politics an important part of their agendas. Among the Nicaraguan critics who have addressed the relationship between art and politics is poet Ernesto Cardenal, Nicaraguan Minister of Culture. Cardenal believes that "literature should fulfill a purpose. It should be at the service of mankind. For that very reason, poetry should also be political."[4] Bilingual Chicana poet Gina Valdés describes the fundamental differences between [writing] poetry in Spanish and English: "Para mí la gran diferencia radica en la conciencia política. El escritor latinoamericano, sea mexicano, chileno o chicano, generalmente tiene más conciencia political que el anglosajón"("For me the great difference is rooted in political consciousness. The Latin American writer, be he [she] Mexican, Chilean, or Chicano [a], generally has more political consciousness than the Anglo Saxon").[5] If we apply these statements to, say, the postrevolutionary love poem in Nicaragua, does it change our reading of these texts? Does the function of the love poem shift from paying homage to the beloved to celebrating the revolution or condemning the U.S. government? For the Chicano movement and now the Sandinista government, the question is, what kind of cultural production should be supported?

Roland Barthes and Fredric Jameson formulate the problem in different terms. Barthes, in "Introduction to the Structural Analysis of Narratives," claims that language, not the person speaking, is what is under consideration in ideological or interpretative criticism. From this perspective, an overlay of codes, including the revolutionary or political, rather than revolutionary fervor on the part of the poet, is the crux of the issue. The larger political context in which the debate itself occurs is described by Jameson in *The Political Unconscious* as a historical dilemma: "Radical politics has traditionally alternated between . . . two classical options . . . the image of the triumph of the collectivity and that of the liberation of the soul or spiritual body . . . between a 1920s Leninist formulation of communism as 'the Soviets plus electrification' and some more properly Marcusean 1960s celebration of an instinctual 'body politic' "(73). Hélène Cixous and Julia Kristeva are closer to the latter. How applicable are these statements to border writing?

If we allow that a multiplicity of codes and the celebration of an "instinctual 'body politic' " are more applicable to border writing, can we also say that the model of border writing allows for the escape of women from the confines of the Oedipal order? In Nicaragua, the duties and attributes of women, as expressed in Sandinista ideology, are no longer those referred to by Chicana poet Marisela Norte in "Salmo para: Ella": "the one who knows how to knit . . . the sleeping woman immortalized in the calendars at the corner baker." There is a new code of duty: revolutionary commitment. This code extends beyond the family. The gap between the codes of romantic love and revolutionary commitment emerges in Julia Aguirre's "En Maladera." Aguirre learned to read during the literacy campaign: "Sentada debajo del atiquilote / escribí en mi diario del campo. En el incluí tu nombre / las veces que llegaste a verme / escondido de tu responsable de escuadra" ("Seated under the atiquilote, I wrote in my rural diary. In it, I included your name, the times that you came to see me, hiding from your squad leader"). The action of sneaking off to visit one's lover betrays a breach of revolutionary duty. In postrevolutionary Nicaragua, how is desire channeled? What is love in this context? Is it revolutionary commitment or is it hiding from the squad leader? The woman here, according to Deleuze and Guattari's model, may be acting according to Terry Cochran's critique of the model, as "a kind of succoring aid" to allow the man to flee from the entrapment of his duty.[6] However, is the woman not more than a helper? Is she not also freed? In love that crosses borders, is not love itself a form of "deterritorialization"? In Luna Robles's "Randazz-o," does the woman help the male flee, or, conversely, remind him of his "duty"?

Considering again the model of Deleuze and Guattari, we may find an example of "reterritorialization" in "Táctica y estrategia," by Nicaraguan poet H.E.M.Z. The narrator explains that his tactics include watching, engaging in conversation, and listening to his lover in order to build an indestructible bridge between them. "Reterritorialization," it will be remembered, refers to blocked desire, that is, the nostalgia for a previous ordering of desire. If by extension, the Gaze could also be defined as a form of "reterritorialization," in that it attempts to fix people and objects in a structure of either looking or being looked at (that is, it blocks desire by forcing it into what Freud calls an ordering of sadists and masochists), then a disruption of the Gaze of a different libidinal order might be associated with listening to one's lover.[7] Looking and listening are tactics in the poem; the strategy is one of waiting. He hopes that one day "she will need him." That a woman should "need" a man is on the one hand a form of "reterritorialization"; it refers to a memory of prerevolutionary culture. In the context of the model of border writing, however, it is also a form of the unblocking of desire: one day, the two may desire each other in a way that was "blocked" by revolutionary duty and the new role of women during the epoch of *Nicaragua libre*.

Border Semiotics

Chicano and Chicana critics and artists including Tey Diana Rebolledo, Tomás Ibarra-Frausto, Marta Sánchez, Amalia Mesa-Bains, Victor Zamudio, and Gloria Anzaldúa have engaged in semiotic debates. Ibarra-Frausto has attempted to imagine a border semiotics. Sánchez has written about Chicana poets using a methodology informed by semiotics. Mesa-Bains and Zamudio have both considered Chicano iconography in the context of memory. Semiotics is a logical choice for a starting point from which to develop a methodology, since much of the Chicano movement has focused on the critical use of signifiers as a way of forging an identity. In a related vein, Anzaldúa has written about identity in terms that resemble Deleuze and Guattari's notion of deterritorialization.[8]

Because semiotics emerged in a European context, certain adjustments must be made in applying its categories to border writing. A Barthian-based semiotics of border writing can be defined beginning with the five codes of *S/Z*: (1) the hermeneutic (who, what, where, when, why, etc.); (2) the proairetic (action or plot); (3) the semic; (4) the symbolic (which is structured in terms of binary oppositions); and (5) the referential or cultural codes (bodies of knowledge: religion, law, etc.). In the border context, all of these codes are deterritorialized. The border hermeneutic is doubled: existential questions about identity and place become legal nightmares of displacement and deportation. The proairetic is overdetermined by at least two orders of referential or cultural codes, derived from both sides of the border: certain actions of everyday life, such as the purchasing or eating of food from *el otro lado* take on a ritualistic significance. When the signifier is deterritorialized, it hovers between two signifieds, seeking refuge in a battle between desire and nostalgia.

Another example of this is altar building, both an everyday activity in the border region and an activity that has become an art form among some Chicana artists.[9] Even the simple action of arranging to meet another person is overdetermined by the political situation: which person can legally cross the border? The border "subject" or Voice of the Person, linked with the semic code, emerges from several languages and cultures. There is a range from monoculturality and monolinguality (only Spanish or only English) to completely comfortable and fluent biculturality and bilinguality (Spanish, English, and possibly Spanglish). The binary oppositions of the symbolic code that may be useful in mapping one culture are not transferable: certain oppositions are not equally emphasized on both sides of the border. For example, the main dichotomy in the region is documented-undocumented, not male-female. This is also the case in Nicaragua, where Sandinista-Contra is a much more crucial dichotomy than female-male. The most important set of codes in the border region constitutes the referential codes, which inform every image of border writing. Border dwellers must be able to switch referential codes; for example, the cultural code of the "mordida" (bribe) in Mexico, if applied in the United States, can result in violent arrest.[10] In the texts I will consider in the following section, the two major referential codes are love and revolution, or the code of political activism.

The Sandinista revolution (1979) and the Simpson-Rodino Bill (1987) have resulted in "deterritorialization" in both regions. In Nicaragua, before the election of Violeta Chamorro, *campesinos* were flown to Moscow by the Sandinista government for military training in the war against U.S.-backed Contras. San- dinistas crossed borders against Contras operating out of Honduras and Costa Rica. Miskito Indians were removed from their homelands by the Sandinista government.[11] In the Mexico-U.S. border region, Latinos are stopped routinely by the *migra* and asked for identification. Thousands are deported every month and even more live in fear of deportation.[12]

The "deterritorialization" in both regions has resulted in a "deterritorialization" of signification. For this reason, a semiotics of border writing must be con- structed with the recognition that desire is deterritorialized. In Nicaragua, before the revolution and until the election of Chamorro to the presidency, the "real" was constituted by that which resisted Somoza's regime.[13] It was preserved as the hope promised by Sandino. In the Mexico-U.S. border region in the early 1970s, the "real" was constituted by the Chicano movement. During the Sandinista re- gime, the Sandinista government became the Law of the Father, the new symbolic order. This order still struggled against a more global Law of the Father, how- ever: U.S. foreign policy. The "real" that continued to resist official symboliza- tion, and which somehow survived in the midst of the war against the United States, was preserved in the love poem in Nicaragua. In the Mexico-U.S. border region, the love poem resists the double symbolization of the official cultures of both Mexico and the United States.

With the defeat of the political movement of the 1960s in the United States, the "real" of the Chicano movement has become problematic. The passage of the Simpson-Rodino Bill is a signifier of a major defeat in a fifteen-year struggle against the exploitative, racist labor policies in the region. Border culture offers a possibility for families separated by the Simpson-Rodino Bill, exiles from the Mexico City earthquake and the "crisis," and Chicanos who refuse to become "Hispanic" to remain in contact. More recently, border culture has offered a ha- ven for disaffected Anglos who would like to redefine themselves as "multicul- tural." A bicultural or multicultural "real" may exist in the imagery of border love poetry; it may resist the Law of the Father(s) of the hegemonic cultures from whose conflicts it emerges.

The Border Love Poem: New Codes or Blocked Codes

We can begin the discussion of the ordering of desire by focusing on one image in Carlos R. Monjárrez's poem "Muchacha": the "flor armada," the armed flower. One side of this binary opposition war/love implied by the image is a reference to the Europeanized, colonized bourgeois woman before the revolution, the woman as a flower. Even in contemporary Western referential codes, women are linked to a romantic view of nature: beautiful, fragile, dangerous, something to be tamed.[14] In this context, nature itself, since the nineteenth century in Europe, has been a seme of harmony to juxtapose against technology. In Latin American culture, war and "nature" or the flower are linked through a very different referential code: the Flower Wars of the Aztecs. Both the European and Latin American referential codes inform Monjárrez's image. The flower has become militarized in his poem, but there is a supplement, a trace of resistance, to this militarization or symbolization. It recalls a moment of a "deflowering" through politicization and points to a future when there might be love without war. Thus, although the image emerges from a context of deterritorialization, insofar as it is a kind of nostalgia for a culture prior to war, it is also an articulation of reterritorialization. In the border writing model, however, it is a form of the unblocking of desire: one day, women and men may not have to be armed.[15]

Unlike the passive, territorialized image of T. S. Eliot's burning rose, the armed flower is activated by the codes of love and revolution. Rather than sacrificing herself to the pentecostal tongues of time, the revolutionary woman, the "flor armada," is prepared to fight. Adelaida Diaz also makes a reference to a flower in the context of a love poem. Diaz, who worked as a domestic servant before the revolution, now is the director of programming at the Popular Cultural Center in Boaco, Nicaragua. In "4 meses," composed in the poetry workshop in Boaco, she writes to her lover that four months have passed since they have been together. Yet, in spite of everything, "las flores de malinche huelen y son rojas" ("the malinche flowers are fragrant and red"). Here, the flower is a signifier of continuity and strength; the border Penelope waits, but not passively.

Robert Jones, a bilingual Chicanized Anglo poet living in the Mexico-U.S. border region, writes in "A Border Rose" that the rose he purchases while waiting to cross into the United States from Mexico is "alien, an undocumented." This poem is dedicated to "Patricia, the Rose Woman." The signifier of the rose functions not only in the context of a love poem, but also as an ironic critique of U.S. immigration policy.

The juxtaposition of the discourses of love and politics appears in a poem written in Nicaragua just before the Sandinista victory. In "Iluminación," Rosario Murillo describes "la victoria" as "ya cerca acariciable" ("already close enough to caress").[16] Here, the experience of the imminent victory is in part an opportunity for "reterritorialization" through erotic imagery. The pull toward the past of the discourse of love is modulated by an envelope of a pull toward the future: further deterritorialization and victory.[17]

The "subject" both in revolutionary Nicaraguan poetry, or the Voice of the Person, and in the writing of the Mexico-U.S. border region emerges from the same matrix of countervailing forces: it is an assemblage. Desire between border subjects is deterritorialized. When bilingual Chicano poet Ruben Medina writes in "Amor de lejos" ("Love from a Distance") to Estela Jurado, he makes no direct reference to love until the last lines: "Vengan, / Vengan / pero atrás de la barrera / y green card en mano / porque amor de lejos . . . / a Estela Jurado." The entire poem is a list of examples of the ability of U.S. culture to make a place for everyone: "the deaf man, because suddenly he will obey"; "the one who argues, because he'll only say I understand"; "the nice ones in English, and sons of bitches in Spanish"; "the ones who dye their hair, the ones who don't need to dye their hair." The distance between the lover is the cultural border described in the poem: the border between the deaf, the nice English-speaking one, those who dye their hair, on one side, and those who obey, those who understand, the sons of bitches in Spanish, and those who don't need to dye their hair, on the other side. The "place of encounter" is "beyond the fence, . . . green card in hand."

In "Todo será distinto," Nicaraguan poet Centeno, like Medina, describes the love between two individuals in the context of the community: "Todo será distinto cuando triunfe la Revolución. El amor al pueblo será nuestro amor. Pero nosotros dos nos amaremos lo mismo" ("Everything will be different when the revolution triumphs. The love of the people will be our love, but we will love each other the same").

In terms of the model of border writing, these love poems of Monjárrez, Diaz, Jones, Medina, and Centeno are examples of border texts. In "4 meses," "A Border Rose," and "Love from a Distance," the lovers are physically separated, a kind of deterritorialization. In both Medina's and Centeno's poems, the personal relationship is placed within a larger political context. The Voice of the Person in their poems is a collective enunciation: in neither case does it refer back to a single subject. In all of these texts, love is a kind of border crossing, between people and countries and between prerevolutionary and postrevolutionary times. Love functions as an opening for an unblocking of desire.

Deterritorialized: ¿Y Qué?

The conscious decision to embrace deterritorialization and to resist the temptation of nostalgia in favor of a new hybrid culture is particularly strong in the U.S.-

Mexico border region. Julia Stein's "Latin American Friend" has much in common with those searching for a new hybrid culture. An Anglo from Los Angeles, Stein writes about herself and an unidentified Latin American friend in historical and political terms; her relatives fought in World War II and Korea, she herself was an antiwar activist. Her "hero-Thoreau" concludes: "Latin American friend, / if you keep walking / and we keep walking / one day we'll meet / in a new America." The desire to be deterritorialized, to become marginal, to make a journey from North to South, distinguishes this text. Stein writes that Thoreau and Twain were ashamed of their country and that she sometimes wants to "drown in a sea of shame." Although not deterritorialized for the same economic reasons as some Mexicans in the United States or for the political reasons of those Nicaraguans forced to the countryside to fight the Contras, Stein is culturally and politically dislocated or displaced. In her poem, the "locus of subjectivity" is a generation of North Americans (referring to the United States and not Canada or Mexico, which are also part of North America) who have traveled to Latin America, who are attempting to learn Spanish, and who are seeking to understand their other half, who is across the border.

Bilingual Chicana poets Marisela Norte and Gina Valdés both explore the border feminine subject. In Norte's "Salmo para: Ella" ("Psalm for: Her"), she writes about herself, but this border "self" is divided into two voices: "Soy" and "Ella es" ("I am" and "She is"). In the "Ella es" section, she includes the following deterritorialized identities: "La que baila el TWIST/La que tiene por profesión ser Rock-n-Rolera . . . La del coiffure francés" ("The one who dances the TWIST / The one who is a rock-and-roller . . . The one with the French haircut"). The "soy" level includes: "la literatura contemporánea . . . La del crédito fácil . . . " ("contemporary literature . . . The one with easy credit). The "Soy" level also includes the following, constructed entirely from Los Angeles barrio graffiti: "LA TINY / STRANGER LONELY DIAMOND / TEARDROP DEMON SHY SAD EYES *MOSQUITA* / GANGSTER DREAMER BABY LOCA CASPER / PEE WEE *HUERA* SHADOW SMILEY JOKER / PRINCESS SQUEAKY CYCLONA SLEEPY DIM- / PLES MOUSEY QUIET *HEFITA* MONA TERMITE / PLAYGIRL . . . LOSER . . . HOMEGIRL." The text does not refer back to a single subject; instead, the two voices refer to the divided "subject." This divided subject is constructed from the two sides of the border woman. One side is linked to Spanish and to traditional images of women: La Llorona, La Muñeca, La criada bien creada. (The Weeping One, The Doll, The Well-Behaved Servant). The other is linked to mass-media images: "La Reina de la Fotonovela" (The Queen of the Photo-Novel), "Esa misma que vende televisores por las noches en el Canal 34" (the same one who sells televisions at night [on evening television] on Channel 34). Similarly, in Valdés's "Soy de aquí / soy de allá," there is a split subject.

Exorcism: A Remapping of Desire

The role of the poet is transformed in a border region; a deterritorialized poet can become a cartographer in a project of remapping desire. France, Nicaragua, and Mexico are countries in which poets have always had an important political role. Rigoberto López Pérez, a poet, participated in the assassination of Somoza in 1958. Poets and artists led the Chicano movement in the Southwestern United States in the late 1960s. Since the first U.S. invasion of Nicaragua in the mid-1800s, Nicaraguan poets have criticized *yanqui* imperialism. In his poem "To Roosevelt," Rubén Darío addressed Roosevelt as "the future invader of our native America." Centeno later warned, "Tenele miedo de los poetas, tirano" (26) ("Have fear of the poets, tyrant"). Chicanos have not forgotten the Mexican-American War of 1848. In all these cases, artists have participated in articulating the desire for revolution rather than colonization.

Although poems are still being written in Nicaragua, the fear of U.S. invasion remained uppermost in the minds of most Nicaraguans until the election of Chamorro and *glasnost*; now, there are even more complex fears. The main focus on the poetry in the literacy campaign of the Sandinista poetry workshops was the documentation of everyday life. In the U.S., border poets continue to document everyday life in the context of U.S.-Mexico relations, police harassment, deportation, AIDS, and fear.

In Nicaragua, the post-Somoza pre-Chamorro poets were no longer critics of their government, but instead served to help consolidate the revolution; in the border region, poets of the Reagan-Bush era maintain their oppositional and autonomous stance. The role of Nicaraguan poets during the Sandinista regime raised questions about the role of poetry itself in postrevolutionary societies and more specifically in multicultural situations. The role of the artist or poet, a critical voice, as it remains in the border region, changed in the context of Sandinista Nicaragua. These changes partially accounted for the form of the contemporary love poem in Nicaragua. The romantic imagery of the past was now integrated into ideological support for the revolution. In the border region, love poetry is integrated into ideological opposition to U.S. immigration policies. In the context of the defeat of the Sandinista government, can we in retrospect read Sandinista love poetry as a product of reterritorialization, a longing for the romantic images of the past, signifying not only nostalgia, but "permanent revolution"?

During the Sandinista regime, the critical voice of poetry was not silenced, but merely displaced. The "utopian" element in prerevolutionary society, the image of future revolution, was no longer perceived as necessary. Everyday life was now tolerable, at least officially, and not something to be subverted. The children of maids now dreamt of becoming professors.[18] A better future seemed possible; building the new society was an occasion for celebration. The prerevolutionary attacks on the social order gave way to gentle subversion, a subtle resistance to the complete militarization of everyday life. As Aguirre testified in her poem "En Maladera," lovers would manage to get together, despite restrictions placed by revolutionary military duty.

In the border region, the critical voice of poetry grows stronger and louder. Everyday life becomes more and more unbearable. Undocumented border crossers risk their lives crossing unlit freeways at night. Bodies are washed ashore on the U.S. side of the border and never identified. A majority of Latino students do not finish high school in Southern California. The future is both frightening and depressing; lovers and families continue to be divided by immigration policies.

In both Sandinista Nicaragua and the U.S.-Mexico border region, the voice of "deterritorialization" and "reterritorialization" became and, in the U.S.-Mexico border region, continues to be a space for the critical voice of poetry. In Nicaragua, it was a space in which H.E.M.Z. could long for the time in the future when the "new" (Sandinista) Nicaraguan woman would need him. The border love poem is not the poetry of the official culture of Mexico or the current poetry movements in the United States. There is a mixture in border love poetry of nostalgia ("reterritorialization") and the ability to situate oneself in cultural and historical terms between cultures (to embrace "deterritorialization").

In the border love poem in Nicaragua, there was a matrix of need, desire, and human interaction that could not be satisfied within a militarized society awaiting invasion. In the U.S.-Mexico border region, the "imaginary," which refused to be subsumed under the dictates of the Reagan-Bush era, resides in a displaced, disguised form. Guillermo Gómez-Peña writes in "El Luchador": "regreso de combatir / contra la migra / me quito el casco y las rodilleras / destapo una dos equis / y me sumergo en la laguna / de una hembra transitoria" ("I return from fighting against the *Migra* / I take off my helmet and kneepads / I open a dos xx / and submerge myself in the lake of transitory woman").

The role of poetry in Nicaragua has changed as the distinction between readers and writers has changed. Before the Sandinista revolution, the audience for written poetry was primarily middle class and urban. Even in the urban areas, illiteracy was estimated at 50 percent. In rural areas, it was as high as 80 percent. By 1984, thanks to the literacy campaign, the figure for the country as a whole dropped to 12–13 percent.[19] In California, reading and writing bilingual poetry is a subversive act since the passage of a proposition declaring English to be the official language of California, legislation that will ensure the continued illiteracy in Spanish in the Anglo community.

In Nicaragua, poetry workshops, an outgrowth of the literacy campaign, created new poetry and a new audience for poetry. Held in the countryside and in urban areas, the workshops produced poetry for publication in the cultural supplements of *Barricada*, the official organ of the government, and *El nuevo diario*, a newspaper that gave critical support to the revolution. *La prensa*, the opposition paper, also had a weekly cultural supplement. Small, inexpensive paperback books of poetry, published by the Ministry of Culture, were made available even in small towns.

In the Mexico-U.S. border region, literacy in both Spanish and English on the U.S. side is a major problem. Most Anglos are illiterate in Spanish. The major newspapers, owned by the Copley press, do not publish poetry and function as conservative interpreters of events for Washington, D.C., and as a warning to Los Pinos in Mexico.

Sergio Ramírez, a poet and a critic, has written extensively on the role of culture in postrevolutionary Nicaragua. In his article "Los intelectuales y el futuro revolucionario," he discusses the need for a culture that is not elitist but popular. The rich ethnic diversity of the country, including the bilingual culture of the Atlantic region, where black, English-speaking Protestants live, must be a part of this new culture, along with the cultures of the Miskito, Suma, and Rama Indians, according to Ramírez. Now that the Sandinista government is no longer in power, historians will begin to analyze to what extent the Sandinista government was able to implement the vision articulated by Ramírez. Because a variety of cultures exist in a nonsynchronous relationship to the hegemonic culture, which is urban, monolingual, Catholic, and Spanish-speaking, the Sandinista government attempted to take advantage of indigenous, bilingual cultures (represented by Indian ethnic minorities), the Caribbean culture (represented by black ethnic minorities), and the culture inherited from Europe.

Ramírez has also written about mass culture and individual creation. In "Cultura de masas y creación individual," he argued that the bourgeoisie has robbed Nicaragua of its culture, and that the past must now be recovered by Nicaragua's artists. He cited the Atlantic coast culture and poetry workshops as examples of how this could occur. In a visit to Nicaragua that I made in 1984, however, signs of mass culture from North America were everywhere; rock and roll was played on the radio and California-designed T-shirts were as common as AK47s.

In the border region, several groups of artists have formed to create a context in which Chicanos, Mexicans, and Anglo-Americans can work together.[20] These groups are bilingual and organize events on both sides of the border. Some Chicano members believe that only by becoming part of a broader cultural alliance can they continue to fight for the rights of Chicanos in the region. Some Mexicans in these groups attempt to build a cultural bridge across the border and to heal old historical wounds between Chicanos and Mexicans. Some culturally deterritorialized Anglo-American members feel a strong sense of identification with a struggle in which they can participate as coarchitects of a new, multicultural future.

In Nicaragua, the literacy campaign was evidence of the commitment of the Sandinista government to culture as a primary need in the creation of the new society. The support for poetry at both local and national levels was an outgrowth of the literacy campaign. In the border region, the city of San Diego threatens every so often to close the oldest Chicano institution in the region, which for twenty years has provided the community with cultural activities and more recently has sponsored the Border Art Workshop. While poetry workshops flourished in Sandinista Nicaragua, experimental art suffers and multicultural collaborations are still rare in the Mexico-U.S. border region.

To return to our original questions: (1) Is Jardine's critique applicable to the revised border model; and (2) does narrative "excess" or repetition hold the feminine border "subject" in place?

In his introduction to *Kafka*, Dana Polan extends Jardine's critique of Deleuze and Guattari's model and suggests that perhaps it requires "a certain reterritorialization of the sister—her reification in a myth of Femininity as a kind of succoring aid to the adventuring male in his quest to go beyond his limits" (xxvi).

Jumpcut.

Anglo monocultural feminist says:
You know, Rocío, sometimes I just get so depressed about my
relationship with Biff.
Chicana multicultural nonfeminist maid says:
Sí, señora.
while thinking to herself:
"Like the Black writer
Maya Angelou
I too am puzzled as to why
the descendants of strong-willed
and courageous
pioneering women of early America,
who literally cleared forests, built homes,
and shot game,
should have completely lost their position
as partners in home-steading,
land appropriation, cattle breeding . . . "
Anglo monocultural feminist continues:
Yeah, but I guess Mexican men really are macho, aren't they?
Chicana multicultural nonfeminist maid is pissed, but merely replies:
Sí, señora.
while thinking to herself:
"In less than 200 years
Anglo women
have allowed themselves
to become dependent
inept, unskilled, and eventually pampered."

Anglo monocultural feminist is slightly defensive but smug:
I might be prejudiced, but it seems to me
that Mexican, Chicano, and Black men
have a lot of trouble understanding women's rights.
Chicana multicultural nonfeminist maid makes an
unsuccessful attempt at multicultural communication:
Sí, señora.
while thinking to herself:
"It is my observation
that the relationship between Chicano men and women
is one of union . . .
our people really like and respect each other . . .
you said that Mexican men are such machos,
yes, but Chicanas can be machas too.
When your very survival
depends on those you live with,
there is a natural fierceness,
along with love and respect,
that evolves out of struggle.
If we had the privileges of Anglos,
perhaps we too
would regress to alienating ourselves
from each other."
Anglo monocultural feminist ends discussion:
Well, I've got to go to my Women's Studies class.
Don't forget to feed the baby vegetables for lunch.
I'll be back around 3:00.
Oh, and by the way,
if you want to speak Spanish to the baby, go ahead.
We live so near the border, he may as well be bilingual.
You do speak Spanish, don't you?
Chicana multicultural nonfeminist maid says:
Sí, señora.
Anglo monocultural feminist is suddenly depressed; she thinks
to herself:
"Every once in a while I feel really kind of guilty
about having a maid
I guess if I really believed in my feminism, I wouldn't . . . " [21]

Jumpcut.

Is the desire for men to be "needed" by woman anything more than a form of reterritorialization? What about the desire of the psychoanalyst in Valenzuela's *Como en la guerra* to be needed by the revolutionary woman/patient? "She" does not act as a "succoring aid" to the analyst; however, she is the pretext for his adventure, his deterritorialization. Yet the revised border model accounts very well for this: "she" is deterritorialized, an Argentine in Spain who must later flee to Mexico. She is a whole generation of political exiles from the "dirty war" of the 1970s; her identity cannot be understood apart from the political situation of her country. Is the desire between humans not a desire for an opening up of new connections? Is the Nicaraguan woman who refuses the role of providing aid to the adventuring male doing so in order to flee from the entrapment of her prerevolutionary role and/or to bring Nicaragua beyond the limits of Somoza and Reagan? When a North American poet speaks of the shame she feels about her country's activities in Mexico and Central America, is she not fleeing from her entrapment through a self-conscious process of deterritorialization? Is the "flor armada" an image of a trapped woman? When Luisa, in *Cola de lagartija*, wishes to free the reader from the terrifying images of the imaginary by offering a restructuring of desire—to deconstruct the binaries of the Law of the Father, is she reified into a myth of Femininity or is she a border shaman, not subject to the myth of femininity? And what about Ursula's discovery of the way out of Macondo?

Will border writers present the world with a new multidimensional holographic ordering of desire and a new relationship between art and politics? Will it be possible for readers from both territorialized and border regions of the world to connect themselves to the disruptive, grotesque, nonlinear, multiple coded schiz-flows of desire? Do women, and particularly border women, need to worry about whether or not a model allows them to be deterritorialized? No. We are already deterritorialized. Do repetitions in the text hold the border "subject" in place? No. Any two signifiers may eventually be linked in border culture. The *Migra* and Washington hold the border "subject" in place, not narrative repetition. The destination of the border writer is to cross the border as many times as possible.

Notes

Foreword

1. See especially Jameson's "Third World Literature in the Era of Multinational Capitalism," *Social Text* 15 (Fall 1986) and Said's *Orientalism* (New York: Pantheon, 1978) and *The World, the Text, and the Critic* (Cambridge, Mass.: Harvard University Press, 1983). For a more detailed critique of these and other "anti-imperialist" postmodernisms, see my "Postmodernism and Imperialism: Theory and Politics in Latin America," *Postmodern Culture* vol. 1, no. 1 (fall, 1990) [an on-line journal available on internet from pmc@ncsuvm.ncsu.edu].

2. See Lazarus's *Resistance in Postcolonial African Fiction* (New Haven, Conn.: Yale University Press, 1990); Harlow's *Resistance Literature* (London: Methuen, 1987); and Beverley and Zimmerman's *Literature and Politics in Central American Revolutions* (Austin: University of Texas Press, 1990).

3. See *Modernism and Hegemony: A Materialist Critique of Aesthetic Agencies* (Minneapolis: University of Minnesota Press, 1990).

4. See *Modernism and Hegemony*, pp. xxxvii-xliv, and "Postmodernism and Imperialism."

5. See *Caliban and Other Essays*, trans. Edward Baker (Minneapolis: University of Minnesota Press, 1989).

6. See Dussel's *Philosophy of Liberation*, trans. Aquilina Martínez and Christine Morkovsky (Maryknoll, N.Y.: Orbis Books, 1985).

7. Ronald Bogue, *Deleuze and Guattari* (London: Routledge, 1989), p. 103.

8. Translated by Russell Moore (New York: Monthly Review Press, 1989). Cited hereafter in text as *EU*.

Introduction:
Border Writing as Deterritorialization

1. This notion of multiplicity of codes within a single language is taken from Mikhail Bakhtin and informs Jacques Derrida's critique of Roman Jakobson's categories of translation. Marlene Nour-

125

bese Philip discusses the relationship between standard English and Caribbean English in terms that suggest how codes may act upon each other in a single language. In Introduction: "The Absence of Writing or How I Almost Became a Spy," from *She Tries Her Tongue, Her Silence Softly Breaks*, she writes: "The place African-Caribbean writers occupy is one that is unique and one that forces the writer to operate in a language that was used to brutalize and diminish Africans so that they would come to a profound belief in their own lack of humanity. No language can accomplish this—and to a large degree English did—without itself being profoundly affected, without itself being tainted. The challenge, therefore, facing the African-Caribbean writer . . . is to use the language in such a way that the historical realities are not erased or obliterated, so that English is revealed as the tainted tongue it truly is" (19).

2. Bloch's formulation of nonsynchrony and the noncontemporaneous is resonant of the "multiplicity of voices," Jacques Derrida's phrase in *The Ear of the Other*. Slovenian video artist and critic Marina Grzinic expands upon Deleuze and Guattari's notion of deterritorialization to include historical displacement (Tertulia, Border Culture Residency, Banff Centre for the Arts, 2 July 1990).

3. Michel Foucault, in *The Order of Things*, has shown in his analysis of Velásquez's *Las Meninas* that painting was already freed in seventeenth century from the task of representing objects.

4. See the discussion of dismemberment in Paul de Man, "Phenomenology and Materiality in Kant" and "Aesthetic Formulation: Kleist's *Über das Marionettentheater*."

5. See the discussion of Baudelaire in Benjamin's *Illuminations*.

6. Gilane Tawadros, "Beyond the Boundary: The Work of Three Black Women Artists in Britain," 138. See also: "However, I am less concerned at this point with Jameson's own position than with the implications of this notion of the 'fragmented subject' for postmodern practice as well as for black cultural practice" (136).

7. In "Introduction: The Absence of Writing or How I Almost Became a Spy" (*She Tries Her Tongue*), Philip does not use the term "border writing" but refers instead to texts written in "demotic" English by black writers.

8. Philip discusses the i-mage in "Introduction: The Absence of Writing," *She Tries Her Tongue*. She explains that the unconventional spelling not only signifies "the increasingly conventional deconstruction of certain words, but draws on the Rastafarian practice of privileging the 'I' in many words" (12). She goes on to relate the concept to meaning and nonmeaning.

9. Conversation with Magdalena Campos, Border Culture Residency, Banff Centre for the Arts, 27 June 1990. See also Osvaldo Sánchez, "Children of Utopia."

1. García Márquez: Cultural Border Crosser

1. This biographical information, as well as the comments later in the paragraph, are from "Interview with Gabriel García Márquez," *Playboy*, February, 1985. In this interview, García Márquez also discusses his friendship with Fidel Castro.

2. Cf. Gloria Anzaldúa's description of the border region as the home of outlaws in *Borderlands* (74).

3. *CA* refers to *Cien años*, and the number following is the page number in the Spanish edition. The English translation will appear parenthetically after the Spanish text; *OHY* refers to *One Hundred Years of Solitude*, and the number following is the page number in the English edition.

4. Cf. Marlene Nourbese Philip's view that the writer must "re-member" in both senses of the term: (1) to recall and (2) to reconstitute the body (from her reading, Border Culture Residency).

5. Cf. Chilean visual artist Eugenio Dittborn's exploration of the deterritorialization of the Chilean social psyche upon the discovery of the undecomposed body of a customs worker who had "disappeared" twenty years before. The body had remained miraculously intact because of the dry climate in northern Chile. The images and texts in Dittborn's installation at the Walter Phillips Gallery (Banff,

19 July – 4 September 1990), including ten "airmail paintings," were literally deterritorialized by being sent from Santiago to Banff.

6. Cf. Lyotard, *The Differend*, in relation to the Holocaust.

7. García Canclini refers to de Certeau's article "Californie, un theatre de passants," *Autrement*, no. 31, (April 1981), pp. 10–18.

8. This was suggested to me by Mukul Khurana, a student in a graduate seminar at San Diego State University in spring, 1990, in the context of a presentation by another student, Brunda Moka, about the relationship between the Indian concept of *maya* and Baudrillard's notion of the simulacrum.

2. Beyond the Subject: From Territorialized to the Deterritorialized Text

1. See Robert Con Davis's discussion of the Gaze in "Lacan, Poe and Narrative Repression," 987.

2. Conversation with Luisa Valenzuela, San Diego, 9 March 1986.

3. For a discussion of the machine, see Deleuze and Guattari's *Anti-Oedipus* and *Kafka* (9–16).

4. Metis filmmaker and critic Loretta Todd discusses Heidegger's notion of authenticity in relation to her culture in the context of Canadian cultural identity. Just as Gilane Tawadros argues convincingly that, despite some postmodernist claims about the subject, black artists are not fragmented subjects incapable of action, and that certain "postmodernist" strategies have long been used by black artists, so Todd defends her view, based on conversations with tribal elders, that the notion of becoming has always been a part of "tradition," making the binary opposition authentic-inauthentic, or even its deconstruction, somewhat irrelevant from her cultural perspective. Her essay on this subject, which was delivered as a lecture in conjunction with the Border Culture Residency in summer, 1990, will appear in a publication of the Walter Phillips Gallery, Banff Center for the Arts.

5. All references to *Rayuela*, translated as *Hopscotch*, refer to the page numbers in the Spanish edition. The English translation will appear parenthetically after the Spanish text, with page numbers in the English edition.

6. All references to *La nausée*, translated as *Nausea*, refer to page numbers in the French edition. The English translation will appear parenthetically after the French text, along with page numbers.

7. See Jessica Benjamin's essay, "Master and Slave: The Fantasy of Erotic Domination," which is relevant here not only in her emphasis on eroticism but also in her discussion of the relationship between the struggle for selfhood and domination. See also Judith P. Butler's commentary, "Deleuze: From Slave Morality to Productive Desire," in her book *Subjects of Desire*. Although one might take issue with her conclusion that "Deleuze appears to undermine his original project to historicize desire, for his arcadian vision of precultural libidinal chaos poses as an ahistorical absolute (215)," her discussion of "the negative desire" (206) is provocative.

8. Luisa Valenzuela, lecture presented at symposium, Latin American Literature: Modern Discourses of Emancipation, San Diego State University, 11 April 1986.

9. For a discussion of Jürgen Habermas's model of the "ideal speech situation," see Seyla Benhabib, "The Utopian Dimension in Communicative Ethics," 87.

10. See his article, "Surrealism, the Last Snapshot of the European Intelligentsia," *New Left Review*.

11. Conversation with Eugenio Dittborn at opening of "Airmail Paintings," exhibition at Walter Phillips Gallery, Banff, Canada, 19 July 1990.

12. *LM* refers to *Libro de Manuel* and the number following is the page number in the Spanish edition. The English translation will appear parenthetically after the Spanish text. *MM* refers to *Manual for Manuel*, given with the page number in the English edition.

13. See G. S. Kirk and J. E. Raven, *The Pre-Socratic Philosophers*, 274.

14. Quoted by Heidegger, *What Is Called Thinking*. From Nietzsche's *Thus Spoke Zarathustra*, Part II, "On Deliverance."

15. Marguerite Waller brought to my attention that Kaja Silverman discusses the relationship between nonlinearity, feminism, and sound in her book *The Acoustic Mirror: The Female Voice in Psychoanalysis and Cinema*. Cortázar's use of different levels of narration in *Libro de Manuel*, printed in different type sizes, serves to further deterritorialize and decenter the narrative voice(s) and the reader/"listener"; his notion of time, then, consists in part of the juxtaposition of a multiplicity of perspectives and their simultaneous but different unfoldings of narratives. Therefore, a simple binary opposition of linear/circular is inadequate as an approach to his narrative structure.

3. Cortázar: The Task of the Translator

1. All references to "Apocalipsis de Solentiname," translated as "Apocalypse at Solentiname," refer to the page numbers in the Spanish edition. The English translation will appear parenthetically after the Spanish text, with page number in the English edition.

2. All references to "Las babas del diablo," translated as "Blow-up," refer to the pages in the Spanish edition. The English translation will appear after the Spanish text, with page number in the English edition.

3. In both senses of the term, to differ and to defer, there is a distinction/distance between the subject and the object in Cortázar's texts.

4. Cortázar inserts articles cut out of newspapers, fragments of newspaper texts, advertisements, and various other items into his text to form a sort of collage between image and text.

5. For a discussion of visual music, see John Whitney, *Digital Harmony*.

6. All references to "Clone," in *Queremos tanto a Glenda*, refer to the page numbers in the Spanish edition. The English translation from "Clone" will appear after the Spanish text, with page number in the English edition.

7. The English translation preserves this passage in Spanish.

8. See René Leibowitz, *Schoenberg and His School: The Contemporary Stage of the Language of Music*.

9. Jacket notes, *Stockhausen's Momente*.

10. Jacket notes, *Stockhausen's Momente*.

11. L. C., "The Developing Independence of the Argentine Working Class," and James R. Scobie, *Argentina, A City and a Nation*, 2d ed.

12. Ariel Dorfman, Lecture, San Diego State University, 1986.

4. That Which Resists: The Code of the Real in Luisa Valenzuela's *Como en la guerra*

1. I am using the term "referential codes" to refer to what Barthes calls the "cultural code" in *S/Z*.

2. Bloch explains the concept of nonsynchrony in his essay "Nonsynchronism and the Obligation to Its Dialectics."

3. See Deleuze and Guattari's *Kafka*.

4. The "dirty war" in Argentina refers to the war against the *subversivos* in which thousands of activists and students "disappeared" during the 1970s.

5. Valenzuela: The Imaginary Body

1. All references to *Cola de lagartija*, translated as *The Lizard's Tail*, refer to the page numbers in the Spanish edition. The English translation will appear after the Spanish text, with page numbers

in the English edition. *Cola de lagartija* will be abbreviated *CL* with page references; *The Lizard's Tail* will be abbreviated *LT*.

2. René Girard, "The Oresteia." Lecture at San Diego State University, 10 April 1985.

3. The English translation of "El verbo matar" ("The Verb to Kill") appears in *Strange Things Happen Here, 26 Short Stories and a Novel*.

4. Eugenio Donato, seminar, UC San Diego, winter 1976.

6. Contemporary Border Writing and Reading: From Aztlán to Nicaragua

1. The Simpson-Rodino Bill was widely criticized by Chicano leaders in the San Diego-Tijuana region. Jonathan Freedman, who won a Pulitzer Prize for his coverage of the border in the *San Diego Union*, supported the bill.

2. See Maria C. Lugones and Elizabeth V. Spelman, "Have We Got a Theory for You?", 573-81.

3. Post-Arte is an international network of mail artists founded by Cesar Espinosa in Mexico City. Mail art has often been the only possible art form available to political activists living under repressive regimes.

4. Ernesto Cardenal, preface to *Poesía nueva de Nicaragua* (Buenos Aires: Ed. Carlos Loehle, 1972). Quoted in *Nicaragua in Revolution: The Poets Speak/Nicaragua en Revolución: Los Poetas Hablan*, ed. B. Aldaraca et al., 1.

5. Gina Valdés, "Fragmento de Diálogos Fronterizos," interview, *The Broken Line/La Línea Quebrada*, año I, May 1986.

6. Terry Cochran, introduction to Deleuze and Guattari, *Kafka*.

7. See Robert Con Davis, "Lacan, Poe and Narrative Repression."

8. See Tey Diana Rebolledo, "The Politics of Poetics: Or, What Am I, a Critic, Doing in This Text Anyhow?", 129-38; Marta Ester Sánchez, *Contemporary Chicana Poetry: A Critical Approach to an Emerging Literature*; Gloria Anzaldúa, *Borderlands, La Frontera, The New Mestiza*.

9. One such artist is San Francisco-based Amalia Mesa-Bains.

10. Progressive elements in Mexico are currently criticizing the corruption of the government.

11. The Sandinista government was subsequently self-critical of this policy.

12. Anglo-American travelers in the region may witness this situation as passengers on the Amtrak. In a *Los Angeles Times* commentary (1990), a Latino businessman described being asked for identification by an immigration officer while riding the Amtrak from San Diego to Los Angeles. He was dressed in a business suit. He concluded that the inquiry was on the basis of the color of his skin.

13. An analogous situation has occurred in Spain, where some complain that "things were better" before Franco's death because there was a clear enemy against which to fight.

14. Paige du Bois analyzes the metaphors used to describe women from the time of Homer to Plato, including the field, the furrow, the stone, the oven, and the tablet, in her book *Sowing the Body: Psychoanalysis and Ancient Representations of Women*.

15. Deleuze and Guattari discuss the concept of "reterritorialization" in *Kafka* (20, 24, 25).

16. Rosario Murillo has been the editor of *Ventana*.

17. Jameson discusses a similar tension between reterritorialization and deterritorialization in "On Magic Realism and Film," 301-25.

18. Conversation with a nine-year-old girl in Bluefields, Nicaragua, 18 August 1984.

19. Sheryl Hirshon with Judy Butler, *And Also Teach Them to Read*, xi. These figures, widely reported in the U.S. and Nicaraguan press, were confirmed by Juan Castillo, a teacher of adult education in Managua, 17 August 1984.

20. Two of these groups are the Border Art Workshop/Taller de arte fronterizo and Las Comadres. The Border Art Workshop was founded in 1985. Founders included David Avalos, Guillermo Gómez-Peña, and Michael Schnorr. In 1989, six of the eight members at that time left the

group because of irreconcilable differences, including Guillermo Gómez-Peña, Emily Hicks, and Rocío Weiss. In 1988, a group of women artists, writers, and educators began to meet and a year later named themselves Las Comadres. The group now has twenty members, roughly half from the United States and half from Mexico. Meetings are bilingual and are held on both sides of the border. Las Comadres includes Emily Hicks and Rocío Weiss, as well as current and associated members of the Border Art Workshop.

21. Fragment from "Our Lady of Border Consciousness," performance by D. Emily Hicks in collaboration with Rocío Weiss, 1988. All quoted sections of this text were taken from Parul Desai, "Interview with Bernice Zamora, a Chicana Poet," 26–39.

Bibliography

Adorno, Theodor. *Negative Dialectics*. Trans. E. B. Ashton. New York: Seabury, 1973.
——"The Stars Down to Earth." *Telos*, 19, 1974.
Aguirre, Julia. "En Maladera." *Poesía Libre, Revista de Poesía*. Managua: Ministerio de Cultura, 4.11, 1984.
Alazraki, Jaime. Introduction. "Cortázar—Towards the Last Square of the Hopscotch." *The Final Island*. Ed. Alazraki and Ivar Ivask. Norman: University of Oklahoma Press, 1978.
Aldaraca, B., E. Baker, I. Rodriguez, and M. Zimmerman. *Nicaragua in Revolution: The Poets Speak/Nicaragua en Revolución: Los Poetas Hablan*. Minneapolis: Marxist Educational Press, 1980.
Anzaldúa, Gloria. *Borderlands, la Frontera, The New Mestiza*. San Francisco: Spinster/Aunt Lute, 1987.
Aronowitz, Stanley. "Film—the Art Form of Late Capitalism." *The Crisis in Historical Materialism, Class, Politics and Culture in Marxist Theory*. New York: Praeger-Bergin, 1981.
Bakhtin, Mikhail. *Rabelais and His World*. Trans. Helen Iswolsky. Cambridge: MIT Press, 1968.
Barthes, Roland. *Camera Lucida*. Trans. Richard Howard. New York: Hill and Wang, 1981.
——"Introduction to the Structural Analysis of Narratives." *Image, Music, Text*. Trans. Stephen Heath. New York: Hill and Wang, 1977.
——*S/Z*. Trans. Richard Miller. Pref. Richard Howard. New York: Hill and Wang, 1974.
Bateson, Gregory. *Steps Toward an Ecology of the Mind*. New York: Ballantine, 1972.
Benhabib, Seyla. "The Utopian Dimension in Communicative Ethics." *New German Critique*, 2.2, 1985.
Benjamin, Jessica. "Master and Slave: The Fantasy of Erotic Domination." *Powers of Desire, the Politics of Sexuality*. Ed. Ann Snitow, Christine Stansell and Sharon Thompson. New York: Monthly Review, 1983.
Benjamin, Walter. *Charles Baudelaire, a Lyric Poet in the Era of High Capitalism*. Trans. Harry Zohn. London: New Left Books, 1973.
——*Illuminations*. Ed. Hannah Arendt. Trans. Harry Zohn. New York: Schocken, 1973.

—— "Surrealism, the Last Snapshot of the European Intelligentsia." *New Left Reivew*, March–April 1978, 47–56.

Bloch, Ernst. "Nonsynchronism and the Obligation to Its Dialectics." *New German Critique*, 4.2, 1977.

—— *The Philosophy of the Future*. Trans. John Cummings. New York: Herder and Herder, 1974.

Brody, Robert. "Two and Threes." *The Analysis of Hispanic Texts: Current Trends in Methodology*. Ed. Mary Ann Beck, Lisa E. Davis, et al. New York: Bilingual Press/Editorial bilingüe, 1976.

Butler, Judith P. *Subjects of Desire: Hegelian Reflections in Twentieth-Century France*. New York: Columbia University Press, 1987.

Centeno, Bosco. "Todo Será Distinto." *Puyonearon los granos*. Managua: Ministerio de Cultura, 1983.

Clearfield, Andrew. *These Things I Have Shared: Collage and Montage in Early Modernist Poetry*. Ann Arbor: UMI Research Press, 1984.

Cortázar, Julio. "Apocalipsis de Solentiname." *Alguien que anda por ahí y otros relatos*. Madrid: Alfaguara, 1977.

—— "Apocalypse at Solentiname." *We Love Glenda So Much and a Change of Light*. Trans. Gregory Rabassa. New York: Vintage, 1984.

—— "Las babas del diablo." *Relatos*. Buenos Aires: Sudamericana, 1970.

—— *Blow-up and Other Stories* (originally titled *End of the Game and Other Stories*). Trans. Paul Blackburn. New York: Pantheon, 1967, 1983.

—— "Clone." *We Love Glenda So Much and a Change of Light*. Trans. Gregory Rabassa. New York: Vintage, 1984.

—— "Clone." *Queremos tanto a Glenda*. Madrid: Alfaguara, 1980.

—— Cover notes. *Cambio de aramas*, by Luisa Valenzuela. Hanover: Ediciones del Norte, 1983.

—— "Diario para un cuento." *Deshoras*. Mexico: Nueva Imagen, 1983.

—— *Fantomas contra los vampiros multinacionales: Una utopia realizable*. Mexico: Excelsior, 1975.

—— *Hopscotch*. Trans. Gregory Rabassa. New York: Random House, 1966.

—— *Libro de Manuel*. Buenos Aires: Sudamericana, 1973.

—— *Manual for Manuel*. Trans. Gregory Rabassa. New York: Pantheon, 1978.

—— "*La nausée*, por Jean-Paul Sartre, traducción de Aurora Bernardez, ed. Losada, Buenos Aires." *Cabalgato*, 15 January 1948.

—— *Rayuela*. Buenos Aires: Sudamericana, 1963.

—— *Ultimo Round*. Mexico, D.F.: Siglo XXI, 1969.

Darío, Rubén. "To Roosevelt." *Songs of Life and Hope*. 1914. Rpt. *Impulse* (1984), 11.4.

Davis, Robert Con. "Introduction: Lacan and Narration" and "Lacan, Poe and Narrative Repression." *Lacan and Narration: The Psychoanalytic Difference in Narrative Theory*. Baltimore: Johns Hopkins University Press, 1983.

de Lauretis, Teresa. *Alice Doesn't*. Baltimore: Johns Hopkins University Press, 1984.

Deleuze, Gilles, and Félix Guattari. *Anti-Oedipus*. Trans. Mark Hurley, Mark Seem, and Helen R. Lane. New York: Viking, 1977.

—— *Kafka: Toward a Minor Literature*. Trans. and intro. Dona Polan. Foreword Réda Bensamaïa. Minneapolis: University of Minnesota Press, 1986.

de Man, Paul. "Aesthetic Formulation: Kleist's Über das Marionettentheater." *The Rhetoric of Romanticism*. New York: Columbia University Press, 1984.

—— "Phenomenology and Materiality in Kant." *Hermeneutics*. Ed. Gary Shapiro and Alan Sica. Amherst: University of Massachusetts Press, 1984.

Derrida, Jacques. *Dissemination*. Trans. and notes Barbara Johnson. Chicago: University of Chicago Press, 1981.

—— *The Ear of the Other: Otobiography, Transference, Translation, Texts and Discussion with*

Jacques Derrida. Ed. Claude Levesque and Christie V. McDonald. Trans. Peggy Kamuf. Nietzsche's *Otobiography*, trans. Avital Ronell. New York: Schocken Books, 1984.

—— "The Pit and the Pyramid: Introduction to Hegel's Semiology." *Margins of Philosophy*. Trans. with notes by Alan Bass. Chicago: University of Chicago Press, 1982.

—— *Writing and Difference*. Trans. Alan Bass. Chicago: University of Chicago Press, 1978.

Desai, Parul. "Interview with Bernice Zamora, a Chicana Poet." *Imagine, International Chicano Poetry Journal*, 2.1 (Summer 1985), 26–39.

Dikjstra, Bram. *Idols of Perversity, Fantasies of Feminine Evil in Fin-de-Siècle Culture*. New York: Oxford University Press, 1986.

du Bois, Paige. *Sowing the Body: Psychoanalysis and Ancient Representations of Women*. Chicago: University of Chicago Press, 1988.

Eagleton, Terry. *Literary Theory: An Introduction*. Minneapolis: University of Minnesota Press, 1983.

Esslin, Martin. *Brecht: The Man and His Work*. London: Eyres and Spottiswoode, 1959.

Felman, Shoshana. "To Open the Question." *Yale French Studies*, 55–56, 1977, 5–10.

Foucault, Michel. *The Order of Things: An Archeology of the Human Sciences*. Ed. R. D. Laing. New York: Random House-Pantheon, 1970.

Franco, Jean. *An Introduction to Spanish American Literature*. Cambridge: Cambridge University Press, 1969.

Freud, Sigmund. *Beyond the Pleasure Principle*. Trans. and ed. James Strachey. London: Hogarth Press and the Institute of Psychoanalysis, 1971.

—— "Instincts and Their Vicissitudes." (1915) *General Psychological Theory, Papers on Metapsychology*. Intro. Philip Rieff. New York: Collier, 1963.

—— *Leonardo da Vinci and a Memory of His Childhood*. Trans. Alan Tyson. New York: Norton, 1964.

García Canclini, Nestor. "Escenas sin territorio, estética de las migraciones e identidades en transición." *Revista de Crítica Cultural*, 1.1, 1990.

García Márquez, Gabriel. *Cien años de soledad*. Buenos Aires: Sudamericana, 1967.

—— "Interview with Gabriel García Márquez." *Playboy*, February 1985, pp. 65–77.

—— *One Hundred Years of Solitude*. Trans. Gregory Rabassa. New York: Avon Books, 1972.

Gibson, William. *Neuromancer*. New York: Ace, 1984.

Girard, René. *Deceit, Desire and the Novel: Self and Other in Literary Structure*. Trans. Yvonne Freccero. Baltimore: Johns Hopkins University Press, 1965.

—— *Violence and the Sacred*. Trans. Patrick Gregory. Baltimore: Johns Hopkins University Press, 1972.

Glantz, Margo. Cover notes. *Cambio de armas*, by Luisa Valenzuela. Hanover: Ediciones del Norte, 1983.

Greer, Germaine. "The Future of the Family." *Sex and Destiny: The Politics of Human Fertility*. London: Seever and Warburg-Picador, 1984.

Hegel, G. W. F. *The Phenomenology of Mind*. Trans. J. B. Baillie. New York: Harper and Row, 1967.

Heidegger, Martin. "The Question Concerning Technology." *The Question Concerning Technology and Other Essays*. Trans. and intro. William Lovitt. New York: Harper and Row, 1977.

—— *What Is Called Thinking*. Trans. Fred D. Wieck and J. Glenn Gray. Intro. J. Glenn Gray. New York: Harper and Row, 1968.

H. E. M. Z. "Táctica y estrategia." *Somos*, 2.17, 1983.

Hicks, D. Emily, in collaboration with Rocío Weiss. "Our Lady of Border Consciousness." Performance text, 1988.

—— "La palabra enferma, una charla con Luisa Valenzuela." *La Opinión*, 22 June 1986, *La Comunidad*, pp. 6–7.

Hirshon, Sheryl, with Judy Butler. *And Also Teach Them to Read*. Westport Conn.: Lawrence Hill, 1983.

Hocquenhem, Guy de. *Homosexual Desire*. Trans. Daniella Dangoor. London: Allison and Busby, 1978.

Horkheimer, Max, and Theodor Adorno. *Dialectic of Enlightenment*. Trans. John Cumming. New York: Seabury, 1972.

Irigaray, Luce. *Speculum of the Other Woman*. Trans. Gillian C. Gill. Ithaca: Cornell University Press, 1985.

Jameson, Fredric. *Marxism and Form: Twentieth-Century Dialectical Theories of Literature*. Princeton: Princeton University Press, 1971.

—— "On Magic Realism and Film." *Critical Inquiry*, 12 January 1986, 301–25.

—— *The Political Unconscious: Narrative as Socially Symbolic Act*. Ithaca: Cornell University Press, 1981.

—— *The Prison House of Language*. Princeton: Princeton University Press, 1972.

Jardine, Alice. "Woman in Limbo: Deleuze and His Br(others)." *SubStance*, 44/45, 1984: 46–60.

Jones, Robert. "A Border Rose." *The Broken Line/La Línea Quebrada*, 1.1, 1986.

Josipovici, Gabriel. *Writing and the Body*. Princeton: Princeton University Press, 1982.

Kern, Edith. *Existentialist Thought and Fictional Technique*. New Haven: Yale University Press, 1970.

Kirk, G. S., and J. E. Raven. *The Pre-Socratic Philosophers*. Cambridge: Cambridge University Press, 1969.

Klein, Melanie. *The Psychoanalysis of Children*. Trans. Alix Strachey. Rev. by H. A. Thorner. New York: Dell, 1975.

Kojève, Alexandre. *Introduction to the Reading of Hegel*. Ed. Allan Bloom. Trans. James H. Nichols, Jr. New York: Basic Books, 1969.

Lacan, Jacques. *Ecrits: A Selection*. Ed. and trans. Alan Sheridan. New York: Norton, 1977.

—— "Tuche and Automaton." *Four Fundamental Concepts of Psychoanalysis*. Ed. Jacques Alain Miller. Trans. Alan Sheridan. New York: Norton, 1978.

—— *The Language of the Self: The Function of Language in Psychoanalysis*. New York: Delta, 1968.

L. C. "The Developing Independence of the Argentine Working Class." *Now and After*, 4, May 1978.

Lefebvre, Henri. *Everyday Life in the Modern World*. New York: Harper Torchbooks, 1971.

Leibowitz, René. *Schoenberg and His School: The Contemporary Stage of the Language of Music*. Trans. Dika Newling. New York: Da Capa, 1975.

Lévi-Strauss, Claude. *Structural Anthropology*. Trans. Claire Jacobson and Brooke Grundfest Schoepf. New York: Basic Books, 1973.

Linderman, Deborah. "Narrative Surplus: The 'Blow-Up' as Metarepresentation and Ideology." *American Journal of Semiotics*, 3:4, 1975, 99–118.

Lugones, Maria C., and Elizabeth V. Spelman. "Have We Got A Theory for You! Feminist Theory, Cultural Imperialism, and the Demand of the Woman's Voice." *Women's Studies International Forum*, 6.6 (1983), 573–81.

Luna Robles, Margarita. "Randazz-o." *The Broken Line/La Línea Quebrada*, 2.2, 1987, 16.

Lyotard, Jean-François. *The Differend: Phrases in Dispute*. Trans. Georges Van Den Abbeele. Minneapolis: University of Minnesota Press, 1988.

Marcuse, Herbert. *The Aesthetic Dimension*. Boston: Beacon, 1978.

Marks, Elaine, and Isabelle de Courtivron, eds. *New French Feminisms: An Anthology*. New York: Schocken, 1981.

Martínez, J. Nelly. "From a Mimetic to a Holographic Paradigm in Fiction." Unpublished manuscript.

Marx, Karl. *Capital: A Critique of Political Economy*. Ed. Frederick Engels. Trans. Samuel Moore and Edward Aveling. New York: Modern, 1906.

——and Frederick Engels. *Manifesto of the Communist Party*. Peking: Foreign Language Press, 1968.

Medina, Rubén. "Amor de Lejos." *The Broken Line/La Línea Quebrada*. 1.1, 1986.

Mitchell, Juliet. *Woman's Estate*. New York: Vintage, 1973.

Monjárrez, Carlos R. "Muchacha." *Somos*, 2.6, 1983.

Moi, Toril. *Sexual/Textual Politics*. London: Methuen, 1986.

Mulvey, Laura. "Visual Pleasure and Narrative Cinema," *Screen*, 16, Autumn 1975, pp. 6–18.

Murillo, Rosario. "Iluminación." *Impulse*, 11.4.

Nietzsche, Friedrich. "Truth and Lie in Extra-Moral Sense." *Friedrich Nietzsche on Rhetoric and Language*. Ed. and trans. with a critical intro. by Sander Gilman, Carole Blair, and David J. Parent. New York: Oxford University Press, 1989.

——*The Will to Power*. Trans. Walter Kaufmann and R. J. Hollingdale. New York: Vintage, 1976.

Norte, Marisela. "Salmo para: Ella." *The Broken Line/La Línea Quebrada*, 1.1, 1986, 33.

Paz, Octavio. *El signo y el garabato*. Mexico: Joaquín Mortiz, 1973.

Philip, Marlene Nourbese. *She Tries Her Tongue, Her Silence Softly Breaks*. Charlottetown, Prince Edward Island: Ragweed Press, 1989.

——"Who's Listening: Artists, Audiences and Languages." *Fuse*, September 1988, 15–24.

Picón Garfield, Evelyn. *¿Es Julio Cortázar un Surrealista?* Madrid: Gredos, 1975.

Plank, William. *Sartre and Surrealism*. Ann Arbor: University of Michigan Press, 1972.

Polkinhorn, Harry. "Chain Link: Towards a Theory of Border Writing." *The Line: Essays on Mexican-American Border Literature*. Mexicali: Binational Press, 1989. 37–44.

Prokop, Ulrike. "Production and the Context of Women's Daily Life." Trans. Guntram Weber. *New German Critique*, 4.3, 1978, 18–33.

Propp, Vladimir. *Morphology of the Folktale*. 1st ed. Trans. Laurence Scott. Intro. Svatava Pirkova-Jacobson. 2nd ed. Louis A. Wagner. Intro. Alan Dundes. Austin: University of Texas Press, 1968.

Ramírez, Sergio. "Cultura de masas y creación individual." *Valcanes y volcanes y otros ensayos y trabajos*. Managua: Nueva Nicaragua, 1983.

——"Los intelectuales y el futuro revolucionario." *Valcanes y volcanes y otros ensayos y trabajos*. Managua: Nueva Nicaragua, 1983.

Rank, Otto. *The Double*. Trans. Harry Tucker, Jr. Chapel Hill: University of North Carolina Press, 1971.

Rebolledo, Tey Diana. "The Politics of Poetics: Or, What Am I, a Critic, Doing in This Text Anyhow?" *The Americas Review*, 15.3–4, 1987, 129–38.

Richard, Nelly. "The Rhetoric of the Body." *Margins and Institutions: Art in Chile Since 1973*. Special issue of *Art and Text*, 21, 1986.

Rowbotham, Sheila. *Woman's Consciousness, Man's World*. Harmondsworth: Penguin, 1973.

Sánchez, Marta Ester. *Contemporary Chicana Poetry: A Critical Approach to an Emerging Literature*. Berkeley: University of California Press, 1985.

Sánchez, Osvaldo. "Children of Utopia." *Third Text*, Issue 7, Summer 1989, 33–40.

Sartre, Jean-Paul. *Being and Nothingness: A Phenomenological Essay on Ontology*. Trans. Hazel H. Barnes. 1956. Rpt. New York: Pocket Books, 1966.

——*Critique of Dialectical Reason*. Trans. Alan Sheridan-Smith. Ed. Jonathan Ree. London: New Left Books, 1976.

——*Nausea*. Trans. Lloyd Alexander. New York: New Directions, 1964.

——*La nausée*. Paris: Gallimard, 1938.

Scobie, James. *Argentina, a City and a Nation*. 2nd ed. New York: Oxford University Press, 1971.

Silverman, Kaja. *The Acoustic Mirror: The Female Voice in Psychoanalysis and Cinema*. Bloomington: Indiana University Press, 1988.

Soustelle, Jacques. *Daily Life of the Aztecs on the Eve of the Spanish Conquest*. Trans. Patrick O'Brien. 1964. Rpt. Harmondsworth: Penguin, 1964.

Stein, Julia. "Latin American Friend." *The Broken Line/La Línea Quebrada*, 2:2, March, 1987, 42.

Sterne, Laurence. *Tristram Shandy*. New York: The New American Library—Signet, 1962.

Stockhausen, Karlheinz. *Stockhausen's Momente*. Nonesuch, 71-71157.

Tawadros, Gilane. "Beyond the Boundary: The Work of Three Black Women Artists in Britain." *Third Text*, 1.4–5, 1989, 121–49.

Taylor, J. M. *Eva Perón, the Myths of a Woman*. Chicago: University of Chicago Press, 1979.

Thompson, E. P. *The Making of the English Working Class*. New York: Pantheon, 1963.

Valdés, Gina. "Fragmentos de Diálogos Fronterizos." *The Broken Line/La Línea Quebrada*, 1.1, 1986, 55.

——"Where You From?" *The Broken Line/La Línea Quebrada*, 1.1, 1986, 28.

Valenzuela, Luisa. "Cambio de armas." *Cambio de armas*. Hanover: Ediciones del Norte, 1982.

——*Cola de lagartija*. Buenos Aires: Brugüera, 1983.

——*Como en la guerra*. Buenos Aires: Sudamericana, 1977.

——*He Who Searches. Strange Things Happen Here, 26 Short Stories and a Novel*. Trans. Helen Lane. New York: Harcourt Brace Jovanovich, 1979.

——Lecture. Latin American Literature: Modern Discourses of Emancipation Symposium. San Diego State University, 11 April 1986.

——*The Lizard's Tail*. Trans. Gregory Rabassa. New York: Farrar, Straus, Giroux, 1983.

——*Other Weapons*. Trans Deborah Bonner. Hanover: Ediciones del Norte, 1985.

——"El verbo matar." *Cosas raras pasan aquí*.

Whitney, John. *Digital Harmony*. Peterborough: McGraw-Hill, 1980.

Wynia, Gary. *Argentina in the Post-War Era*. Albuquerque: University of New Mexico Press, 1978.

Young, David, and Keith Hollaman, eds. *Magic Realist Fiction*. New York: Longman, 1984.

Index

Compiled by Robin Jackson

Theory and History of Literature

D. Emily Hicks is associate professor of English and comparative literature and a member of the Latin American studies faculty at San Diego State University. She serves as coeditor of *The Broken Line/La Línea Quebrada*, a bilingual journal of art and literature.

Neil Larsen is associate professor of Spanish and Latin American literature at Northeastern University and the author of *Modernism and Hegemony: A Materialist Critique of Aesthetic Agencies* (Minnesota, 1989).